M000021088

HIGHER GROUND

HIGHER GROUND

A Memoir of
Higgins Classical Institute

Ann B. Tracy

DOWN EAST BOOKS
Camden, Maine

Copyright © 1988 by Ann B. Tracy
ISBN 0-89272-243-6
Library of Congress Catalog Card Number 88-51489

Design by Lurelle Cheverie
Printed at Capital City Press

2 4 5 3 1

Down East Books
Camden, Maine 04843

For William A. Tracy (1889–1969),
who helped make the school,
the author, and the research money.

CONTENTS

CONTENTS

ACKNOWLEDGMENTS

F irst, to Pat Hoffmann, best of editors and friends, a thousand thanks for a thousand things, not least a keen eye and an honest voice. I am indebted to all alumni and friends of Higgins who answered my questionnaires or permitted me to talk with them or looked at chapters, and most concretely to those who lent or gave me yearbooks and other memorabilia: Audrey Delano Allen; Jake Bishop, who also wrote me a 119-page answer; John Bradeen; Gladys Bunker Bridges; Doris Spencer Carle; Peter Chase; Philip Colman; Dorothy Mace Dennis; Wayne Duplisea; Florence Emery; Raymond Farnham; Michael Gallant, whose historical instinct caused him to buy a most useful collection at a yard sale; Phillip Hamm; the late Geneva Higgins; Evelyn Keith, whose gift of her husband's book has been beyond price; Lee Kennedy; Ruth Merrill Kinney; Erma Joy McGuirl; Alden Mitchell; Martha Bragger Northrup; Thomas E. Parker; Madeline Dunham Patterson; Sandra Rich Rhoda; Alberta Rich, curator of the Rich Collection, the best repository of early yearbooks; Avery Rich; Wayne Rich; Pauline Dunham Riley; Janice Rich Rockwell; Richmond (Joe) Roderick; Cecil D. Ross; Madeline Thurlow Rugowski; Charlotte Burgess Sanborn; Mary Mace Siemion; William Tracy, Jr.; Maria Bartlett Verrill; Randal White; R. Leon and Alma Williams, who have been supportive in a variety of ways; and Perry Wortman, who has lent and read and encouraged.

I am obliged to Dean Houng Liu, Thomas Morrissey, Patty Bentley, Julie Davies, and William Nicholson for practical support, and to

Graeme Francis and Shirley Nock for certain clerical aids. P. A. Lenk made my work at Colby College Special Collections a pleasure. I have enjoyed the hospitality of Eileen Curran, Marlene Nightingale, Mary Jane Schildberg, Darthea Tilley, and Bonnie Wood. Mary Higgins supplied the addresses that made the questionnaire possible. Susannah Dicks was the first to read the earliest chapters and give me encouragement, while Bernice and George Dicks's word-processing skills and forbearance, respectively, saved me time and pain at the end. Greta Hoffmann steadied me through the craziness of three days' printing-out. For three of the headmaster photos I am indebted to Colby College and for the others to my talented friend Robin Brown, who generously contributed time, film, and expertise to the copying of old yearbook photos. The text will show how much I am indebted to Hugh Smith for his recollections, though he has not lived to see the book.

I

A NECESSARY INTRODUCTION

Historia, quoquo modo scripta, bona est.

I n the seventeenth century, when inquiring minds still swung between magic and science, one popular experiment professed to "revivify" a plant from its own ashes. Even Sir Thomas Browne, that famous exploder of popular error, avers in *Religio Medici* that the thing can be done, that the "art of man" can "from its cinders recall [a plant] into its stalk and leaves again." (Indeed, the manuscript version seems to imply that he has done it himself.) I, for one, hope that it's all true, that those Renaissance dabblers revivified not only stalk and leaves, but bud and blossom and the very scent of the rose. My intentions in this book, you see, are analogous. I propose, from faded photographs and dead jokes, from memories and memorabilia, from letters and ledgers, to conjure up the late Higgins Classical Institute, alive and educating before your very eyes.

Perhaps I should first make clear my own background and prejudices. My father, William Tracy, was the eighth principal of Higgins. During Christmas break of 1939 he married Brenna Blaisdell, one of his teachers, and a year later I was born and brought home from the hospital nursery to their apartment in the girls' dorm. When I woke to reason I found that other teachers were my extended family, students my sitters, faculty children my earliest friends, the shape of the school year the shape of my year. Before I could write on paper I used to piece together **HCI** with colored toothpicks. In retrospect, I ask myself why not Ann, a name that might have been designed for toothpick rendition? I conclude that HCI seemed like the only thing worth writing. Born and bred in the briar patch, Br'er Fox.

Any faculty child might say the same; we carry common stigmata —eating too fast, for instance, or requiring ceremonies to make the year go round. But I have an additional steeping in the essence of Higgins, for the man whose policies shaped the school for thirty years was doing a concentrated domestic job on me; the pattern that was stamped on Higgins students was woven into my fabric. I am in a position to interpret.

That was the background. The prejudices are given away by my use of "alive" to describe a school. The organization of this book presumes a consistent institutional personality that permits us to talk about tone or sports or attitudes toward romance in all periods at once, so that what we say of Higgins in the 1930s will, barring detail, be true for the 1900s and the 1960s. Schools are vivid, individual presences. Why do you think that Lifers, the Mr. Chipses and the David Powlett-Joneses, don't just gather up their meager belongings and opt for a change of scene, adolescents being much the same and in generous supply everywhere? Delderfield might better have called his novel *To Serve It All My Days*—or perhaps *Her*, since schools, like ships, are usually assigned feminine pronouns.

Readers who themselves have been seduced by institutions will have found my remarks so far perfectly sensible. Those who have never heard the siren song a boarding school croons may have written me off as a lunatic. Believe me, mine is not a singular madness. All over America (and how much worse must it be in England), little pockets of obsessives who have been marked by intimacy with boarding schools are even now finding themselves unable to resist articles, novels, and films, however trashy, about private education. Once I met at a dinner party a respectable Canadian scholar who confessed that he had earlier fled from a prep school job *because he loved it too much*. Or consider the testimony from Derwin Emerson, who taught at Higgins during its last and worst years. Though teachers were hard-pressed and perpetually thrown upon their own resources, supplies, and ingenuity, he told me when I saw him last summer that if through some miraculous intervention Higgins ever opened again, he'd leave his good high school job and his good lab equipment and rush back again to "teach with nothing."

But on to business. Higgins's history will reveal itself in the coming chapters, but some capsule background will be useful. Before Higgins was called Higgins, before it acquired, at the turn of the century, the buildings that meant Higgins to its graduates, it was known as Charleston Academy; even earlier it had had a brief and ill-fated career as a theological institution. Eighteen thirty-seven is the date officially recognized as the beginning of Charleston Academy, for it was in 1937 that Higgins celebrated its centenary.

Through the first seventy years of the nineteenth century, before the Free High School Act in 1873 (and still, in large degree, after it), academies were the backbone of Maine secondary education, for much of the state was too sparsely settled to make high schools feasible. For this and the information that immediately follows I am indebted to Principal Philip Keith's *The History of Secondary Education in Penobscot County in Maine* (hereafter HEPC), published by *The Maine Bulletin* in April 1948. To found an academy, a group of interested citizens would raise money by subscription and petition the Maine legislature for a charter of incorporation. If the legislature liked the plans, it might give a grant of land or money to the new school, which was governed by a board of trustees. Public high schools, both before and after 1873, were a chancy business—some had only a two-year program, some had only one or two teachers, some were teaching at an elementary school level. Academies, though intermittent collapses and closings were not unknown, generally could be counted on for four years of suitably advanced study, and perhaps as many as half a dozen well-educated teachers. Recall Wareham Academy, which Rebecca of Sunnybrook Farm is permitted to attend because of her intellectual promise (and where she is taught by the daughter of a Bowdoin professor), while a closer high school is reckoned sufficient for the needs of her dim friend Emma Jane. The 1873 act and consequent withdrawal of state aid seemed fatal for the academies, and indeed the legislature had made provision for academies to be converted into free high schools. Some followed this course, but a number did not. Academy names survive in both categories—for instance, Hebron Academy, Fryeburg Academy, and Gould Academy in the private sector; East Corinth Academy and Foxcroft Academy in the public. Maine was used to its academies and valued their more sophisticated curricula, so their survival rate exceeded expectation. The School Administrative District (SAD) Act, eighty-four years later, would do to Higgins what the 1873 act might have done to Charleston Academy, save for the intervention of the Reverend John Higgins.

A biographical preview of this man cannot be omitted, for his early life was good Horatio Alger: at sixteen he left Charleston and the rural poverty in which he had been raised to work in his uncles' Manhattan carpet factory, where he rapidly acquired responsibility, wealth, and sophistication. In the midst of these earthly delights he was naturally dismayed to feel that God was calling him to preach. Astute in business, he tried to strike a compromise by paying the salaries of other clergymen, but God, who knows quality, was having none of it. At the death of his daughter, feeling, no doubt, a good bit like Jonah, John Higgins gave in and left New York, the consternation of his millionaire uncles ringing in his ears. He began to preach his way around backwoods Maine. Again, he was a notable success.

Perhaps it was his natural philanthropy; perhaps it was the example of Dwight L. Moody, whom he was inclined to emulate; perhaps God once more spoke a word in his ear—we shall never know for certain exactly what compound of motives led John Higgins to acquire, endow, and upgrade his town's academy. He did not, stories say, intend that it be named after him. He did intend that its character be formed by his principles and priorities. "That there be and hereby is established in the town of Charleston in the County of Penobscot, an institution of learning by the name of Higgins Classical Institute," says the Act of Incorporation, "for the promotion of Christian education, and the instruction of youth in such languages, arts and sciences as the Trustees hereinafter named shall direct." There would be no dancing at Higgins for seventy years.

In 1891, when the Reverend John Higgins laid his hand on Charleston Academy, thereby altering its history and its name, Colby College already owned three "fitting schools"—private academies from whose ranks were to emerge suitably prepared, Colby-bound students. Higgins became the fourth. Colby had title to the real estate of these academies (indeed, when the Higgins dorm burned in 1956, it was necessary for the trustees to obtain their official emancipation from Colby in order to raise money for rebuilding), held their endowments, placed its presidents and deans on their boards of trustees, and in large measure supplied them with headmasters.

Coburn Classical Institute in Waterville, Ricker Classical Institute in Houlton, and Hebron Academy in Hebron were the three original Colby affiliates that the erstwhile Charleston Academy joined as Higgins Classical Institute. They were, as readers familiar with Maine geography will note, spaced strategically about the state. Of Colby's four fitting schools, only one, Hebron Academy, now survives in what I might describe as its proper form. Coburn, the oldest, never recovered from the burning of its classroom building in 1955; fifteen years later it merged with the genteel Oak Grove School and moved to that campus. Ricker, which expanded first to a junior college and then to a four-year college, dropping its prep school segment along the way, seems to have collapsed under the weight of its own ambitions. And though the Faith School of Theology, which in 1975 took over the Higgins campus, operates a K through 12 Christian school that by previous agreement retains the Higgins name, nobody mistakes it for the real thing.

Hebron, long the most prosperous of the fitting schools, survived by changing its tone and focus early. Authentically preppy, it converted to boys only—the other three schools stayed coed—in 1922, and appealed increasingly to an out-of-state clientele that was not decimated by the formation of consolidated high schools in the sixties. Higgins, on the other hand, like Coburn and Ricker, specialized in a student population that made "fitting school" a particularly meaningful term. Its principal mission was the education of girls and boys who would not otherwise have had much schooling, who would perhaps have stayed on the farm or worked in the woods and never known the joys of Caesar or the terror of public speaking or how to conduct themselves at a tea. Nor would they, certainly, have become the executive vice presidents and teachers and mayors and state senators and contractors who so kindly answered my questionnaire. Of course, such students were not the only ones who went to Higgins—its reputation was good and its rates the lowest in the state—but they were its *raison d'etre*. Because Maine towns, if they had no high schools, were obliged to pay the tuition of their students elsewhere, families received bills for board and room only, expenses that could be further defrayed by the student's own labor. All but the most professional work was done by students, not for their characters but for their economic survival.

"This will leave them $4 per week each to pay," a letter of my father's announces to one family after he has made his calculations. "This amount covers all school expenses. I hope I make this clear. It will cost you $142 for each student per year besides the work and scholarships. . . . I shall hold this help until I hear from you." Not bad for a prep school education, even in 1942. For parents paying in full, the cost was $365 a year. Another letter makes an even better offer (and a delightful unconscious pun), this to a father who for lack of funds has planned to withdraw one of his daughters: "If Faith has a small balance left, we will permit her to return to school. I am very sorry about Hope. . . . If you will deliver 50 barrels of potatoes, I will give Hope work and scholarship enough to pay her full expenses for the year. I shall be glad if this makes it possible for Hope to return."

The notion that going to Higgins gave them a lifelong break comes across strongly in the alumni responses. Not that good luck is always easy to live with. "I was tremendously homesick," writes Harry Nason ('27), "green as grass, having never known inside toilet and bathroom or running water or electric lights. Mr. Tracy and Mr. Smith were my mentors in those days of great changes in my life. Mr. Tracy took me for rides in his Dodge touring car. Just when it seemed I couldn't stand it any longer, he seemed to know." But, in the end, most of the students, thanks to the benevolent clairvoyance of the staff and the friendliness of their fellows, seemed to survive and to find the Higgins ad, "A Home for Boys and Girls," more truth than hype. "I always felt that I was one of the Higgins family, no bias, no conditions, but a peer in every form, shape or manner," Harry Nason adds.

Indeed, the fervor of loyalty provoked by Higgins, and not only in its innately ardent teenage charges, now almost passes comprehension. A friend named Forrest Royal once justly observed to my father, and has subsequently been much quoted, that Higgins was not a school but a religion. It may even be that he said it with some asperity, being himself a graduate of Ricker, but his tone is now lost. In any case, he was right. Quite an astonishing note of reverence comes across in alumni responses to my questionnaire; it is the tone I knew in my childhood, when "For the good of the school!" was a rallying cry of my father's before which all domestic arrangements and other considerations gave way, and which I had nearly forgotten in my own less pious adolescence and subsequent time away from Higgins. When I was very small, I used to mis-hear a rather pedestrian line in the school song, "Cheer, oh, let us cheer her," as "Cheer, O *Letters*, cheer her"—that is to say, that the H, the C, and the I, themselves should rise up and join in adulation; I saw it clearly. Years later I found, for the first time, a comparable sentiment (in a hymn, which Forrest Royal would have thought a predictable context): "If we forget to praise Thy name, the stones themselves will sing." I remember, too, that Ethel Beck, daughter of the founder, used to declaim, "The Lord will raise up a man for Higgins." I am now uncertain about what occasions caused her to say this—the hiring of new principals, perhaps?—but there was no mistaking her conviction that our school was under the special providence of God.

Such flights of enthusiasm may lead a skeptical reader to suspect either that Higgins was a delusion of mass hysteria, or that it was real but that neither my alumni respondents nor I can be trusted for a dispassionate account of it. All I can say is that a dispassionate picture is not a whole one. This revivified rosebush of mine will have its roots sunk in as much solid fact as I can scrape together, but that's not what makes the perfume. Facts are only the substrata of truth. I've pretended to myself as well as to officialdom that I can stop being an English professor and take up being a social scientist for a year. I've been lying. Lean closer, reader, and I'll confess it in your ear: this isn't just a history—it's a love song.

II

PLACE

I remember it all—buildings, rooms, mess hall, class-
rooms, trees, football field, shower room, vegetable
room in the basement, even the potato storage bin.

—WILLIAM NOEHOFF ('33)

harleston is a small town even by inland Maine standards, seven hundred inhabitants spread over thirty-six square miles. There are no residential streets; houses are built beside roads that go somewhere—Route 15, Route 11, Puddledock Road, Christian Hill Road. For perhaps two miles along Route 11 the population thickens; that is to say, houses are separated by lawns, not fields. Sixteen street lights celebrate this clustering of neighbors. Here too we find the town's public buildings, which have not changed radically in the last fifty or seventy-five years, though there have been gentle shifts, emergences, subsidings. Charleston is not one of those twitchy hamlets that continually insist on tearing down their post offices and building new. Although internal revision has turned the postmistress's window from south to north, and the eccentric notions shop with which federal business cohabited in my childhood (a store with overhead pipes from which fat cobwebs hung like yarn and dingy yarn hung like cobwebs) has long since sunk into its own dust and been swept away, the mail goes in and out as it always did.

The Grange Hall and the combination Masonic Temple and Town Hall (where one drops his ballot through the slot of a black

8

wooden box)—substantial, dignified, white clapboard buildings—are wisely considered sufficient to their purposes. Charleston supports only two religious denominations, Baptist and Pentecostal, though owing perhaps to the ebullient nature of fundamentalism it has twice in this century supported two Baptist churches simultaneously. Charleston once had a glove manufactory, an observatory—the highest point in Penobscot County—and a hotel. By my time, business had dwindled to (besides the mummified notions shop) a garage, one or two general stores, and a lunchroom patronized chiefly by Higgins students. The least occupationally stable building in the town center has been by turns a Baptist church, the Higgins gymnasium, a potato house, and a chicken house. Built in 1957, the newest public building (aside from the elementary school) houses the fire engine, the one-room library, and the town clerk. Charleston's only sidewalk runs the length of the Higgins campus and belongs to Higgins. Higgins is in the center of town; it *is* the center of town.

Charleston village sits not quite at the crest of Charleston Hill. If we look east, like the school, we can see for some miles, perhaps for a township or two, but all we see, after a few houses, is an expanse of tree-tops and a big sky; all we hear is wind and birdsong and now and then the sputter of a motor—a tractor, say, or a chainsaw. We are not much distracted by traffic, especially in the summer when school is out; in winter there is human traffic. My family once owned a public nuisance of a cocker spaniel who slept in the middle of the road all one summer with no cause for regret.

Eventfulness, however, is a matter of perspective. Children in West Charleston used to stand in awe of "the village," be nervous about coming to it. Despite appearances, Higgins was not, or mostly not, a rural exile to which urban adolescents were sent unwilling. Often it was a cultural mecca to which even more rural adolescents aspired. There was an understanding on a certain Maine island, for instance, that good boys and girls who studied hard would be allowed to go to Higgins; slackers would be deported to the mainland high school, no money wasted on them. "Coming from a small town as I did, it was without doubt the highlight of my life," says Harvey Davis ('29).

Higgins catalogues from 1894 to 1959 tout the "cordiality, thrift, and high moral tone" of Charleston's citizens. This is surprisingly true. By and large they possess, as well, intelligence, aspirations, senses of humor, and a remarkable tolerance for the senile and insane, who have always been allowed to roam the streets like traveling players. Charleston's inhabitants are not readily taken in by fads or fanaticism: I've seen a Baptist congregation sit patient as stone while a young whippersnapper of a minister explains that they are not to use the Lord's Prayer, that it's intended for the exclusive use of Jews in the Millennium. They don't believe him for one minute, but they know that ministers come and go, while God endures. They endure too.

The closest thing to book-banning that Charleston ever had was a librarian who used to cross out all the bad words in pencil until the number of acquisitions—or perhaps the level of modern profanity—got beyond her. Nobody supported her in this tiresome habit; neither did anyone, as far as I know, try to make her stop, for that would have hurt her feelings. Although the polls register one Socialist ballot in each election, nobody in this Republican town has ever tried, as Hollywood might expect, to identify that voter and burn a cross on his or her lawn. They would think cross burning uncivil, wasteful, and more than slightly blasphemous. But of course they are cordial, thrifty, and moral: they are themselves Higgins graduates.

The Higgins campus has changed more over the decades than the town itself, or we notice the changes more because the space is smaller. Therefore, let us choose a time frame for this tour, understanding that we can look backward or forward; let us consider Higgins as it looked from the late thirties to the mid fifties. This is a good representative period, coming as it does in the middle of the school's life span. It includes the last of my father's principalship as well as all of Philip Keith's and Charles O'Connor's, and the first half of Leon Meader's, and it is the period that I best know by observation.

Standing in the main road, facing west, the athletic field at our backs, we see before us the green rectangle of the Higgins campus. It is bounded on the west by the Institute (or classroom) building, the gym, and the boys' dorm, all in a row; on the south by the weedy field assigned to softball; on the north by the girls' dorm. These three trim acres, sectioned by concrete sidewalks (823 linear feet) and gravel drives, around which couples stroll and bad boys run punitive laps, constitute the biggest and best-kept lawn in town. It may well be the biggest and best-kept lawn that some of the students have ever seen, for graduates, asked to identify their favorite spot at Higgins, often name it. "The front lawn is bigger than our east field," says one of those fake-hayseed letters home popular in Higgins yearbooks, but the awestruck tone is not so far off the mark.

I remember the lawn as a kind of outdoor stage, where players wonderful to the childish eye sometimes appeared: athletes standing on one another's shoulders in pyramids; girls posing in long satin dresses for Senior Banquet; mustachioed and scimitared operetta performers being photographed for their parents; a boy called Tiger Lyon flying a new and enormous gas-propelled model plane of his own manufacture. Sometimes in the winter we had snow sculpture. Snapshots from my childhood show small snow replicas of the Higgins buildings, a cannon, a horse. In 1938 Willis Parker and Bill Oliver sculpted a man in a boat.

Like the lawn, the sidewalks that intersect it are an attraction in themselves. "S is for the sidewalks," says an acronymic poem in the 1944 yearbook. Poured in blocks perhaps three feet square, portions of the sidewalk heave and tilt slightly with the frost so that deltas of moss and silt gather in the low corners. They are too irregular for roller-skating, but each block has a personality. In the spring they re-emerge through the melting snow with all the seasonal promise of crocuses, and we rejoice to see them again.

Higgins has plenty of space besides the lawn. To the west, behind the buildings, lie open fields of no designated purpose, bordered with apple blossoms and catkins in the spring. At the southernmost wooded edge, unwary nature lovers may find themselves rambling through an open sewer. (This is an intimate tour and will spare no details.) Dogtooth violets grow lavishly at its marshy verge, and children straying from the grade-school classroom in the Higgins basement at recess occasionally fall into it and are scolded by their teachers and made to spend the rest of the day outdoors. The same woods contain, in the bad, unecological forties, a small dump or two where Higgins deposits institutional-size empty cans, the severed lids of which are prized by local children as a kind of savage proto-frisbee.

Behind us, across the road, the athletic field lies a yard or so below street level, and on its far side the ground dips again, so that we see

the crowns, not the trunks, of small trees. On a generous terrace between the field and the street, a row of old maples stand far enough
apart to allow for benches, thick weathered planks nailed to posts.
Lucetta Doore ('14) remembers those benches, so they've been
around for a while. We do not know who planted the trees. They
look substantially older than the fifteen trees planted around the
edge of the softball field on Arbor Day 1905. The benches are a good
place for watching football games with small faculty children who
might get trampled at field level, and even better for courting or
dreaming or adolescent chatter in the sun.

If we begin our circuit of the campus at the north end, we come
first to the girls' dorm. The old wing, with its porch and its mock-
orange bushes, was once the home of the Reverend John Higgins.
Here the widowed Mrs. Higgins later entertained the seniors at formidable banquets amidst massive sideboards and gilt mirrors from
Queen Liliuokalani's palace, relics of her previous marriage to Lawrence McCulley, judge of the Supreme Court of Hawaii. In 1926 the
trustees purchased the building, continuing to call it The Higgins
House until it was expanded in 1937, after which it became simply
"the girls' dorm."

It is an unusually homey dormitory, perhaps because it was for so
long an actual home, or perhaps because until the mid sixties the
principal and his family lived in the ground-floor apartment. It sur-
prises me now to see, in snapshots, the family clothes reel planted beside the headmaster's door, right where the parents drive up, but an
odd balance of unpretentiousness and formality is typical of Higgins.
Snapshots reveal a wealth of homely domestic detail besides the
clothes reel: a sandbox (mine) beside the drive, woodpiles and a stray
bucket near the garage, and a row of flowers, nasturtiums I think, beside the just slightly decaying door sill (where fuzzy caterpillars wearing the school colors of orange and black demonstrate that nature
itself is pro-Higgins). In this environment the most unpolished freshman must have felt that he had a fair chance, for all he had to wear
a tie to dinner and watch his grammar.

The dorm is designed to hold thirty-six girls, two to a room,
though there may have been more than two in "the suites," two long
rooms over the center section converted from attic by the addition of
dormer windows. The rooms are big and airy, with two windows

each. A letter from my father to an incoming student (8/28/40) responds to a decorating query: "The woodwork in your room is painted cream. The paper is tan with green and orange tints." The third-floor rooms on the old end have the added charm of sloping ceilings and enormous built-in drawers that skinny, wicked girls occasionally remove in order to slip into the attic for a life-threatening smoke. Girls caught at this trick are sent home.

The usual entrance for students and teachers is in the new west wing, facing the rest of the campus. A small portico of some social importance shelters the door. Between the pillars and the wall, and again between the pillars and the front opening, the carpenters have provided a wide, sittable ledge. In clement seasons girls perch there thick as herring gulls on a rock, their faces turned steadfastly south toward the boys' dorm. Boys are not encouraged to join them on the ledge, but may lead them away for walks. ("No couples from 4:00 P.M. to 6:00 P.M." read the forthright regulations for 1948–49. "Do not go outside limits—town hall to potato house—without a teacher. Do not hang around boys' dorm.") A round light over the door officially summons young ladies home when the dangerous shadows of evening begin to gather.

Just inside the front hall, where young men are permitted only under rigidly chaperoned conditions, we find a communal living room with a fireplace and a piano. It looks comfortable and a little shabby, though it is called the Reception Room and now and then rises to the formality of an instructive tea. Two tall windows to the right of the fireplace look not outdoors but into the principal's sunporch. They are close to the floor on the Reception Room side, rather higher on the sunporch side, a reminder that the dorm was built in two stages, and uphill. These windows have their uses. The student mailman, for instance, can deliver the girls' mail without trespass; he simply walks onto the sunporch, opens the window, and shoves it through. Actually he doesn't need to open anything; at mail time the window has a thousand hands. Also, if the principal has a small child—Patty O'Connor and Neil Meader would bear me out on this—it is sometimes requisitioned by students or faculty and hauled bodily up over the window ledge.

The porch opens directly into the principal's big kitchen, another note of informality. It is an inconvenient kitchen, I realize now, the appliances ranged around three walls and too far apart. The table at which my parents and I usually took our meals sat against the west wall, smack up behind the girls' piano. We seldom made it through a meal without music, mostly "Chopsticks" and "I Love Coffee, I Love Tea," played over and over with unflagging gusto, and I think sometimes simultaneously. "Eat quick before somebody comes," my mother would warn in lieu of grace, but by dessert some swift-footed student would always appear in the doorway, wanting a permission. In this kitchen in 1946 three kind and dignified headmasters—my father, Hugh Smith, and Philip Keith—condescended to dance the Hokey Pokey at my instruction. The memory of that sight has tickled me ever since.

Anyone who supposes that the middle of the room, away from the piano, would have been a better place to put the table is reckoning without the propensity of female boarding students to stop up drains and flood the ceiling underneath. I enjoyed these floods myself, wearing my rubber boots inside the house and watching my mother go berserk with a mop. In fact, I liked all the oddities of life in that principal's apartment: the fine slope of the dining room floor, down which one could coast a tricycle; the moan of the wind as it rounded the little juts where sections of the dorm joined; my school cot in the corner of my parents' bedroom. I can imagine, though, how little my mother and the principals' wives who followed her must have enjoyed conducting family life in a dorm.

Other than the kitchen, the room most frequented by students was my father's office, a small square area separated from the dining room by a curtained arch. From this room, with its rolltop desk, most of the school's business was conducted; my mother provided clerical assistance, for at the time Higgins had no office staff. Pocket money was given out there, I think, and "permissions"; students must have liked it better than the Institute office, where they would have gotten mainly chewings-out. I liked it better, too, for it was not at all austere or off limits, and I could sit on the linoleum and emboss bits of scrap paper with the Higgins seal or go through the wastebasket for envelopes containing advertisers' samples.

We had, as well, a pleasant living room with a fireplace and from one to three bedrooms, depending on needs and circumstances. Much of school life is implicit in that qualifying phrase. My family used either one or two bedrooms, depending on how accurately my father had figured his acceptances and how soft he had been about hard luck cases or students who had decided at the last minute to return after all or some friend whose daughter could not be turned away. If he had more girls than the dorm proper would hold, more even than he could farm out to suitable townspeople, then we would surrender the outlying bedroom and retreat into the one just off the living room; and after graduation my mother would chip the gum off her headboard and wonder, perhaps, what had possessed her to marry a school.

The problem of where to put the adolescent sons of the principals bore on the bedroom question as well. The Keiths, for instance, sent John to live in the boys' dorm. I believe that this was considered proper, for I dimly recall a raised eyebrow or two when the Meaders chose to keep Buddy at home. Buddy, however, though attractive and not impervious to female charms, thought girls were people and knew how to be friends with them; it did not occur to him to think of himself as a fox in a chicken house.

Outside the dorm are pleasant bits of flora—baby's breath, flowering bushes, a small garden with poppies and phlox and a rose bush, even devil's paintbrushes and daisies growing wild in the depression around the new wing. Behind the barn, at the north edge of campus, are clotheslines under which the girls can sunbathe in some privacy during inland Maine's brief, hot spring. From these clotheslines, Frances Ward ('38) tells me, her brother Lowell's underwear was swept away on a fierce January night and never seen again.

But the fifteen amorous feet of driveway by the portico, just where the road turns south past the other buildings, is the outdoor spot of prime importance. Here it is that shoals of couples stand furtively embracing in the after-dinner, after–study-hall, after-basketball dark. Here boys who have walked girls home (permissible occasions grow more frequent as the years pass) take their reluctant leaves, disengaging themselves as the female teachers catch up. Higgins students are expected to conduct themselves in seemly ways, to moderate passion with principle, and to try not to be made greater fools than necessary by their hormones; smoochers are not so much on the road to hell as on the road to silliness, distraction from work, frivolity. Sometimes kindly female teachers walk slowly enough, weather permitting, to allow lovers a few extra moments of bliss. Perhaps they take into account that not even the most ardent of couples can break into truly dangerous flame with the snow up to their hips.

Just south of the barn, behind the couples' trysting spot, is an empty field. Students of both sexes are playing softball there in an old yearbook snapshot, and I remember some boys once tossing each other in blankets. In the 1950s it provides parking for the growing number of cars. In 1964 Perry Wortman will build a principal's house on this spot, a pleasant, modest, white ranch house. There is nothing much to say about it, except that perhaps my mother, Evelyn Keith, Mildred O'Connor, and Mary Meader would have killed for it.

Tibbetts Hall, the boys' dorm, is dark red with white trim. Bilaterally symmetrical, it has two of everything—two front doors, two sets of stairs down to the dining room—because it was at first coeducational, though strictly segregated by gender. Alumni inform me that boys and girls were discouraged even from trespassing on the opposite sex's side of the porch, a fine distinction. Now boys lounge happily in twos and threes on the slightly curling wooden steps, and though they do not look toward the girls' dorm, it would be discriminatory not to speculate that they too may be hoping to be noticed. At some point in our time frame the old steps are replaced by concrete ones, which are less sat upon. That must have happened by the early fifties, for it was down the new steps that two faculty children, renowned for their maniacal inventiveness, rolled their baby brother, and all the ladies cried, "Right down those *concrete steps!*"

Inside Tibbetts Hall the corridors are brown and echoing, like hospitable caves. Neil Brown ('56) writes, "I found the old boys' dorm to be very comfortable, because of its wooden structure and pleasantly worn look—like that of old leather. It seemed a very warm and cozy place, despite its considerable size." It must be confessed that by "warm" Neil will almost certainly have been describing ambience, not temperature. From Ellis Holt ('27), who remembers scraping a wastebasketful of frost off his window so that he could see through it, to Jake Bishop ('55), who describes the morning he had to shovel out his room after a nor'easter, there is a consensus that Tibbetts Hall was no spa. I have found in yearbooks some evidence of a specialized genre of student verse that we might call "janitor poetry" (e.g., "Far from home we live in our dorm / 14 blankets to keep us warm / It does no good to complain cause it's cool / Merle, our fireman, is stubborn as a mule." [1973 *Scroll*])

The rooms, especially in the early years, sound spartan as well as cold. Originally they had double beds, one to a room, that could be folded up against the wall ("on occasion with the occupant still in it," adds Ellis Holt), but as these inevitably broke they were replaced by single cots, so no sweeping post-Freudian renovation was necessary. One feels sorry for the poor freshman, though, thrust into bed with a possibly hostile stranger on his first night away from home, and a story survives about two roommates, brothers, so angry at one another that they were discovered sleeping one on a desk, one on a trunk, the double bed empty between them.

Faculty apartments are located on both ends of the first floor. These usually consist of two or three rooms, but can be expanded by annexing another room on the corridor, if one doesn't mind emerging into public territory en route to the study or bedroom. Married faculty members get more space than single (who rate only one room), and families get more yet. Dependents are calculated into salary, though—"$1800 plus keep for wife and child." Records show one man's cash salary down by $230 the year he brings Higgins a wife to house and feed, and a cook who in the 1940s makes $23 every two weeks after his son's school expenses and his wife's keep are deducted.

In the basement, reached by either set of stairs, we find the dining room and the kitchen. Before meals, girls and boys crowd on their separate staircases with attendant faculty members, waiting for the signal. John Moore ('47) admits to having enlivened one such wait by dropping a dead mouse down the stairwell into the bosom of his English teacher. The dining room, like the corridors, is slightly cavernous but not unpleasant. Tables for ten, with bentwood chairs, can be pushed together for state occasions like Senior Banquet, their linoleum tops covered then with white tablecloths. Near the kitchen is a spoon closet, aptly named, where coed workers duck for a hasty kiss. The outsize kitchen looks efficient in an old-fashioned way and is generally clean, though cleanliness varies slightly from cook to cook. The stove shifts from wood-burning to coal to gas to wood again as the economy changes. Outside, behind the kitchen, there's an alley atmosphere cleverly transported to the country—garbage cans, rotted steps up the embankment, the ground hard and sour and gray-green from mop water.

Tibbetts Hall was named for an earlier Tibbetts Hall that stood on the same ground and looked almost exactly like this one. The Reverend John Higgins built the first in 1902, naming it after his lifelong friend Charlie Tibbetts. An old photo shows it to be, if anything, slightly more handsome than its successor, with decorative balls at the top corners of the porch and pillared porticoes at the north and south ends. The first Tibbetts Hall seems to have had a granite rather than a brick foundation and to have sat a little lower to the ground, requiring less than half the number of front steps. Perhaps it did not have a finished basement, for the kitchen and dining room were then housed in the original wooden Academy building, which had been attached to the back of Tibbetts Hall for that purpose. The 1900–1901 catalogue promises that the first Tibbetts Hall will have, when completed, forty double rooms and a trunk elevator, that it will measure 115 feet by 42 feet and cost ten thousand dollars exclusive of furniture, and that it will be in fact the "best type in the state." It burned in its twelfth year, a dismally short life for such a paragon of a building, and John Higgins was not there to cope with the emergency. He had been dead four years.

Lucetta Doore ('14), who was in school then, remembers the boys in their zeal "saving" china wash bowls and pitchers by throwing them out the windows. (In the 1956 fire, boys would repeat this folly with phonograph records.) The school managed to stay open, and the townspeople loyally raised the then astonishing sum of three thousand dollars toward the new dorm, as well as taking boarding students into their homes. (Could eagerness to move the students back out have added stimulus to the fund drive, one wonders?)

The second Tibbetts Hall lasted forty-one years and burned in April of 1956. I saw that fire myself, and details remain vivid: all of us standing on the lawn in the late-lingering, crusty snow and watching the dorm's polite and tidy burning, floor by floor, room by room; one student's cry of "Don't take that ladder away, the coach is up there!" and the cheerful response, "Let him burn!" as the ladder was removed; firemen snowballing out the flames on an adjacent roof; the post-conflagration rat phobia, which caused the "Around the Campus" column in a spring *Scrawl* to announce alarmingly, "Rats in the girls' dorm—BEWARE. Your life isn't worth a cent!!"

The 1956 fire led to Higgins's only professional fund drive. It was headed by Leone Dakin Nutting ('21), who put out a very slick booklet called *Oblivion or Opportunity*, and even if nobody pledged the enormous sums suggested in the booklet's "formula that will assure success," one gets the sense from reading the ledger of pledges and payments that some of the fifty- and twenty- and maybe even ten-dollar donations meant some deprivation to the givers. Higgins alumni on the whole were not wealthy and were unaccustomed to alumni solicitations, but the drive was a success in any case.

The three-story masonry and steel building that replaced Tibbetts Hall II was low on charm but high on fire resistance. Leon Thorsen ('26), a Higgins trustee, saved the day financially by drawing up the plans himself and supervising all problems of construction, but he was not an architect and the dorm looks a good bit like a shoebox. Efforts to soften its contours with ivy have made it look like a shoebox abandoned to the forces of nature. Inside, the walls are painted cinderblock, and such grace notes as closets were a long time in coming. Perry Wortman added the final touches in 1964.

But I should not speak lightly of the newest dorm, for the lounge, directly across from the front door, was named for a dear friend and classmate, David Gray, and the dorm itself was named for my father. He must have been deeply gratified at the dedication, though good New Englanders do not go in for effusion. Before that he had once or twice, in the bosom of the family, remarked that through all his years at the school, his going into the army and his coming back, his retiring, all anyone had ever given him was one letter sweater. The dorm must have made it right. My friend Bobbie Simpson, who was assigned to do a piece about my father's life in the November *Scrawl* that year, endearingly asserts that in having Tracy Hall named after him, "he was awarded one of the greatest honors a man could receive." Nobel Prize be damned.

The second Tibbetts Hall, to get back to our tour, is built on higher ground than the gym and the Institute, and just where the sidewalk goes downhill, at the south end of the dorm, some architect or builder with a heart has added two brick and concrete excrescences, like elongated steps or backless settees. (You can just glimpse the highest one in the photo.) It's possible that they have some anti-erosion function, but everyone regards them as recreational. Measuring from memory, the one nearer the dorm is perhaps six feet long, two feet wide, eighteen inches high where the ground is lowest; the other is smaller. A reader to whom this seems a tedious description of two slabs of brick and concrete has never sat there with his or her beloved, concrete cool and rough under the thighs, grass brushing the feet, gazing past the forsythia bush.

Between the dorm and the Institute lies a tennis court. Tennis courts have been there since 1899, though interest in tennis has waxed and waned. Doris Spencer ('18) remembers that her friend Jack used to climb onto the roof and whistle for her to join him in a prebreakfast tennis game. The court was cracked and weedy clay when I first remember it, but later it was blacktopped and tennis picked up again. Across from the court, on the lawn, sits the flagpole, which, like the sidewalks, is more of a presence than the urban will understand.

Behind the tennis court lies the gym, built in 1929. No building on campus was so long and so passionately desired. When the Institute was built in 1902, the students said that they were sure it would be very nice, and yes they looked forward to it, but they had been very fond of the old Academy Building and would miss it. No comments about the dorms are on record, but presumably students were already comfortable somewhere; indeed the accommodations at the old Trustee House, hotel by summer and dorm by winter, may have been more luxurious. But the gym! Cries and fulminations echo down the years: student publications, trustees' minutes, draft letters of my father's—they all go on about it. A gym of sorts existed in the Trustee House stable; photographs show gas lamps on brackets, a vaulting horse, and rings hanging from the rafters. It purportedly contained one hoop and a basketball as well. Another makeshift gym was set up in one room of the Institute basement, for I find in Principal Philip Keith's master's thesis an allusion to a physical culture class in 1904 doing exercises there to music. But these were not proper gyms.

In 1905 the Oak Hill Lodge of Good Templars gave Higgins its old lodge for a gym; it was dragged onto campus and put between the Institute and the boys' dorm, roughly where the 1929 gym stands now. It helped, and everyone was grateful, but still it wasn't a very good gym and certainly not large enough. The Winter 1909 *Scroll* notes that an oyster stew supper and social have been held to raise money for gym improvement, and that there has been a tag day as well, ten cents a tag. The writer remarks with as much cheer as he or she can muster that now the gym is "nearly as large as regulation." But by 1910 the cheer has worn off; a student editorial in the March *Scroll*, entitled "Higgins' Greatest Need," asserts that a gym is it. The writer craftily argues that "A boy who has spent an hour in a gymnasium after school with the basket-ball or medicine-ball, will not feel like throwing a dumb-bell or a jug down the corridor during study hours to mar the disposition of a teacher." Evidently nobody fell for this misleading assessment of student energies, but I am very much taken with the period quality of the missiles. Apparently what changes over the decades is not adolescent behavior, but what one throws. In 1915 the students are still grousing: Principal McLellan himself has coached the basketball team, which has done better than expected despite having "no suitable place to play in."

In 1919 the school tried another solution, using what had been the Free Temple Baptist Church as their gym. The Free Temple and the Free Will churches had in 1917 joined to become the United Baptist Church and moved to the Free Will's building. (Only the two women's groups, the Mission Circle and the Ladies' Aid, declined to merge.) Free Temple had been the Reverend John's church, which is perhaps how the school came to get hold of it, and logically it would have been the church to which Higgins students were sent on a Sunday, so some of them may have had the odd experience of using it first for worship, later for basketball. It must have been larger than the donated lodge, but it was as far from campus as the Trustee House (not very nice for sweaty players in the winter), and still not large enough for many spectators. Ted Emery's editorial in the 1922 *Scroll* says that it's too small, too far away, too cold, and you have to stand up to watch a game; he thinks Higgins needs a new gym. Leon Williams tells me that the baskets had to be in opposite corners. He has passed on as well the once famous attempt of a new student and good ball player, Wendell Thornton ('24), to be polite on first seeing the Free Temple makeshift: "It's nice and *high*," he said.

On June 17, 1927, the Board of Trustees admitted that Higgins did in fact need a new gym and instructed my father to contact an architect and to buy lumber if he could get it for thirty dollars per thousand board feet. The building of the gym seems to have been a remarkably communal project. One graduate of the class of 1934 wrote, "My father donated many loads of field stones when they built the gym—that cleaned up the old rock walls and made our fields easier to till and we were happy to be a part of the building." Charles ("Shine") Higgins ('40) tells me that the bricks for the gym came up from Bangor on the electric cars and sat on the siding until the farmers and their sons were free at the end of the day. Then they brought their rigs and unloaded bricks and hauled them up to the building site, hard work after a day in the fields. The 1930 *Scroll* photos show all the teams posed before the raw brick entrance, wallowing proudly in the loose sand.

As I write I am looking at an old picture of the gym's interior. I take this to be quite an early photo, for there are no dents in the ceiling from too enthusiastically hurled basketballs, no bleachers yet (just rows of folding chairs), and the gold trim on the stage curtains looks bright and new. Light from the windows reflects off the shiny newness of walls, ceilings, girders, floor. The floor, by the way, must have been somehow defective—there comes to me a faint memory of improperly cured lumber—for it was relaid in 1938. Treasurer Frank Higgins's journal specifies that the 1938 floor used 4700 board feet of hard pine and that, after it was sanded, two women and one man washed the floor for three days each before it was varnished. I don't know in what way the performance of the women was unsatisfactory, but a loose memo in Frank Higgins's famous copperplate says, "Next time hire men to wash" and notes disapprovingly that two mops (the women's mops?) had been left in the varnish in nearly empty cans.

The stage at the north end is a well-loved feature of the gym, and one that Ted Emery's editorial had recommended. It serves not only for school plays but for the giving of awards and diplomas. The off-stage areas on either side are adequate (though I believe that actors, like basketball players, tended to arrive already dressed), but any upstage area of substance must be created with scenery; the stage is one enormous tongue-and-groove room. We always give one-indoor-set plays, for we live in Maine and know when not to fight nature. A cover lifts to reveal a row of footlights. The curtain is theatrically heavy and dusty, decorated with the school's monogram in tarnished Old English letters above scallops of gold fringe. By my time it is a muted brown, but it may have faded from something livelier. During basketball games a net is stretched in front of the curtain to prevent shots that miss the backboard from rolling onstage.

Downstairs, on the south end of the basement, beside the indoor jumping pit, we find that malodorous bastion of masculinity, the Smoker, a spot so murky, so redolent of sweat and tobacco and who knows what, that even in the empty summer it seemed too alien a turf for little girls to tread. I remember my own high school contemporaries grouped around its doorway with their cigarettes, suddenly too confident and slouchy and inclined to shout wise remarks. No doubt it was loved for just such reasons, so I shall pass on the remarks of an initiate who can do it better justice than I. Ormonde Brown ('47) writes:

> My favorite spot on campus was the "Smoker." . . . This is where you got to know the real person inside the student. This is where friendships grew among the boys. Conversations from "how to roll your own" (during the war cigarettes were sent overseas) to what made Chaucer tick became great entertainment and relaxation. . . . This was really the only place on campus where you had a lot of laughs and entertainment in an informal atmosphere. Some boys who didn't smoke would even come down for the "fun of it." This was the spot where nicknames were born.

He notes as well that there were ritual whacks of initiation until the veterans came back from the war and refused to play.

Male teachers as well as boys—no provisions were made for female vice—were obliged to use the smoker, at least during school hours. I remember how longingly a teacher of mine would look out the window toward the smoker as class wore on, how he would shake out a cigarette when the period was almost over and put it behind his ear, and how he would dash down the front steps at the bell, matches already in his hand. We did not dislike him, but we watched his suffering with pleasure and interest.

The red brick heating plant (new in 1931) sits behind the gym, shaped like the gym but smaller, and almost buried under mountains of coal. My brother reports being impressed by the large and handsome school seals on the boilers, but the heating plant is rather a bad-luck spot. Besides the predictable disasters caused by inattentive student firemen, a student died there in 1944, of which more later.

And while it was being built, one of the workmen was hit on the head by a falling brick. (He kept right on working, but for the rest of his long life he was a little chuckleheaded, inclined to sing elaborate songs about kissing old maids and widows, and to forget what he was about.)

Now we come to the *piéce de resistance*, the Institute itself. That the classroom building is by tradition called "the Institute" is significant. If you handed a pencil to any graduate from the class of 1902 on and said, "Draw Higgins," you'd be likely to get a sketch of the Institute, its triple-arched entrance and three peaks. Here is the focus and embodiment of the school. The granite slab inset over the arches is chiseled with the school's name and its date of foundation. The Institute building needs no ivy to make it look like the right sort of school, though it has worn a bit since the camouflaging of Tracy Hall, and wears it well.

Its predecessor (almost but not quite identical, like the predecessor of the second Tibbetts Hall) burned on December 12, 1930. That fire is of particular interest to me, for I suppose that I owe my existence to it. In 1930 my father had been head of Higgins for better than a dozen years, had made a reputation as an educator, was in his early forties, and not unnaturally was thinking of moving on. He was considering the headmastership of a school rather more upscale—Gould Academy, I think, though I may be wrong about that. And then the Institute burned. How could a man with an ounce of loyalty or sentimentality (and he had more than an ounce of both) desert his school in such a crisis? He didn't, of course. Indeed, he turned his salary back to the building fund for a year and settled in for the duration of his career. My mother came to Higgins to teach in 1937.

Not much was saved from the fire—some school records, a few artifacts from the library and the chapel. The fire, which started in an overheated basement stove, traveled up an air shaft to the attic. Fire departments from Dover and Bangor were on hand an hour and a half after the fire was discovered and might have confined the damage to the roof had there been sufficient water. Fire Chief Nason told the *Bangor Daily News* (12/18/30) that "it was a wicked sight to stand about and see the fine building go to destruction for lack of water."

The school, again, managed admirably, holding classes in reception rooms, in the gym basement and on the stage, and study hall in the dining room. Everyone took gym just before lunch so tables could be set. Boys and girls alternated use of the gym—boys got it oftener—one sex exercising inside while the other went on what must in January have been pretty grim hikes.

The old Institute, which cost $100,000 in 1902, was designed by Wilfred E. Mansur, at that time one of Maine's most distinguished architects. It differed most conspicuously from the new in that it possessed a cupola with a bell, a bell that Sabra Lee ('18) tells me you could hear far out in the country. And Lucetta Doore ('14) says that in her senior year—emboldened by status, no doubt—she and Violet Lovejoy used to climb up to the cupola and study beside the bell. Phillip Hamm ('35), who watched the fire and remembers seeing the belfry tip over and go down through the building, says that the bell apparently melted, for no trace of it was found. The old third story was more commodious, two real windows in the center instead of the little round one, three windows on each outside peak; there were laboratories up here ("the best in the state," boasts a school catalogue) that were moved to the basement in the new building, and meeting rooms that were not replaced. Some subtler internal changes resulted, too. Harriet Lord ('30), who attended classes in the old building and taught in the new, complains that for her the new chapel always faced the wrong way.

But part of the old Institute is also the new Institute, for the fire left portions of the first floor standing. The brick pillars and the granite sign, for instance, are original, and you can see a slight difference in the color of the brick, like a water line, where the old and new join. We'll go up the granite steps, over the giant door mat with HCI in the middle, and through the entrance that Brad Brown ('47) remembers, lighted in the early winter dark, as the finest spot on campus. The entry hall contains only a World War II Roll of Honor on the left wall and opens into the main corridor, which runs north and south.

The woodwork is light oak, generous in its moldings and baseboards; the walls are of plaster covered with a kind of stout oilcloth painted in two shades of glossy brown, slightly more chocolate below an ornamental oak strip, slightly creamier above it. Oak-framed steel engravings of famous monuments—the Colosseum, the Arch of

Constantine—ornament the walls at dignified intervals. The State Department of Education's accreditation committee will insist in 1960 that Principal Perry Wortman redecorate with "a judicious use of color," bulletin boards, and pictures "of interest to young people." They would have been baffled to see me loitering through the halls alone during first-day break in my freshman year, running my hands over those absolutely right brown walls, staring at those perfect engravings, marveling that I'd really lived long enough to start at Higgins, that my time had come.

The south end of the corridor is one of the good sitting places, like the concrete slabs on the side of Tibbetts Hall. Six tall windows with oak window seats offer perhaps the most idyllic spot in the building, especially when the windows are open in spring. Day students remember with the greatest affection sitting there to eat their lunches, and I can assure you that moments spent there, even without lunch, linger fondly in the memory. It is from these windows, too, that high school boys sometimes throw pennies down to the elementary school children who attend the model classrooms in the basement and play outside the building at recess, as tourists throw coins to little native swimmers, to see them scramble and dive. Both throwers and catchers revel in this sport, but the elementary school teachers deplore it and send complaints to the principal.

This seems a convenient place to detour and explain the Institute basement. Besides the science laboratory (where in 1956–57 my peers were assembling glorious confections of gunpowder, especially one memorable bomb in a trombone mute), the basement contains two elementary school classrooms of three grades each, a book storage closet, and the facilities known as "the girls' basement" and "the boys' basement." Even in subprimary I thought it ludicrous that we asked to "go to the basement" when any fool could see that we were already in the basement, but one marvelous boy (who at his academic best maintained only an intermittent hold on the principles of coat-buttoning) took yet a firmer view of its silliness than I did. "I gotta pee," he'd announce, shooting up his hand. "Now, that's not what we say in school, is it?" the teacher would remind him for perhaps the fiftieth time. "We say, 'I need to go to the basement.' " "Yeah," he'd reply, "but I gotta pee."

The model classrooms were so called from their days as a corollary to Higgins's Teacher Training course, a program that lasted until 1932, when legislation stiffened state requirements for certification. Perhaps Higgins would have rebuilt differently in 1931 had it been able to see ahead, or perhaps its friendly relations with the town would have compelled it to keep up the cohabitation in any case. Having spent six years in these classrooms myself, I can report that they are attractive, with decent windows on the west side and dark oiled floors with engaging cracks full of fuzz, good for dragging one's pencil point in (and sometimes breaking it). The corridor, on the other hand, is gloomy, dank, and on some days, thanks to the chemistry lab, filled with the smell of rotten eggs. "Hydrogen sulfide again," the youngest child learned to sigh, feeling sophisticated. It was almost worth the stench.

Back from the detour, let's look at the first floor. The library occupies the southeast corner. As we come in, the long wall to our right is lined with glass-fronted barrister bookcases. One alumnus told me that only four or five years ago, fifty-five years after his graduation, he saw and could not resist buying a set of bookcases like the library's. On top of the bookcases sit three plaster busts, the larger two each a full thirty-six inches high, and the basketball trophies. The busts were given by the classes of 1906, 1907, and 1908; they represent Shakespeare, Longfellow, and a third literary-looking gentleman who is perhaps Tennyson, perhaps Whittier. Shakespeare is smallest and therefore probably the gift of 1906, for students would dislike falling short of their predecessors, and Shakespeare is the most obvious choice. Longfellow is unmistakable, a replica of the bust in Westminster Abbey, though the 1908–09 catalogue unnervingly refers to busts of Shakespeare, Tennyson, and Zeus. Perhaps Higgins once possessed a bust of Zeus (an odd acquisition for a Baptist school), but the Longfellow bust appears in a photo of the old Institute's library. The third bust is marked on its back, in what looks like my father's writing, "Gift of the Class of 1907," and the 1907 *Scroll*, which ought to know, says that there are busts of Shakespeare, Longfellow, and Whittier. It's worrisome. Alumni were unable to help me identify these, though several old grads spoke with warmth and wit of other busts they remembered better, and John Nicholson ('41) provided my favorite speculation—Venus, Socrates, and Mr. Tracy.

On the north wall hangs the piece that a number of alumni do remember with particular love, a huge—perhaps five feet by seven feet—arrangement of butterflies and insects in a heavy frame, given to the school by the founder's nephew, Franklin Higgins. Butterflies lie in a great golden horseshoe, their colors surrounded and set off by specimens in iridescent blue and pale green. Rows of beetles (and a brace of mean-looking scorpions) add aesthetic weight, but mostly it's butterflies, mounted on stained cotton batting, and a few moths. It draws the eye first and longest.

On the opposite wall hangs the wild-eyed head of an elk, a gift from the same source; from time to time over the years it holds a wicked cigarette between its dry lips. Near it a copy of Giovanni Bologna's Mercury stands tiptoe on a pedestal. Most of the library equipment (and not much else) was saved in the fire of 1931, but some things have disappeared—Johnny Bradeen's model of Caesar's bridge, the "fine specimen of blue heron" presented by Frank Gillingham ('09) and Principal Wortman, the portraits of Charlie and H. L. Tibbetts, the framed photo of the University of Pennsylvania. Although, I fear, more of an artifact than an intellectual resource, the library is nevertheless the finest artifact on campus. Until 1965 called Tibbetts Library, it was in that year appropriately renamed for Philip Keith ('21), a book-loving man who was principal from 1948 to 1953 and indeed gave his whole life to Higgins. By 1965 the library seems to have been more in use.

Other than the library and a home-economics room, the principal room on the first floor is the Chapel, which occupies the entire north end. It is called the Chapel, not the auditorium, even though it contains no religious trappings, and what we do there is also called Chapel—that is, when it isn't called Prize Speaking or National Honor Society or Friday Night Movies. There's a low platform at the west end, with a tall chair for the principal in its center and shorter chairs for the faculty on either side. It is possible that the faculty do not enjoy the scrutiny of two hundred pairs of eyes as they confront the student body (boys on their right, girls on their left) in its sections of folding wooden seats. The boys' side has the flag and a portrait of the Reverend John Higgins with his nice little round beard; the girls' side has the piano. Here, every morning before classes begin, the school assembles. There are announcements, a prayer, a few hymns— "Are Ye Able, Said the Master," or "Oh Jesus, Thou Art Standing," or perhaps "Follow the Gleam"—slightly more restrained numbers than we sing at church. It may be that we pledge allegiance to the flag, but I forget. And often there are Chapel Talks by the principal or once in a while by a guest speaker. I find the first reference to Chapel Talks in the 1908–09 catalogue:

> These talks are for the purpose of enthusing the minds of the students for honest, earnest, and thorough work in their studies; to call attention to current events and signs of the times; to acquaint them with men who are in the public eye; to raise the ideals by pointing each mind to the nobler motives and deeds in life as illustrated by Christian men and women.

My father was called in once while I was at Higgins and gave what I suspect was a good, mainline, representative Chapel Talk; it was about how Abraham Lincoln's dying mother said to him, "Abe, be something," and how we should take the same message to heart.

Information from my brother's time and later suggests that speakers then were fewer but more dramatic. He remembers a quick-change artist, and a sports columnist telling Eskimo jokes. Rae Smith ('72) recalls a speaker whose larynx had been removed because of smoking-induced cancer—the moral of that talk is clear—and Michael Gallant ('71) reports having passed out when a Vietnam medic gave a Chapel Talk with color slides.

I imagined when I sent out my questionnaire that Chapel Talks would be a good source of philosophy and educational policy, and that my father at any rate had probably liked doing them and thrown himself into them. I found out what of course I should have known, that mostly the students had not been listening. There was some consensus that my father's message was often tersely practical—"Someone is taking Mr. A's apples from his orchard; I expect it to stop"—varied by observations like "The first man to lay down his shovel is the poorest workman" and "I hope you're all homesick, because that means you have a home worth missing."

Pithy though it is, this is pale stuff compared to the talks he gave me. I suppose that because I was his own daughter, he wanted to make sure that life wouldn't catch me with my guard down, and of course he was able to speak more freely at home. In any case, he skipped "the nobler motives and deeds in life" and dealt out nuggets of alarming cynicism, like, "The quickest way to make a man your enemy is to do him a favor," and "Your neighbors can forgive you anything except success." These pronouncements he usually ended by warning, "—and that's the way of the world." I was a disappointing audience for truth, as I invariably burst into tears at the prospect of one more bad news bulletin from the universe. Though this distressed him, paternal affection urged him on. He would say kindly just before each revelation, "Now I'm not scolding" (this was the misapprehension he had decided I was under), a foreshadowing that merely permitted me to begin weeping one line earlier. However, I must say that as an adult I am seldom shocked or disillusioned by human behavior, and for this immunity I am indebted. I should say as well that in the teeth of his own philosophy my father went right on doing favors furiously, dragging hungry-looking children into lunchrooms, helping boys through college, devising unsuccessful schemes to stand the floppy and indigent on their feet through discreet self-help investments.

On the second floor of the Institute are the classrooms—nine, says a catalogue, though I can't think of more than six—and, until Perry Wortman's time, the principal's office, a small room with a paper-storage annex, a file cabinet, a roll-top desk, and a table. There is no secretary, which means that the principal, who also teaches, is blessedly obliged from time to time to run out and answer the phone. The biggest room on the second floor, occupying the whole south end, is the main study hall. Here boys study for two hours at night, while girls work in the smaller room next door. These supervised study halls are deemed crucial to the functioning of the school, a major reason why parents should send their children. They must have been a long, itchy, weary, hungry business for some, but no doubt even the least intellectually inclined did study a certain amount by default of other entertainment. It is not unusual to hear alumni attribute the more sterling habits of adult life to those study halls.

Food, or the prospect of food, seems to have made study hall more tolerable. One repetitive golden memory from graduates in the twenties was that Leon ("Ben") Williams ('28) would come around after study hall, selling hot dogs out of his foot locker. In fact, those hot dogs are memorialized by an anonymous verse in the 1928 *Scroll*:

HOT DOGS TONIGHT

Ben Williams is a popular boy,
Toward half-past nine each night,
The ways the girls all rush to him
Is an amazing sight.
When they hear his melodious voice
Loudly shout, "Hot dogs!"
You'd think that each and every one
Descended from the frogs.
They hop and jump and skip and leap,
And borrow lacking money;
Then they crowd around poor Ben
Like bees around wild honey.
Poor Ben slings mustard and makes change
And sometimes conversation.
Then the girls go back upstairs
As pleased as all creation.

My father was proud of Ben's initiative and is reported by Myrtle Paine ('27) to have said, "Give that boy a basket of chips and he'd make a living," a nice piece of foreshadowing, for Leon Williams now owns a large and prosperous lumber business. In my own time at Higgins there was a seller of ice cream during study hall break who was crucial to a complicated scheme of boy-girl note passing via the fire extinguisher, though none of the participants can now recall the details of how it was done.

Beside the second-floor stairwell, one more short flight leads up to the attic. It's a good attic and a lot of people never see it. It's locked, and you have to be given the key by the principal—you have to *be* somebody, in short, with a purpose. (Or alternatively, I suppose, you have to pick the lock and be a proper malefactor.) This is where we come to get the portrait whose eyes, we are sure, follow us, an artistic touch for the mystery/comedies we favor for class plays. I know now that this is a portrait of H. Warren Foss, principal from 1896 to 1903, which was presented to the school by the class of 1904. The Reverend John's was the only portrait rehung in the new Institute. The attic is well floored, open, raftered. The light from the windows catches motes of dust, but the place doesn't feel dirty. There's an agreeable absence of spiders: perhaps all that exposed asbestos insulation isn't good for them. It probably isn't good for us, either, but we won't stay long. There's a big enclosed water tank—a couple of friends and I un-did some expensive plumbing there with the purest of intentions one day; you can see why the attic is locked—and piles of textbooks, foot-ball gear, band uniforms, boxes of crepe-paper streamers.

It may seem that the attic is an unlikely place to end a tour, but not this tour—for what is this whole book, after all, but a tour of the attic?

III

STUDENT BODY

Dormitory life was something of a shock (all those people!). At home in Sebec I had one older sister, and the nearest neighbor was nearly a mile away. I was both shy and a little cocky—if anyone crossed me, I fought. I had a lot of fights that first year.

—WILLIS PARKER ('39)

Higgins was designed by its founder for Maine students, especially those to whom secondary education was not otherwise available, those whose towns had no high schools and whose parents had no money. The boys and girls at Higgins resembled the popular stereotype of prep school students chiefly in their sense of privilege and consequent superiority. By keeping costs down and permitting needy students to work much of their room and board, Higgins attracted a core of ambitious, low-income boys and girls, who, far from being charity cases, were by their own labor giving themselves a bona fide prep school experience and were justifiably proud of it. Some students worked a lot, some a little, some not at all, but the family incomes were not necessarily very different, for Maine is not a prosperous state. (Even now it ranks only thirty-sixth in per capita income, and that statistic represents progress.) An illness, a new baby, a bad growing season, one more child in high school—any one of these could make the difference between being able to pay and needing help. Sometimes alumni whose parents had managed to pay part or even all of their expenses still knew exactly where the money had come from. Margaret Bishop ('41) told me that she had worked her way, but she thought that her father had sold a cow or two. Robert Houghton ('37) told me that his father, who raised tulips and glads as a hobby, paid for his education with the Memorial Day flower receipts. I need not belabor the advantages of having a school full of students for whom the price of education is so concrete.

Some students who could have attended public schools found the opportunity to board a relief from hardship, especially early on. Walter Elden ('27) wrote to describe his schooling difficulties before he went to Higgins:

> My first two years at high school were spent at Bradford High. I lived five miles from the school and attended it by horse and wagon through all kinds of weather, stabling my horse in a barn not far from the school. During the winter after too much snow for my horse to travel I used to get up early in the morning and snowshoe or ski across country in time for my classes until the road was suitable for travel. . . . Early after school had closed Mr. William Tracy came to see me and my folks and after he had found out how I had labored to get to school he offered me a chance to go to Higgins and work my way. My father accepted the offer and I heard Mr. Tracy tell Dad that my sister had been such a good student while learning her teachers course that he was sure I would be the same. I studied my lessons hard and enjoyed my stay at the Dorm.

Myrtle Paine ('27) and her brother, whose home town of Atkinson had no high school, could have gone to Foxcroft Academy, but "this meant living with an eccentric aunt. We did not want to do that." For them, too, dorms were a haven. Students accustomed to farm chores must, in all periods, have found boarding school life a welcome respite.

In 1941, to pick a year at random, only eight of the 179 students came from outside Maine. Out-of-state students were not actively turned away, but a kind of natural selection kept their numbers small. Not many non-Maine parents, however ill-disposed, seriously consider exiling their own flesh north of Bangor for the winter.

Maine students, on the other hand, were actively sought out. Former principal Perry Wortman explained to me, when I interviewed him, why he had mutinously asserted that Higgins was not a prep school but a public high school with a boarding section: prep schools have students beating down their doors to get in, whereas at Higgins you had to go out and drum up the students yourself. True enough, you did. When students are in danger of getting no education at all, nothing in their world may lead them or their parents to suspect that a prep school education is possible.

"Soliciting students," the process was called, or sometimes "road work" (as in "Due to traveling conditions we have done very little road work"). Thanks to alumni, I can provide some recollections of how it was done.

> Mr. Tracy came to see my parents on a hot July day; my brother and I were out in the field picking wild strawberries. The family liked him but Dad felt he could not afford to send us both, we were just a year apart in age. Mr. Tracy said my marks were good enough for a scholarship and we could both work and we did. —FRANCIS WARD ('38)

> I graduated from H.S. and worked for two years on the Canadian Pacific R.R. I needed to sharpen up my educational program. Bill Tracy came to my home, offered me a $150 scholarship and a job. That's all I needed. I was a poor boy and this was opportunity, a truly American dream. . . . I had lost my dad in a railroad accident when I was 8 months old. This offer was pure frosting! —RAYMOND FARNHAM ('31)

> I'll never forget his first visit to our home to talk with mother and Brad about attending Higgins (Brad went all four years, I went three). His black Buick automobile, the stick pin in his tie and his friendly manner convinced both Brad and mother that Higgins was the place to go. I stayed in the kitchen and listened to the three of them talk. I was envious. . . . —ORMONDE BROWN ('47)

> I had worked through potato harvest and had gone five miles back into the woods, living alone in a log cabin and cutting cord wood. One weekend when I came for groceries I met Mr. Tracy and he asked if I would like to come back for a postgraduate and play basketball, live in the dorm and work my

board and room at the kitchen duty. If so he would then loan me money to go to Colby and I could work on his farms in Cary in the summer. I wasn't that good at basketball but I had been given an opportunity to join society again and save face as a lumberjack. Mr. Tracy was always helping students to get their lives back on track and establish some worthwhile goals.
—WILDER PEARL ('37)

Such road work, although arduous, must have been joyful. Imagine the gratification of pulling the rabbit out of the hat, making the magical offer and seeing the recipient light up at the prospect of an education and ultimate escape from poverty. Although the passages above make it sound as though students thus solicited dropped into my father's hands, and to some degree they seem to have, he could never forbear the fun of making a crafty sales pitch. He used to tell my mother and me how he'd subtly change his conjunction from "*if* your girl comes to Higgins" to "*when* your girl comes to Higgins." Nothing pleased him more than to sidle up to a boy whose mind the thought had never crossed and say, "I understand that you're interested in going to boarding school," and then watch the boy's growing conviction that boarding school was exactly what he wanted.

With these tricks in mind, I asked Hugh Smith (who solicited at various times not only for Coburn and for Ricker, but for Higgins under four principals including my father) what his sales gimmicks had been, how he had gone about the job. Why, he said, he just told the truth about the school and then people came if they wanted to. His method was clearly sufficient; I should have remembered that my father in fact relished strategy for its own sake. He had a fine baroque turn of mind that revelled in loops and turnings and psychological fake-outs and previously unconceived shortcuts in mental math; he never got over the delight of once having achieved some financial end by foreclosing a mortgage on himself.

My favorite story, perhaps, about the acquisition of students shows not only Hugh Smith's straightforwardness but the difficulties of dealing with taciturn Mainers. He had dragged a boy and his father all over campus, telling them everything he could think of and evoking not a question, not a smile, not a comment. He could hardly wait to have the fiasco over, but, dutiful, he stuck out his song and dance to the end. Then the father opened his mouth for the first time. "Well, d'you want to come?" he said to the boy. "Yes, I do," said the boy. That was the whole discussion.

Although Higgins advertised in the usual ways—listed in the Porter-Sargeant guide to private schools, planted its catalogues in doctors' offices, and so on—it also relied upon its graduates and trustees and assorted well-wishers to spot prospects. My father's sister Geneva kept a canny eye out for candidates in the Houlton area, for instance, and several alumni artlessly told me that they knew about Higgins, of course, because their eighth-grade teacher had gone there, but they couldn't imagine how Mr. Tracy had heard about *them*.

On July 13, 1942, my father writes to a teacher who is resigning to take a more convenient job, "Students are coming in just medium. If you see any students down your way, I would appreciate any help which you could give me in obtaining them." In an undated draft from about the same period he appeals to an appended list of sixteen men, some of whom I recognize as alumni, to hunt up a few more boys: "I am asking your cooperation and help. For the first time in the last decade our boys' dormitory is not filled. This condition is due to the high wages which are attracting boys from school. I need 12 more boys. Can you contact one or two desirable boys? I or a member of my faculty will call on them if you deem it advisable." At about the same time, too, he writes to a Bangor man and cancels a $23.50 debt to the school "in payment for the work which you have done in obtaining students for Higgins."

Other schools were soliciting the same territory in one way or another, but the principals seem for the most part to have competed like gentlemen. A number of extant letter drafts recommend to applicants beyond the capacity of Higgins's dormitories that they try Coburn, or sometimes Coburn and Ricker. Those schools seem to have had the closest ties with Higgins, but one draft responds to a polite offer from Fryeburg, which has found itself with a surplus of girls that year: "Thank you for your offer on girls. However, my girls' dormitory is full. There may come a year when I would appreciate such an offer. In turn I will gladly recommend students to Fryeburg if you should have a year when enrollment was not so good."

It is also possible to make out from the drafts a form of etiquette observed when a student from School A writes to School B for a catalogue: the head of B writes to the head of A for permission to send it, and A replies that of course he would not wish to keep the student against his or her inclination. Now and then someone broke the rules, as in the spring of 1940 when the principal at Ricker seems to have overstepped, making surreptitious contacts with Higgins students on a visit to campus and sending them letters after he left. This poaching provoked a much-redrafted shout of outrage and a withdrawal of a previously issued invitation to come back the next year.

Not that all Higgins students waited to be discovered. Wilmot Oliver ('39), now Dean of Instruction at Ocean County College in New Jersey, had finished only one year of high school when his father made him drop out and work in the woods. He took his future into his own hands one day in the summer of 1936 and approached my father in a potato field in Cary, the northern Maine settlement where they had both been born and brought up, and where my father returned frequently to help with the family farm. "William," he said, "do you think that I could get an opportunity to work my room and board down at Higgins this fall?"

> William's response to this question was, "I am going back to Higgins this week and I'll be back in two weeks and I will talk to the Board and determine whether or not we can work this out." This was the longest two weeks of my life. When he did come back and indicated that I could attend Higgins and work room and board I was indeed the happiest boy in Aroostook County. However, I had several seemingly insurmountable obstacles to over-come at that point in time. First of all, my father insisted that I stay home and work for him. Secondly, I had no money with which to buy clothing and bedding required to attend a boarding school. It was at this time that my mother interceded and told me that she would take care of my father's opposition and that she would purchase the necessary clothes from the Puritan store in Houlton on credit and pay for them by picking potatoes during that fall. It was indeed a red letter day for me.

Like all boarding schools, Higgins relied to some degree upon the blessing of families who sent it successive generations, or even all the siblings of one generation. The Maces from Aurora, for instance, went to Higgins: Douglas, Asa, Bertha, Charlotte, Frank, Mary, Dot, and Ansel—all eight of them. Their mother, a fine flamboyant figure who wore a turban, would every year or so come bearing us another of her lively brood, present it with a flourish, and say, "You think my other kids are smart, this is the best one I got." Ruby Marden ('18) came back in the thirties and put her three children through Higgins by supervising half the dorm and being pastry cook. Harriet Lord ('30) moved back to Charleston so that her four boys could attend as day students.

To say that nearly all of us were from Maine is not to say that we were especially homogeneous. Students raised in lumber camps, on farms, in villages, on islands, or in small cities brought with them different areas of experience and ignorance. The novelties that alumni say they first met at Higgins include plumbing, the Bible, arguments without fisticuffs, black people, football, electricity, male teachers, and crowds. Jake Bishop ('55) remembers a boy who couldn't get the hang of hard-boiled eggs, so the teacher or senior who headed his table had to peel them for him. But sophistication usually varied within a restricted range. Slightly off the upper edge of the range would have been a girl six or seven years older than I who came from New York City and *owned an evening bag*. Slightly farther off the lower edge would have been a girl whom Eleanor Mills, a music teacher at Higgins in the late thirties, recalls as having been so terrified of flushing a toilet that someone else would have to pull the chain while she fled its redoubtable roar.

We were all polished enough to know some facts about Europe but none of us had ever been there. Some of us expected to get there sooner or later, even without joining the military, and some of us neither expected to nor wanted to. We all wore some vague facsimile of current fashion, but few, perhaps none, of us could have imagined the pale green suede ball gown that a student of my own, years later at Cushing Academy, casually produced for a dance. Neal Brown ('56) writes:

> Being poorer seemed to make little difference, because most of us were from families with either immediate or recent roots in the lower socio-economic classes. Being rich was rare, and therefore, was likely to distinguish one from his mates. Of course, there were occasional expressions of envy and jealousy

of the more affluent student, but this was rare. HCI was by no means seriously afflicted with the problems of snobbery and class distinctions for which the elite prep schools of the east were, and remain, noted.

And neither sophistication nor economic variables seemed to affect the things that were valued by the student body—brains, a fine singing voice, wit, a pretty face, athletic ability.

It would be misleading, of course, to imply that Higgins was peopled entirely by pure-hearted rustic types. Like any boarding school, it had a migratory smattering of hard cases whose earlier schools had declined to keep them. Often we rather liked them. Indeed, some worked out and ceased to migrate. Others, exotic incorrigibles with nicknames like Catman, March Hare, Tinkerbell, flashed across our horizons, leaving behind them an agreeable whiff of brimstone, and were gone. After offering brief instruction in lock-picking and other useful skills, they would commit, or be the victims of, unspeakably depraved acts, and would be sent away, or run away, yet again. There were a lot of only mildly troublesome students, too—troublesome at home, that is, not at Higgins. "My father thought going to school two days a week wasn't sufficient, so he sent me to Higgins," says Pete Minott ('38).

Though students came from all over the state, one geographical subgroup deserves special mention for its importance to Higgins. Always, and I think increasingly over the years, Higgins drew students from the Maine coast and more especially from the islands—Swans Island, Matinicus, Beals Island, and so on. By the sixties the school was running a bus to the coast so that the students' fathers needn't lose a day's lobstering. Those islanders were an asset to the tone of the school. Perhaps I can remember only the ones I liked, or perhaps they were well and thoroughly presorted, but they seem to me to have been consistently likeable, talented, and upright. The boys arrived, my brother tells me, with their footlockers full of stripfish, that coastal Maine delicacy produced by salt-drying raw fish in the sun, and induced a schoolwide taste for it by passing it around the bus on athletic trips.

The landlocked life of central Maine was an adjustment for the merely coastal, let alone the islanders. George Smith ('52) admits that he was "rather homesick for the coast of Maine. No fault of the school." Lucien Green ('32) writes, "I used to hitchhike home every weekend as I wanted to see the ocean." The 1950 *Scroll* comments, under Charles Stinson's graduation photo, "Charlie has made many friends here at Higgins but we believe his heart has been at sea all the time. Best of luck in your travels, Charlie." I have no statistics, but my impression is that students raised in sight of the ocean were somewhat likelier than inland students to go back to their home towns after graduation and stay there, or if they traveled, to head east out to sea rather than west into the continent. The last time I saw George Smith, now a pilot on the Panama Canal, he was chuckling about a favorite teacher's objection to his attending a maritime academy rather than a regular college. The teacher hadn't understood, George said kindly; the Smiths had always been seagoing people.

Another significant subdivision (and the largest minority group at Higgins, though it was not then fashionable to speak of it in those terms) was its female population. Higgins was always a coed school; I am only now realizing the degree to which it was, nevertheless, a dominantly male school. I didn't notice this during my childhood or my own studenthood there; my imagination was too much engaged, I suppose, with the personalities and adventures and dramas of my own sex. Certainly the male boarders outnumbered the female almost three to one, but that we perceived merely as better pickings for the girls. Inferior facilities for girls' sports did not rank high, from my unathletic point of view, among the curses of womanhood. Yes, it was worse that girls had fewer privileges, less freedom, and that rankled, but it wasn't a big surprise. But now, reading letters and responses, I can see the degree to which—in my father's mind at least, and it molded Higgins for thirty years—the heart of the school was its male boarders. They worked at harder and more varied school jobs, made more trouble, got expelled for more outrageous offenses, went to war and got killed, rescued furniture from burning houses, injured themselves on the football field, wrestled with their instructors, and permitted themselves to be kicked up and down stairs by the submaster. What could girls offer in competition with such visceral activities? When my father speaks of boys, in his letters, he does so with confidence: "All boys sometimes do that"; "Now and then a boy just needs such-and-such." His letters about girls are specific and tentative: "Miss F— is rather an odd youngster. . . . I am not sure that I helped Miss F—." He never generalizes about girls, for although he liked them, encouraged them to go to college, and taught them the same rules of integrity and square dealing that he taught the boys, I think that he always found their motives and reactions murky, not subject to predictable rules of cause and effect.

Officially recognized minorities—blacks, Jews, Indians—were welcome at Higgins but did not show up in appreciable numbers. Except perhaps for the last of these, they were not in ready supply in central Maine. It's hard after even this slight passage of years to look back without dismay at attitudes that in their own time must have been not merely respectable but mildly liberal, but fair play requires us to try. My father, for instance, used to make a point of having black students at Higgins for their educational value: if his boys and girls at Higgins had black friends and classmates, then they wouldn't go out into the world and be mean or fidgety or stupid about blacks—I take this to have been the idea. There can be no doubt at all that most Higgins students knew—maybe even saw—their first blacks at Higgins. So the black student was there not so much, I suspect, as a token gesture toward his race, as a *rara avis* who would make the school a richer place, and I must say that blacks were a great hit. Indeed, if black students did not turn up in the natural course of events (and usually they wouldn't have), my father sent off to Washington and acquired some. By the mid forties this scheme was beginning to bear second-generation fruit. I find a letter to a dean at Howard University, thus: "I am very pleased that you want to send your son back to the old school. . . . You certainly have a fine reputation in this town, Mr. W—. Everyone knows you and everyone has a good word for you. We want the children of alumni with such records."

It was my father's practice to acquire two young men so that they could room together. And inevitably (he would say a little wryly), in their second year they had paired off with prospective white roommates. So he would write to four sets of parents—did they object to biracial rooming?—and then, I suppose, after that pair graduated he would send for another two. When I began to think about this book I was consumed with curiosity as to what organization in Washington could have been supplying blacks to boarding schools, and I wondered a little, too, whether this importation might have been some private eccentricity of my father's, so I began to ask around. I spoke to Mary Jane Keith first: Had her father kept up the custom of sending off to Washington for two blacks? Yes, she said, and if by chance one of them didn't have anybody to room with, her father would assign her brother John to live with him. But she didn't know who supplied them. Next I tried Hugh Smith, who had after all worked for Dad as well as run Coburn. "Do you know where in Washington Dad used to get his blacks from?" I asked him. "Nope," he said, "I always got mine from Boston." So we may surmise at any rate that Higgins was not peculiar in its practice. I think now that the School Guidance Center in Washington may have been the agency; I find a letter thanking a Mr. Herbert Beal for his friendly attitude toward Higgins.

Beryl Segre ('61) and I both believe that she was the first black female student. I don't think that there was any deliberate effort to exclude girls up until then; boys just seem to have been more easily acquired. I find a letter written in the summer of 1948 confessing that Dad has been hesitating about an application from the correspondent's daughter: could she possibly bring a friend, someone of her own race with whom to room? "If your daughter comes here, we want her to be happy," he says, having alluded to the sensitivity of the female sex. It is not clear to me whether he expects the applicant's own sensitivity to undo her, or whether sensitivity is a euphemism for nasty reactions on the part of the other girls. But I suppose he would not have been surprised by a black girl a little after Beryl Segre's time who one day broke down, flung herself on her teacher's neck, and wailed, "Oh, I can't stand it here with all these white people!"

I have lingered on blacks as a steady, identifiable minority group partly because I find it difficult to write about minorities at Higgins. There were few minority students in the strict sense, and at the same time the school was bristling with eccentric minorities of one, students whose isolated circumstances had allowed their personalities to expand untrammeled. Furthermore, their isolation meant that they came at possible prejudice from an odd direction: they had never known anybody to be prejudiced against and they were fairly keen on novelty. The few Jewish students, for instance, seem to have passed unremarked; nobody had anything against Jews, and they weren't conspicuous enough to be interesting. There were too few of them to warrant transportation to a synagogue, so they went to the Christian, usually Baptist, services, where they were much offended by the irreligious behavior of their Protestant peers. Catholics were of some interest because they crossed themselves on the basketball court before taking foul shots; local Protestants regarded this as quaint. And I remember, because it marked a moment in my education, Mary Jane Keith's indignation when a faculty wife picked up a Catholic medal lost by some student and laughed at it.

Except for three English refugees during World War II, two of whom were younger than high school age, Higgins didn't get into foreign students until Perry Wortman was principal. They were an extremely popular innovation, by all accounts, and must have done for their contemporaries what blacks had done earlier. I recall hearing plaudits for Parviz Moarefi, Iranian, a whiz at math, who when asked how he coped with compulsory church attendance explained peaceably that he sat there with the Baptists and said his own Moslem prayers, and for Andy Koo, a Chinese schoolmate of my brother's who suffered much from the cold and could fight with his feet. James Arunga was there from Nairobi; he taught Doreen Dugal and her siblings to eat fried bananas when he went home with her brothers to Indian Pond. Mariano Delgardo had come out of Cuba in a rowboat and consequently wore an aura of political glamor. Peter Paricharn, from Bangkok, was a class officer, beloved for teaching his friends rude expressions in Thai and for having a Buddhist shrine in his room. (His teachers objected to the incense but not the Buddhism, my brother says.) In fact, I know of only one foreign student who was not a success—an Iranian girl, a great disappointment after Parviz. Having failed to make the cultural transition, she stole from the other girls to punish them for kissing their boyfriends, and was sent away. It was later yet that Higgins recruited a sizeable population of Passamaquoddy Indians. In fact, that story belongs to the account of Higgins's last days.

As one might expect, the composition of the school changed somewhat through the years. Until perhaps some time in the 1950s, when the wave of GIs had passed, there was a tremendous age range among the male students, though less noticeably so among the females. Student-body photos from the twenties and thirties show children in knickers beside men who, though students, look as old as the faculty, and meaner. All these lived in the dorms together, their ages ranging from perhaps twenty-five down to twelve. On the upper end were men who had decided after all (or after war) to go to college, but who found themselves inadequately prepared. On the lower end were not only the handful of students who were sometimes admitted to an arrangement called the "Junior School" (i.e., seventh and eighth graders who boarded at Higgins), but students whose mothers, in less academically regulated days, had wearied of them and sent them off to elementary school at four. One graduate told me that his brother, one of the latter cases, had spent much of his time and energy in hiding his absence of pubic hair from his more mature dormmates.

Postgraduate students, boys mostly, were an important element in the decades I remember. They were a great boon athletically (bigger, more experienced) and socially (older, newer, more glamorous), and I suppose that they may have been a sobering element in the dorms psychologically, though not, I fear, alcoholically. In the sixties and seventies their number dwindled. High school standards had risen, college admission standards had dropped, and changes in athletic policy (see Chapter IX) meant that they were not sought out for teams.

Over the years, too, more high schools and better transportation meant fewer rescues from rural hardship, though certainly Higgins students never inclined to be wealthy. In the 1950s, however, Higgins still looked to a number of parents like a traditional, plausible, even rather classy alternative to keeping their children at home; enrollments were high. My schoolmates seemed to be there because they'd been running wild at home, or their parents were divorced, or both parents worked, or one taught in the local high school, as well as because of some inadequacy in public education.

Then, with an almost ecological finality, Higgins's natural clientele suddenly disappeared, just dried up. The sixties and seventies were a bad time for boarding schools, and several factors contributed. First and worst, in Maine, was the SAD (School Administrative District) Act of 1957, which mandated that towns band together to form district high schools. In 1954, more than fifty towns were paying tuition to Higgins; by 1968 half of these towns belonged to SADs. That threw the burden of private school tuition back in the parents' laps: scratch the poor. The onset of the recession meant that even better-off parents had to be unusually desperate before they spent money on private education when public education could be had: scratch the middle class. It was an unpopular time for structure in education and an inauspicious time to tell your offspring that he or she was going to boarding school for a bit of polish: scratch the upwardly mobile. The effect of all this was a scramble to find a new market.

One strategy was to acquire more day students. In my own time at Higgins, Bradford students had joined the original base of Charleston students as nonboarders. After the further acquisition of students from Kenduskeag and Glenburn, day students began for the first time to outnumber boarders. But the SAD Act also made the retention of day students a problem. Bradford and Kenduskeag joined a district and were lost; Glenburn in the end was enticed back. Perry Wortman told me about the morning of his Glenburn gamble, when he sent a bus on speculation, having solicited Glenburn eighth graders without getting a commitment from them. He watched the bus roll up to the school, not knowing whether it would let out one student, in which case he would have wasted precious money, or forty, in which case he would have pulled a coup. Twenty-five or thirty students climbed out and enrolled, so his credit was well saved.

The other and more glaring shift of population in his time was toward students with assorted difficulties more personal than economic. These students and their improvement were the most gratifying components of what he identified as his best ten years, the ones at Higgins. So toward the end, again, Higgins was engaged in doing something like what it had set out to do at the start—rescuing the perishing, to quote a good fundamentalist hymn. I may be exhibiting early symptoms of a crotchety, backward-looking old age when I confess that what tickles me most about Perry Wortman's notable success with the halt, maimed, and learning impaired is that Higgins hadn't a shadow of therapy (speech or otherwise), special education, remediation beyond one reading course, or anything else except what it had always offered—classes and expectations. "I haven't got time for special cases," Perry would say firmly to a dejected and much therapized applicant. "If you come here, you're normal." And pretty often they would be, or near enough.

Here are a couple of his favorite success stories. A boy who had previously been educated by home tutoring was discovered, while he was at Higgins, crying and threatening to run away. What was wrong? Perry asked. He couldn't do his algebra, the boy said. "Oh, well, try it," said Perry, who couldn't think of much else to say, and these words inexplicably turned out to be the magic ones. The boy came back the next year, saying, "I won't go to school anywhere else." Better yet was the student whose parents had been told to forget him educationally, after three years at a special school had yielded one high school credit. The boy was nineteen already and Perry tried hard not to take him, but the father persisted, saying that he thought Perry had horse sense, an educational approach that hadn't been tried. The boy graduated from Higgins with his class, science project and all, and subsequently made it through a four-year business college.

Not all students at Higgins then had trouble on that scale, to be sure, but I notice that when my brother and I entertain each other with our wildest Higgins stories, it's the faculty from my time and the students from his who star in the anecdotes. I remember particularly that he knew a boy who used to entertain his friends by breaking Coca Cola cases over his own head, and that one of his teachers, out shopping in Bangor with five or six absolutely random female students, was asked whether Higgins was a school for children with speech impediments. Students from broken or difficult homes, too, were of particular interest to Principal Wortman, who, after years of being a fervent public school man, began to perceive boarding schools as valuable in protecting students from their own families. "Higgins: A Home for Boys and Girls" continued to be a significant description.

Hugh Smith has written to me:

> I always put the alumni of a school in two classes. First, those who went to college and made names for themselves in their field, and secondly, those who went back to the communities they came from and helped make them better places. Of course, the second group outnumber the first.

The Richs, Alfred and Harold, tried the outside world and then came back to Charleston and raised their families and made the community a better place. Alfie Rich's son belonged to the first class. He worked on the first computer that General Electric Co. built. Both classes are important to society.

His quite proper assumption is that four years' exposure to the school should make a student something better than merely four years older. "Value added," my college is calling it these days. Certainly, in the case of Higgins students, the years could be expected to lay on some polish, raise some sights. I heard from one Higgins graduate who had been raised in lumber camps in a numbered Maine township but, after Higgins, went to Parsons for a design degree and wound up on the Los Angeles Times. "All my memories of Higgins are so dear to me," he said, "more than later education—it was so different."

Generic enrichment was the aim; I never had the feeling that Higgins or Coburn or the other schools with which they consorted were trying to stamp their students with a hallmark to distinguish one prep school's product from another's. Rather, when a student went out into the world, the world was supposed to say, not "There's a Higgins man" (or a Higgins woman), but "There's a good man." But of course it was nice if the world happened to ask where the goodness had been cultivated.

IV

TONE
AND PHILOSOPHY

*There is no place for the private school unless it has
the missionary spirit—unless it feels that it can not
only educate boys and girls but can make better men
and women of them than the public school.*

—HUGH SMITH
Speech to Waterville Clergymen, Late 1940s.

mong the virtues to which Higgins successfully aspired,
democracy is perhaps the most conspicuous. I wish that
there were another word for it; "democracy," in an academic context, conjures up misleading visions of student
government, group decisions about rules, even misguided extremes
of first-naming and back-slapping across the ranks. What Higgins
had, rather, appears even at this remove to have been an atmosphere
in which individual merit alone really did determine social standing.
Says a 1922 *Scroll* editorial by Eleanor King ('23), "A strong democratic spirit is fostered in the school. When a student comes to Higgins he must do his own work and not lean on someone else; he gets
exactly what he deserves, no more, no less." Any social credit ac-
crued by one's parents ("Her folks are good people / not much good
/ no good") was necessarily left behind, nor could Solomon himself
have sorted out comparative standings from five dozen separate and

subtle village hierarchies. Everything was ripe for the rise of true merit.

As for financial distinctions, the intrusive query launched at new boys in British public schools—"How much a year does your father have?"—would have seemed to Higgins students not only irrelevant but laughably naive; the answer for most would have depended on weather, pollination, market prices, and a dozen other variables. Furthermore, as F. Allen Shaw ('52) observed, "Money did not affect social life in the Higgins structure. There was little to spend it on." Just to make sure, I asked alumni whether being richer or poorer had affected their social standing. Most of them claimed, emphatically, that it hadn't, though a few of the poorer students confessed to inner shrinkings about their wardrobes or said that having no money for dates had inhibited their social lives. Martha Bragger ('35) writes:

> I felt somewhat poorer than the average student, but I tried to remember that my father was not well and the apple crop did not do well due to the trees being killed by the severe winter cold. Also it rained during blossom time and the bees neglected their usual good work pollinating the fruit trees. I got the impression it was hard to scrape up money for my board, let alone decent clothes.

The likelier possibility, that richer students had been the victims of reverse discrimination, was not proposed by any of the alumni. I remember, though, some baiting in the early fifties of an out-of-state dorm girl who had bragged that she was going to make her debut. Sometimes in Civics class, Sabra Lee ('18) tells me, my father would say, "Some of you are used to a higher life style than we, but I think by association we will learn from each other." Note that this speech puts the "we" on the side of the less prosperous life style, so one can see who the deviant, and hence the potential victim, was. An unsigned editorial in the 1931 *Scroll* ("What Is Higgins?") faces the issue but concludes that all is well. The emphasis is mine.

> Higgins Classical Institute has always been famous for its democracy. Some of the students are poor, but there is no barrier, real or imaginary, between the boys who work their expenses and the well-to-do. Intellectual rivalry among healthy students is fatal to class distinction. The son of wealthy par-

ents meets his match in the classroom and on the campus in a fellow student who is working his way. *On the other hand, the ignorant contempt for the rich which sometimes manifests itself in young people is quickly corrected.* The good scholars are not all self-supporting and the poor boy often finds his intellectual rival in his well-to-do comrade. Such association is good training for American citizens, therefore it is the constant care of the governing board to maintain this democratic spirit.

So far we have considered only horizontal equality. The relationship between the different strata of the school, the students, the faculty, and the staff, is captured best by St. Paul's analogy (I Corinthians 12) about all the bits of the body—eye, ear, foot, hand—together composing the body itself and having "the same care for one another." But after that the analogy breaks down, for at Higgins the hand really would fill in for the foot, the eye for the ear, and so on: although chains of authority existed, firm demarcations based on what work one did and where one stood socially in consequence did not. Let me offer two illustrative vignettes from Higgins life. In the first, Mary Jane Keith, then the headmaster's daughter, is once again called out of her high school classes in the spring to start the lawnmower for the janitor, Mr. Percy, who is not good with machines. (She is good with machines and mows all summer.) In the second, Ruby Hillman, talented and very much beloved pastry cook and dorm matron, is sitting on the foot of my bed, listening to the newest of my father's bedtime stories from the continuing saga of Whitey the Owl, his own invention. She comes over for it as often as she can get away at my bedtime, and nothing could seem more natural to any of us. To notice it even now tarnishes the memory a little, but I know that in other sorts of schools the headmaster would fear to lose dignity by letting his anthropomorphic bird-fantasies fly past the bounds of the nuclear family.

Many, perhaps even most, of the students were performing some kind of janitorial duties. The faculty were not, as a regular thing—though of course they kept their own quarters immaculate; there was no maid service—but they were on their own for the unexpected. Nobody was going to call the sole buildings-and-grounds man, who probably lived off campus anyway, to come running with a mop and cope with floods and vomit and other domestic miscalculations.

Quite a few male graduates remembered as one of their keenest pleasures being up early for coffee with the janitor. I quote Willis Parker ('39) as representative.

> The janitor at one period was Mr. Percy (Tom). During the period that I peeled vegetables (mostly potatoes, several bushels per meal) I used to get up early and go down to the kitchen and have an early cup of coffee with Mr. Percy. He made it himself, using a battered old blue enamel-ware pot—fill it with cold water, throw in a handful of ground coffee, boil it up, and then break an egg in it to settle the grounds. I can almost taste it—strong enough to float a chain-hook.

I might add that the trustees' minutes for August 1930 make it sound as though the local board members were themselves digging up and laying pipe from the pond, and they probably were.

Kitchen work was not the exclusive domain of kitchen staff or even authorized student workers. Two of my own classmates, Phil Eaton and David Jewett, sometimes used to surprise the cooks with a night off and make the dinner themselves, and certainly faculty who found themselves saddled with devoted or abandoned or infirm students at vacation turned to and cooked. For some the kitchen felt like home; one 1926 graduate told me that he used to hang around the kitchen with Mr. and Mrs. McLean because they cooked things that reminded him of the lumber camp where he was raised.

Sometimes students were allowed to teach a little. Several alumni recalled the special privilege of conducting a class or taking a review session. The opportunity to make a valid adult contribution to community life lends dignity, and especially, perhaps, in the earlier days of the school, the contributions were down-to-earth and highly practical. For instance, John Bradeen ('28), who apparently had some facility as a nurse, says that he "took time from classes sometimes to help someone, especially those who had whooping cough, scarlatina, and measles." In a school with no infirmary or nurse, where resident adults must spend the day at classes, a student volunteer is worth a good deal. "Bill Paine had measles," he goes on. "[He] fainted and rolled downstairs. When he came to, he broke out." A good brisk atmosphere for nursing. Bill Paine himself is remembered fondly by several graduates as the supplier of maple syrup to the school, and

Robert Houghton ('37) sometimes shot deer on weekends home and brought back venison for the school larder. Stanwood King ('50) tells me that he spent many happy hours building the school a track pit for the long jump, and that he "sort of formed" a track team, there being no coach.

It was not to the school alone that the students supplied practical benefits. The town was part of the school family, and the school was part of the town. The boys seemed always to be plunging into burning buildings in the most impromptu way and emerging safely. When the Stan Higgins house, just across from the school, burned in the mid forties, students got virtually everything out. Indeed, it was boys from the school who barged in on the family at the table and, excusing themselves, announced that the house was burning. The Keiths have supplied me with dramatic details. Students (girls too, I think) dragged sacks of grain to safety. They rescued canned goods from the cellar even after the lights went out, coming up only when the atmosphere got really murky. They rescued the animals, housing the younger and more vulnerable of them in the school furnace room. One of the boys' reception rooms was given over to household goods.

The good will was reciprocal. Although Earle Stevens ('48) recalls a ritual "potato attack" after potato harvest, when town boys would wait outside evening study hall to throw waste (or "pig") potatoes at the dorm boys, serious relationships seem to have been good. Certainly they were good between boarding students and town parents. Harriet Lord Stanley ('30) says that when her boys went to Higgins, she woke up one morning to find that she had seventeen kids for breakfast. Another day she came home to find two boys, not hers, having coffee and donuts at her kitchen table; they explained that they'd been out hunting, were cold and hungry, and knew that she'd have asked them in if she'd been there. Pete Minott ('38) says that he went home once with Charlie Dunham, a local boy, and never looked back; Dunham's was home. Ellis Holt ('27) has a memory of more aggressive caretaking of Higgins by the formidable Dyer family, who quelled a troublemaking visiting football team by standing over it. (" 'What's going on here?' Mr. Dyer asked quite gently. The boys looked up at him, and up further at his sons, and as quietly replied, 'Not a thing, mister.' ")

Work—not only the necessity of it, the universality of it, the possibility of contributing by it, but the sanctity of the activity in itself—was also crucial to the tone of Higgins, at least in my father's time. This glorification of work was not to be confused with educational theories about "Work Experience," though at first glance there seems to be a resemblance. "Work Experience" was play-acting by Higgins lights, an affectation to be regarded with contempt. Hugh Smith said in his speech to the Waterville clergy,

> I . . . got my first work experience on the south end of a cow when I was about six years old. Every New England farm boy of forty or fifty years ago got plenty of work experience. The Schools of Education have just discovered that it was educational.

His tone is typical. "Experience" limits; work is a way of life, a desideratum like justice and honesty. My father believed that labor was a cure for everything from weak character to hangnails, and if this seems a kind of fanaticism (as it sometimes did to me), I can only say that his passion for work did not mark him as peculiar in his time and place. The nineteenth century was not far behind us, rock-hard fields were all around us, and evangelism led us on. "Work, for the night is coming," we sang in church, and "Be strong! We are not here to play, to dream, to drift; / We have hard work to do, and loads to shift." We were supposed to be laborers worthy of our hire. It was not only adults who believed this. An older boy was heard lecturing a newcomer who'd tried to slide out of a promised task: "You want to do what you say you'll do; if you want to stay around here you want to be able to *do* things."

There is evidence from the alumni that working not only kept them in school but built their confidence, made them feel competent members of the world. Ronald Bishop ('49), who swept floors, waited on tables, washed blackboards, scrubbed pots and pans, and did, he thinks, every other job available, thus financing his entire Higgins education except for $153.00 that he earned at a dairy farm to pay the leftovers at the end, says:

> I'm grateful that I had a chance to go to Higgins, that my Dad was wise enough to make me work. . . . that was a very meaningful experience, and I treasure the fact that I was able

to have been dutifully employed in all of those different jobs, that *I got to be a somebody* because I was able to do those jobs well. He had taught me how to work and how to complete my tasks and not leave things undone and to achieve perfection as best a thirteen, fourteen, fifteen year old boy can do that. I think that whole experience at Higgins was very much a reinforcement of that kind of thing.

If work at Higgins turned Ronald Bishop, already knowledgeable in the ways of labor, into a somebody, imagine what it did for the less initiated. Nobody stood over the workers with a whip, but they were expected to do their jobs properly. Willis Parker ('39) says, "My first year, in the Fall, I had the job of sweeping floors in the Institute. My rooms were the Math room and the Office (both Mr. Tracy's). I recall his offhand remark to my father that I was doing all right, but he thought I might have done better in a *round* room. Father suggested that a little more attention to the corners might be appropriate." His later remark, "I loved the place and I grew up there," may have no direct bearing on his work experience, but I notice that before he left Higgins he was being trusted to tend the heating plant.

It may seem odd that I have gone on this long about the tone of a private school founded by an evangelical minister without mentioning either culture or religion. The truth is that neither one was anything like so important at Higgins as democracy and hard work were. The school seems, in retrospect, curiously *a*cultural—not at all *anti*-cultural, but monumentally unsophisticated about the arts. It valued intellect, and the students themselves admired brains in other students and were complimentary about mental feats. People who might have been despised for bookworminess in public high school got a fair lot of social credit for it at Higgins. Students who could sing and act and play instruments were popular for those skills, too, but music was mostly an individual talent, like basketball, not something that the musically ungifted masses learned to understand (though the catalogues assert that history of music and a knowledge of harmony were taught in conjunction with piano instruction). Higgins could never have afforded an art teacher as well as a music teacher, and one can see that bands and operettas contribute more to school morale than drawing lessons. Still, it would have been nice if someone had managed art appreciation.

A primary difficulty, I think, is that none of the heads were humanists; they were mathematicians and chemists and such, and had little training or sophistication in the arts. My father, for instance, was fond of Kipling and liked to quote his poetry, and he never got over having seen Ethel Barrymore in *Death Takes a Holiday*, but he would have thought it self-indulgent to go raring off to the theater in hopes of repeating the pleasure. Our walls were decorated with reproductions of *Sir Galahad and His Horse*, *Jesus on the Mount of Olives*, Maxfield Parrish's *Hilltop*, and a pleasant collection of tinted photographs of trees and lakes. Nobody we knew had anything better. If you don't count the little turntable on top of our console radio (where we played "The Stranger of Galilee" and "The Ninety and Nine"), the first bona fide phonograph entered the house with my adolescence, and we're not talking high tech. I think that I recall one making a similar debut in the Keiths' house when Mary Jane was in her teens; theirs had been a wind-up model.

Of all the principals, Philip Keith was almost certainly the most culturally oriented, for he loved poetry and music and went to see Shakespeare at summer theaters. But this was a private taste, something for his leisure; for the school he emphasized sports. The Keiths' tinted photos showed a preference for mountains. I recall Leon Meader once telling a Gertrude Stein and Alice Toklas anecdote, so he was in some kind of touch with the world of arts, but his real passion was nature—canoeing, hunting, and fishing. His wife played the piano and was rightly considered a bold and original decorator, but although I was in and out of their house all my childhood, I do not remember any cultural revelations. They seemed to be about like us. The principal obsession of Perry Wortman, a Phi Beta Kappa chemist, I take to have been the science of education itself, its process and evaluation and statistics. I can't speak for Foss and Chase, but by that point it was too late to do much about Higgins's cultural tone.

As for religion, the school clung pretty well to identifiably Christian principles, but I suspect that whatever evangelical habits the Reverend John Higgins may have been able to impose wore away shortly after his death. He is said to have insisted during his lifetime that the trustees and instructors all be Christians. The Portland paper's account of Higgins's impending centennial adds this story:

> During a series of evangelistic meetings at the school, someone made the remark: "The students cannot get their lessons

with so many meetings." Mr. Higgins's reply was: "To get Jesus
is far more important than to get lessons."

He died early in the school's history, however—1910—and although
subsequent heads would probably all have agreed, if pressed, that
getting Jesus was more important, on any particular night they
would perhaps have plumped for lessons. His "no dancing" edict
stuck longer.

There were compulsory once-a-week Bible classes for freshmen
and sophomores, I see from a catalogue printed as late as my own
time, and I think they really must have happened, for I have a little
mental snapshot of the Reverend Claude Nutter walking down the
Institute steps while all the rude students in the windows chanted,
"Claude, Claude" (or perhaps "Clod, clod"; it was meant to be ambivalent). Ellis Holt ('27) remembers his Bible lessons from Dr. Ramsdell, and says that "their basic purport was to identify the number of
books of the Bible, and classify them into books of History, Poetry,
Letters, and such."

Elbridge Hamm ('26) remarks of religion at Higgins generally,
"Although the Scriptures were read, morality rather than religion
was stressed, which I feel Mr. Tracy knew would be more likely ab-
sorbed by his teen-age students." Another member of the class of '26,
on the other hand, felt that Higgins had religion and to spare. He
told me on tape,

> I had no religious preference, I mean I was just sort of
> brought up in the woods, a nature boy. I loved and respected
> Mother Nature and she was sort of my god, or goddess, but
> when I got to Higgins I found out that it was a hard shell Bap-
> tist school and going to church Sunday was compulsory and
> also there was Christian Endeavor on Tuesday night and hav-
> ing bible study classes during school— I think old Reverend
> Ramsdell was the minister at the time—and that kind of
> bothered me because that was something entirely new.

It will not do, however, to understate any more than to overstate
the degree to which the school's tone and philosophy had a religious
foundation. Nobody should suppose from the restrained quality of
religion at Higgins that its heads were token Christians, the sort of
people who say "We're all Christians," but mean "We all wash our
necks and pay cash." Nothing of the sort. But they were New Englanders and of northern European stock to boot, and they didn't get

emotional about anything if they could help it, God included. My father, for instance, got baptized as an adult, so evidently he meant it. He tried hard to regulate his conduct by Christian principles, and he went right on thinking about the Bible to the end of his life, now and then announcing some new insight into the cleverness of Jesus. Further, he would not play cards or see a movie on Sunday (though he would fish), and he very much wished to be, and was, an influence for good with his students. In our church, though, we believed that all earnest Christians were *ipso facto* "born again" (we even sang about it in Sunday School—"Happy Birthday to you, aren't you glad you've got two?"), and when we ran into an excited adult convert, we were pleased for him and wished him well and reckoned that he'd steady down after a little. In a context of so much reserve, how could a school have manifested its religion except in moral behavior? "I try to have a Christian school," Hugh Smith said of Coburn, "and Jesus Christ was the first great democrat with his new commandment, Love Thy Neighbor as Thyself."

However, after these apologetics, I must admit that my father had one kinky rule about religion: if you made ice cream, you didn't have to go to church. Any number of former ice-cream makers told me this. There was always homemade ice cream for Sunday dinner, manufactured by the laborious turning of an old-fashioned crank in a wooden freezer (wooden, I know, for I remember the Sunday the dasher broke and there were great slivers in the dessert), and I suppose that my father hit on the best way to make cranking a volunteer activity. It wouldn't have been right to deny student kitchen workers their religious prerogatives, though that might have increased the appeal of church going. The Reverend John, perhaps, would have said that it was more important to have Jesus than to have ice cream.

Eleanor King's 1922 *Scroll* editorial, already quoted on democracy, is good on "Christian principles," too.

> They are apparent in many ways. Each student is expected to be honest and upright in his school work as well as in his life outside school hours. Our athletics are clean and the students do their best to keep them so. These standards go a long way toward the development of character.

I'm not sure, myself, that cleanliness in athletics is next to godliness, but of course I can see that viciousness on the field is un-Christian.

David Lassell ('60), who was at Higgins in those pivotal days when chapel and dancing coexisted, described Higgins then with a phrase I cherish. "It was a normal ungodly school," he says. "No better or no worse than the average." Thirty or forty years earlier, when we were a little bit godly, even rather godly, we would have been more religious than the public schools and some of the private schools, though not as religious as today's Christian schools.

The atmosphere at Higgins, besides being democratic, pro-work, acultural, and moral, was an appealing mix of the formal and the homey. Marian Boyer ('37) writes, of formality, "I particularly remember how important it made me feel to be called 'Miss Boyer.' I think calling the students Mr. and Miss made us feel good about ourselves." On the homey side, Wilmot Oliver ('39) writes:

> I remember my experience in the dormitories at Higgins with great pleasure and joy. I also recall that Ma Hillman was the proctor on the girls' side of the dorm and she was like a second mother to Zeke Parker, Roland Hutchinson and me. As a matter of fact, during our second year at the school we purchased a special airplane cloth in Bangor from which she made parkas or windbreakers. She even put fur on the hood. She will always be remembered with great affection.

Probably the major element in making Higgins the home it claimed to be was the seriousness with which the staff stood *in loco parentis*. The term seems too often to be merely a justification for high-handed restrictions, but ideally it should confer the obligation to love as well as to discipline. "I shall really be glad to see you youngsters come trooping back again," my father writes to a student in August of 1943, and he means it. Taken literally, *in loco parentis* is a full-time, no reserves, all-out job, but it has its rewards. Someone once said of Hugh Smith at Coburn, "He gives the boys all he's got and they tell him all they know." And he did, too—left his room open for them with a radio and magazines available, took them shopping for their suits, nursed them, ferried them around, and bore their vacation visits kindly. And he did the same at Higgins and Ricker. No doubt he learned some fascinating things in consequence.

Alumni, being queried, remember many faculty kindnesses beyond the strict requirements of duty, though the gratitude they felt for human decency is a terrible indictment of what treatment teenagers expect from adults. One graduate, for instance, reported the gentleness with which Larry Eaton told him that his mother and father had separated. To anyone who knew Larry Eaton this would not be surprising, but implicit in the gratitude is a vision of how the thing could have been mismanaged. ("All students whose parents still live together raise their hands. Not so fast, you.") Another graduate was grateful that my father never talked to him directly about his learning problems, just demonstrated confidence in him obliquely; so much for counseling.

Informal conversation was most welcome. Dozens of graduates cited communication—"Talking on a one-to-one basis," said Ronald York ('45) and his wife, Joyce Robinson ('46); "Just chatting like an equal—not talking down to me like a child," said Inez Carey ('61)—as a principal gift from teachers. My mother let Miriam Sweet ('40) come to her room and talk out her homesickness. Louise Gerrish took time to comfort and encourage dozens (maybe hundreds) of students even though she lived out of town and commuted to work.

Other students were grateful for unexpected help with schoolwork. "A teacher took time out to help me pass an English test," Clyde Bowley ('57) remembers, and Elizabeth Chase ('46) points out that Leah Brown helped her with compositions even though she was not her teacher. Charles Folsom ('51) mentions "Hugh Smith's after hours Algebra lessons in his room, with huge four posted bed and all." The phrases "time out," "even though," and "in his room" catch the tone of faculty generosity.

Unclassifiable kindnesses were cited: Mr. Danforth gave one alumna free music lessons. Leola Mitchell bought treats and didn't play favorites. Florence Sawyer ('21) accepted a friend's invitation to eat in the dorm, not knowing that someone had to sign for the meal. My father saw her embarrassment and signed. Charles Cummings ('41), who was on the football team, had lost a fingernail loading potatoes. He wanted a protective bandage and his own coach brushed him off as being too tough to need it. Joe Roderick, who by then was coaching for the opposition, bandaged him up. A number of people also mentioned being nursed and being given rides—rides to school in the cold, rides to see sisters in the hospital, rides to Dover for variety, even rides off campus to relieve the cravings of female smokers.

Other students remembered the kind of thing one always covets from parents, even real parents: respect, confidence, trust. "Made me think I knew something," one anonymous graduate responded tersely when asked for the best thing a teacher had done. A number of students savored the compliment of having been allowed to teach a class on some occasion, and John Thibodeau ('57) was delighted that Miss Trafton trusted him to fix the school typewriters and that he was allowed to help with the construction of the dorm.

A number of students noted that they had been helped on the road to self improvement in one way or another—made to stand straight, "shape up," study, grow. Teachers taught that sort of thing on their own initiative. Joe Roderick, for instance, who was short, took particular pains not to let tall boys slouch. "Toe in!" Leola Mitchell was always shouting at Frances Ward ('38), who says, "Thanks to her I don't walk like a duck." The teaching of manners was a somewhat more official responsibility. Doreen Dugal ('66) tells me that her brothers learned table manners at Higgins with such speed that they astounded their mother on their first weekend home, for she had been cracking them with a wooden spoon for years to no avail.

It could be uphill work. I remember hearing about a big, good-hearted, clumsy girl who was hard to train. Galumphing down the corridor one day, she smacked into Leola Mitchell, Dean of Girls. "Pardon *me*," Miss Mitchell said, in what she hoped was an illustrative tone. "Oh, thas all right, Miss Mitchell," said the girl. Now and then a student was outright recalcitrant. There was a list of table do's and don'ts in Perry Wortman's time, Doreen told me, which included breaking your bread into quarters. One farm boy resented this. "All right, it's in quarters now," he'd say, folding a slice over twice and shoving it all into his mouth.

Besides manners, other legs-up in life had to do with college—the suggestion, say, that one should plan to go, or the strong-arming of the college in question. Dad secured a scholarship, job, and room at Colby for Carl McGraw ('36) on very short notice. Don Matheson helped at HCI "and afterwards" with his further education, says Paul Goss ('50), and Ernie Ross ('51) says that Matheson always urged his athletes to keep on with their educations.

Being a responsible substitute parent wars against the administrative temptation to homogenize (or at least to perceive as homogeneous) any institutional group. "I usually permit a student to establish himself as dependable or as not dependable," my father writes in September of 1940, checking up on a doubtful case, but he ordinarily dealt in finer discriminations. We can seem him trying to figure out why a particular boy is lazy, or whether a boy is not lazy at all, merely dull.

> L— is very faithful in doing any physical labor. He is a good boy and I certainly hope that he improves scholastically.

> C— is lazy but he has grown fast and this growth undoubtedly takes a lot of his energy.

> B— decided that he was a ladies' man and I didn't realize that that was the fact as soon as I should have. If he returns this winter he will have to forget this lady situation and go to work.

> J—'s conduct is good but he does not study. He will sit looking off into space dreaming. I will call his attention to his work and in five minutes he is dreaming again. I am working honestly with your son but I do not feel that I am accomplishing too much. Possibly the trouble that he had with his blood affected his vitality more than we know.

I'm afraid that real parents sometimes took advantage of his sensibilities. A long series of threats one winter—*Pay your daughter's bills or we'll send her home*—is followed by a defeated admission that "M— has remained to complete her winter term. Naturally I wouldn't see her put out in the snow." But no parenting, *in loco* or *in domo*, is foolproof. "The best advice I can give you is to take G— out of school and put him to work," says another discouraged letter. Sometimes, too, a child just slips through the quasi-parental net; he had not realized, my father says in December of 1943, that W— was not contented. W— has the job of carrying mail, "which is easy, pleasant work"; he was given double windows for his room as soon as he complained of the cold; and it is too bad that he has lost money to a thief so far not identified. He will give the boy closer attention. After three months of closer attention, he reports that W— is inclined to be despondent and to complain about other places as well as Higgins, but "he will probably outgrow this characteristic." In the meantime, one imagines W— with his mailpouch, cold, broke, and disgruntled.

The real proof of pseudo-parental attachment, however, was not the treatment of students actually at Higgins (after all, happy students are good business) but the continuing concern for them after they'd left. I find a letter from my father begging a boy to take a post-graduate course somewhere, anywhere, not necessarily Higgins, rather than go to college unready. Another assures a family that he has not ceased to care about the welfare of a girl who has chosen to spend her senior year at an out-of-state school. A letter to a boy who is cooking in the army promises recipes and advice from the Higgins chef.

Then there are more practical matters. My father somehow got a mortgage on the Colby College bookstore and was able to award the running of it to Higgins grads attending Colby, like an English lord dispensing ecclesiastical livings. He lent his own money, too, for term bills, or gave it outright, and so did Hugh Smith, who also sometimes let boys work their meals at Coburn while they went to Colby. Wilmot Oliver ('39) says my father lent him a hundred dollars to go to college his first year when nobody else would lend him a nickel. Harriett Lord ('30) writes:

> I was as green about what to do about college as I had been about everything else; of course I was poor; so more or less arbitrarily, Mr. Tracy and Hugh Smith arranged for me to go to Ricker Junior College when I got through at Higgins. They enrolled me and found me a chance to work my board in Houlton. I don't remember many of the details—not even signing entrance papers. They just told me when and where to show up the next fall. I had no money, but no one ever presented me with a bill and when I worried about money, as I sometimes did, I went first to Mr. Tracy and asked about any money arrangements that had been made and he told me Mr. Smith was looking out for me. When I went to Mr. Smith, he told me that Mr. Tracy was looking out for me. . . . I understood that Mr. Tracy and Mr. Smith had helped many young people, mostly boys, to go on to school, but I never knew any details about them or even about me!

A letter of condolence from Jake Bishop ('55), which my mother kept, says, "But the point is, Mr. Tracy believed in his boys, and the dollars he siphoned off and the treatment of us as men was what kept many of us going."

Higgins and Coburn and Ricker were not altogether typical in their nurturing of students. I didn't see anything like it, frankly, in either of the prep schools I taught in myself, though one of them had a very endearing institutional personality. Hugh Smith writes,

> I don't think that prep schools in general paid much attention to their students. I know one of my Colby friends that sent his son to M.C.I. asked me to help him get a college scholarship for the boy, who was a very good student and a fine boy. I did and he got it and kept it for four years.

Is it any wonder, on the whole, that Higgins students were swept by an ecstasy of school spirit that set them cheering when the trolley from Bangor approached campus, and drove them back for weekends when they were away in college, at least through the twenties and thirties and forties? I can remember my father's pleasure at hearing his students spontaneously break into the school song as they came back to their dorms after some evening activity. Even in my own conscientiously blasé days at Higgins, the unlikeliest people would fall on each other's necks with rapture if they chanced to meet during vacation, and my mother told me that it had always been so. As Forrest Royal said, Higgins was a religion. Ted Emery ('22) is known to have asked, some years after his graduation, "Do they still love Higgins as much as we did?"

V

PRACTICALITIES

The poor spook moaned and hung his head.
"I'm Tom, I'm Tom!" groaned he,
"At H.C.I. I kept the fires
 In the days that used to be."

His voice called up those by gone years
 And thoughts of my cold room.
Nor more was said, and he turned his back
 And drifted off into the gloom.

—A.L.F.,
from "Our Janitor's Future," 1930 *Scroll*

WhEN in the summer of 1980 my brother and I cleared out our parents' house, we found, among other Higgins documents, about a peck and a half of dunning notices addressed to our father. Blood loyalties at once overbore archival consciences, as is so often the case with family editors, and we burned most of them before we sent the Higgins material on to the Colby library. We left in a small sample, however, and I have before me a representative and pleasant note from Shep Hurd, manager of Dakin Sporting Goods in Bangor, dated March 1, 1948:

> I am sending you a statement of your account and since we have not had any check from you at all this school year, I would appreciate it if you could help us out. March 15 seems to be the time when the Government wants their money with no ifs, ands or buts about it.

Two things are noteworthy: Dakin has gone a long time unpaid, and Dakin is not being rude about it. Partly this reflects the civil, offhand way in which business is often conducted in Maine, as though it doesn't matter very much. (Now and then I still slip back into home habits and face a polite ninety degrees away from a shopkeeper, making my queries about his goods seem purely conversational. In New York State this unsettles the clerks and exasperates my friends.) Partly the tone of the letter reflects Mr. Hurd's long experience with Higgins: "help us out" is a canny phrase.

I can see now that we did not need to cover up for our father by burning the unpaid bills, for they were not simply the effect of his absentmindedness, though no doubt that contributed; in fact, he could not pay his bills because he could not *collect* his bills. Higgins was consistently the least expensive private boarding school in the state; a list of comparative rates for 1953–54, for instance, has Hebron, at the top, charging $1500, and Higgins, at the bottom, only $625, or $333 below the average. The low fees were designed to allow the children of the poor to get a good education, but it's at least as hard for the poor to pay a small fee as it is for the more prosperous to pay a large one.

Salaries as well as business debts sometimes went unpaid. Hugh Smith writes,

> When I first went to Higgins [1920–21] they had no regular times of paying us or any other bills. Town tuition[s] . . . might come in any time that some of the small towns collected. . . . I collected the money from the individuals for everything but the town tuitions, which your father collected. Finally they decided to pay the teachers $100.00 a month of their salaries and the balance when it came in. One summer I ran all summer to get seven hundred dollars that was owed me.

A number of letters survive from the Depression years, written by parents or occasionally by the students themselves, enclosing a dollar, five dollars, ten dollars, or just explaining why even that much is impossible. Those letters are so sad that it seems intrusive to quote from them, but the acuteness of the crisis, the evident goodness and honesty of the writers, and the implications for Higgins finances argue for their preservation. Some of the letters come in series. One mother writes in June of 1933, planning secretly to cash in her insurance policy and pay the bill, for her son "has done well, and got good rank, hasn't he, and we think H.C.I. a wonderful place, and school." In July she writes again:

> I am so sorry Mr. Tracy, but all of us have been out of work, until now, my husband has found work in N.Y. and we lost about all we had in the bank Crash, and the insurance fell through. But beginning next month $10 every two weeks, until it is paid. A man in Boston is sending J— this fall if he goes, and you wouldn't hinder him from going, would you, we couldn't send him, not until we get you paid, and perhaps a little later we can send you more a month.

Another mother writes, "I feel so much like a beggar sending my boy to you all this time with so little money. This has been the hardest year of all for us." Four years later that family is still struggling to pay its debts to Higgins:

> I am ashamed of the way I have had to use you in regard to the school. In 1937 we had so many troubles that it was impossible to pay even our expenses. From Thanksgiving until August we had four deaths in our near family. I picked up a germ that came near taking my life and B— was ill. The lobster business was bad this fall. B— had a large catch but the price was lower than it had been in twenty years.

The son has been working away at the bill as well. A 1933 note from him says, "Am sending you my first check. It is lots different working in a gravel pit than going to school. I feel sure I will appreciate school more after working nine hours a day."

A number of parents, like the lobstering family above, are impoverished by low prices for their produce or by the inability of their own debtors to pay them.

> Much to my regret and humiliation, as well, it will be impossible for me to pay the boy's term bills now. I had plenty potatoes but with the prevailing low price it was impossible for me to clean up my fertilizer bill. I will do the best I can just as soon as I can. [undated]

> I had hoped to be able to pay something before this. We had hoped to sell our potatoes before this but the price has been so

low we sold only enough to pay our fertilizer bill and the expenses of digging. [1/23/35]

We have three car loads of apples to dispose of ere we return to Exeter and trust since things in general are moving faster our apples will also. I assure you that we are doing our utmost to keep M— at school. [3/19/34]

A dairyman will send money as soon as *he's* paid. A parent who runs a fishing camp sends fifty dollars ("only a *miserable bit* of all I owe") and will send more if the fishing business gets better. Some parents try barter. "Would it be possible for you to take some wood on our bill in the spring?" "Mr. Tracy I have a dozen nice chickens to sell this fall that would weigh five or six lbs. and I was wondering if you could use them, I thought it would help me out on the girls' expenses if you would take them." The painful letters go on and on.

My husband is into the camp and won't be out for some time and just as soon as we can we will pay you the amount he promised you for E—'s expenses. I myself have been sick and our expenses are very large. Thank you for being so kind in waiting. [5/22/32]

Since coming out of the woods last October I have not done a days work and cannot find any to do anywhere. [2/33]

My bank is closed now and I have only 37 cents. I hope it will open soon so I can send you a check. [3/23/33]

Dear friend, I am sending a check for fifty bucks I will have the other soon. [4/20/33]

Of course Mr. D— expects to go back on the rail road this month, but even then we would not have the money for school for a month as he has been so long out of work. . . . I have to leave it to you whether H— can stay or not. [4/1/35]

I am sending you ten dollars on A—'s bill and if it is allright with you I will send you the rest by February first. We are having a hard time to keep him at your school but I do want him to stay there if it is possible. [1/8/37]

Find enclosed money order for four dollars, haven't been working steady, this is all I could send now. [2/11/37]

My Dear Mr. Tracy, I am sending you a check for $30 for Dec. 31—that will be $5.00 short but I will make it up in Jan. Taxes insurance all come together this is for Nov. and Dec. Hope you are fine and I wish you a Merry Xmas. [12/12/36]

No doubt you noticed that I have been slow about paying my bills. Well to tell you the plain facts money has been very scarce with me this winter, as I have worked but very little since I came here last fall, and to keep the girl I have in Boston and the two at H.C.I. going it takes quite a little.

But I have a few seed potatoes to sell a little later soon as the roads open up, and I think I will be able to pay you some more then.

I wish to thank you for all favors. [4/7/34]

Sometimes in the end (though less often, apparently, than one would suppose) the parents have no recourse but to take the students out of school. A mother who has already tried without success to sell her radio writes in January of 1933, "Again I am sending W— Jr. back to school without any money. . . . W— has done such good work that I can't bear the thoughts of keeping him home and will do the best I can to get some money as soon as I can." She goes on to say that if Mr. Tracy can't take him back without any money, he should send him home at once, that very day. It looks as though poor W— Jr. has had to carry the note. We do not know how that transaction turned out, but in January 1935, she writes about her daughter,

A— is going to pack her things and bring them home tonight if that is satisfactory. Potatoes seem to have been going down instead of up. . . . I cannot see my way to pay her bills so will remove her now. . . . I am almost crazy to think of taking her out of school but what am I to do? . . . Thanks for all the favors and your kindness to her. It will be some time before I'll have any money for you but will settle all accounts before either child starts in again and if anything happens to me they will see that it is paid. Hoping you and Mrs. Tracy will come to see us sometimes.

I include the last sentence to suggest the characteristic lack of acrimony in these financial exchanges.

This story has a happy ending of sorts, for in 1942 Dad writes to the mother, "I have never questioned your bill. A bill is as good as the intentions of the person who owes it. I was very glad to hear about W— and A—. It hardly seems possible that youngsters can grow up and have homes of their own while I am still thinking of them as children." And then, as apparently requested, he gives the balance still owed ($38.50 for A—, $101.10 for W—) and, one imagines, gets it.

I am very much struck by the way the payments keep coming in after the education has been completed. In 1935 an old student sends fifteen dollars toward a 1933 bill; in 1938 he sends two dollars and asks if there is any work around the school that he can do to pay off some more. A boy sends ten dollars on account for his old bill, adding that he can't go to college yet, that he needs to work for a few years first; his father writes the school to promise that as soon as he gets his girl through the last year of nurse's training, he'll turn his attention to helping the boy pay the Higgins bill.

With whole families pitching in to pay, though, it is hard for the school to tell who's responsible. One irate boy, whose father has received a bill, writes:

> I wish to say that Dad has nothing to do about it. The deal was made between you and me and that I should pay when I have some money. I haven't been working and therefore I can't pay. My Dad has all he can do to keep the family. . . . as you and I made the deal, I think we should settle it. I will try and do my best, if I get some work.

Another boy's grandmother has written to assure the school that she has assumed the cost of her grandson's schooling and that, although the money may be irregular, it will come; six years later Dad writes to her, pointing out that $113 is still due and gets back a sharp reply from her daughter, the student's mother: Grandmother is having a brain tumor operation that very day and cannot be disturbed by any legal proceedings; the writer herself has never undertaken to pay for anybody's education, so too bad.

We do not have parental letters from other periods—the Depression and post-Depression letters must have been saved for their historical interest—but it is well to remember that there is always an economic depression of sorts in rural Maine. My father used to tell the story of an old woodsman who, asked how the Depression was affecting him, said that he hadn't noticed it. Letters from the early forties, a hypothetically more prosperous period, show that a lot of people are being dunned for small and long overdue amounts. Poor is still poor. There are ramifications, too, from the stress of the thirties. One late-thirties graduate writes in 1941, cheerful, saying that he's joined the Naval Flying Cadets and will be able to pay his three years' total in November; but in November his mother writes to report that he is working in the mill to hold things together at home, for his father has had a nervous breakdown. Correspondence suggests a high incidence of illness and psychological collapse.

"As long as anyone is paying as fast as he can it is all we expect," Dad writes in an undated letter sometime in the early forties. For those parents who are not paying at all and haven't seen fit to mention their lapse he has a sterner word, but I don't know whether it worked. There seem always to have been a lot of unpaid accounts. "In addition to this bill there is an unpaid balance of $147.50 from last year. We appreciate the fact that you will ultimately pay but we need money to settle our own bills," he says to one steady customer with a large family.

It's hard to imagine how the school kept going at all under the circumstances, but I suppose that much of the defaulting was on board and room and that the tuition payments from no-high-school towns came in rather more steadily. The state, too, seems to have paid a small per capita subsidy to "the academies of the state," though the more students you had the less you got per capita; in 1947 Higgins lost $597 in state money by enrolling nineteen more students than in the year previous, thus putting itself into a different bracket. Also, the Commissioner of Education could issue occasional special grants to private schools, though after a legislative change in 1933 the grants were made less frequently. There would have been a little, but only a very little, income from investments. No regular system of alumni contribution existed. Alumni were asked for money only in the greatest emergencies, and although some of them came through wonderfully on those occasions, they had no steady, supportive habit of giving to the old school. Individual trustees were sometimes a great boon, on the other hand. Judging by the trustees' minutes, Franklin Higgins kept lending the school money and then cancelling debts or portions of debts. Leon Thorsen ('26) gave five thousand dollars out of pocket to help the school in its later days. Leon Williams ('28), toward the end, took third mortgages on everything and lent the school ten thousand dollars without much confidence that he'd get it out again.

Sometimes, too, trustees saved money by doing jobs that would otherwise have been salaried; for instance, Leon Thorsen planned and supervised the construction of Tracy Hall. Now and then there were bequests, though not a lot of them.

We have not so far in this chapter talked about that principal financial arrangement, crucial to the whole notion of the school—student labor in exchange for board and room. Most students worked some, even if it was work around town (picking potatoes, shoveling snow, splitting wood) for spending money. Some students worked incredibly hard. Many students would have worked more if they could have gotten more work, but there are only so many jobs to do around a school, even if you maintain a high level of tidiness and cook a lot of peeled vegetables. Compensation wasn't high, but neither were school expenses. Robert Bearman ('46), who has been so obliging as to include figures, says that he swept floors in the Institute for $2.50 a week, and that he did kitchen work and waited on tables for $5.00 a week.

It was common for each student to do a variety of jobs at Higgins, probably in the interests of fairness; some jobs were much less pleasant than others. Mailman and headwaiter, for instance, would have been relatively pleasant occupations. At the bottom of the list would be the only job that Walter Elden ('27) found acutely unpleasant—helping the cook butcher some hogs that the school had been raising on kitchen garbage. Besides butchering hogs, we hope a one-time occupation, Walter Elden did a number of other jobs. He writes,

> After pushing the lawnmower miles around the campus, putting ten tons of coal down a chute into the coal bin and bucksawing furnace wood at Higgins I felt a part of the school; I might say a working part.

Merrill Clement ('43) tells a similar tale, though things sound marginally softer in his time:

> I did every job at school except wait on tables. I washed dishes, silver ware, dished up desserts and cakes, peeled pota-

toes, swept floors every where at different times. I even tended furnace at the boiler house. We used some wood and some coal.

Girls had fewer jobs—kitchen work and cleaning in their own dorm were it, I think—but they weren't protected from the unpleasantness of labor. Their options were limited, rather, by a conventional perception of "woman's work" (silly, for farm girls), and probably even more by rules about where they could be and when. Margaret Bishop ('44) told me that she was in charge of the girls' bathroom, and her peers always yelled for her when it overflowed. Besides that, her hair was always greasy from helping to fry donuts every morning before breakfast. Martha Bragger ('35) worked in the kitchen "every other week—washed glasses and silverware in scalding hot water and homemade lye soap." Alternate weeks she cleaned in the dorm.

Though Margaret's brother Ronald ('49) says that the work at Higgins was easy compared to farm work, it should be clear that these kids were doing, in a lot of cases, hard, nasty, sometimes dangerous adult work, and nobody was worrying about whether they got eight hours sleep if their job happened to require them to be up. Says Carl McGraw ('36), "Huck and I peeled all the vegetables—a bushel of potatoes every day and one other vegetable, e.g., a whole 50 lb. bag of onions *before breakfast*." Students in charge of the heating plant would have kept odd hours, too—Jake Bishop ('55) remembers a friend who had a cot and a study table in the boiler room—and the Keiths tell me that a night fire watch was organized in flammable Tibbetts Hall, the older boys volunteering to patrol in two-hour shifts all night. I find no record of ill effects from this irregular life and the injuries seem to have been few, though John Moore ('47) writes, "It's frightening to recall that I climbed those high ladders to the 3rd floor to put on storm windows."

It's frightening, too, to reflect that food, warmth, and safety were dependent on, and expensive equipment entrusted to, teenagers, that traditionally scatterbrained and irresponsible species. (And if you imagine that our fathers were more stable in their youths, reread *Seventeen* and see what Booth Tarkington has to say about it.) Tending the furnace seems to have been a particularly sensitive assignment. Willis Parker ('39) wrote to describe a close call.

During my tenure as night fireman, I would have to keep a good head of steam during basketball games in the gym. One night I went down to the boiler room at half-time and fired up, but the pressure wasn't quite up and a couple of guys were down there smoking (it was also the boys' smoking room). I asked them to close the draft doors in ten minutes and hurried back to the game (I think maybe Nettie was involved in my hurry). Some time later I had an uneasy feeling, and went back down to check. As I opened the boiler room door I glanced at the gauge, and the needle was just coming on to the pressure that would "blow off" the safety valves (this was the ultimate crime for a student fireman). I kicked shut the draft doors, yanked open the fire doors, and she didn't blow! But I can still feel the relief that I felt when that needle came back down!

His friend Bill Oliver ('39) fared less well. He says, "Probably my most unpleasant memory of Higgins was the weekend when I was tending the boiler room and somehow or other I inadvertently allowed the water level to go down in the tubes to the point where they burned out. This did cost the institution a great deal of money and for me it was a very traumatic experience."

The remarkable thing was not the odd mishap, but the fact that the school ordinarily functioned so well on student labor, that one could take it for granted that students would do their jobs more or less competently and on time, though now and then someone would be snapped out of the work force for flaws indigenous to his or her adolescence. We can see from letters to parents that workers were sometimes mouthy ("At the time we sent your bill, J— and the chef weren't quite agreeing on some of the details of running the kitchen and so J— wasn't working"), or lazy ("On three separate weekends, I went over to the Institute and emptied his wastebaskets myself when we were having services in the Chapel on Sunday"), or loud, silly, flirtatious ("Then at times she would sing and was generally noisy. . . . In addition to this, when some boys came around she was more interested in talking to the boys than in working"). But these are the exceptions. Mostly the horseplay was kept within bounds and the jobs got done.

Next after money, the necessity that gave most trouble was water. Higgins was not, of course, on a city system, there being none available; it was dependent upon its own sources, and these periodically ran dry, proved inadequate to new demands, or were rendered inaccessible from difficulties with pumps or pipes. Amphitheater Pond was originally devised as a water supply for Higgins, and the school seems always to have been digging wells. The trustees' minutes for the summer of 1941 are suspenseful as the well drilling goes to 665 feet without adequate water, then to 1087 feet. "Too far down for practical pumping," Frank Higgins concludes in his treasurer's journal, and in 1943 another well was drilled near the girls' dorm. By Philip Keith's time, only ten years later, another well was required, and again in Perry Wortman's tenure a new well was necessary. Water emergencies appear regularly in *Scrolls* and reminiscences. I quote here from a long anonymous poem in the February 1912 *Scroll*; it is called "The Little Injun," evidently razzing the pronunciation of "engine" by a student called West, whom I believe to be the William West who was later a dean at Howard University.

> *One Sunday morn*
> *The water was gone,*
> *And nary drop could we find;*
> *When we came from church,*
> *We were still in the lurch,*
> *And such distress in our mind!*
>
> *With hands so black*
> *From water's lack*
> *Our pitchers far we'd bear,*
> *"On the water wagon,"*
> *But our steps would lag on*
> *The next to the top-most stair.*
>
> *A week had passed*
> *Until at last*
> *We feared we must depart.*
> *We vowed we'd not stay*
> *Another whole day*
> *Unless the water would start.*

Til a sudden thought
Came like a shot;—
They bethought them of the well.
To Bangor town
They sent right down,
And after quite a spell

The creature came,
Now known to fame,
"The little injun," says West.
It thumps and thumps,
And pumps and pumps,
And seems to be doing its best.

The water came;
We did exclaim,
It was good enough to last,
And sure enough,—
Oh, it is tough!—
That water's a thing of the past.

The "injun" will puff,
But not enough,
And then will stop for breath.
We dare not drink
And we almost think
'Tis a matter of life and death.

Men come from Bangor;
It stirs our anger
That they don't know what to say.
No one comes near,
Or has any fear
For us who are wasting away.

The "injun" is pumping, And our hearts are thumping,
As we crave for the boon it may give.
It surely's a caution,
With no water for wash'n',
If it continues, how can we live?

The water wagon remains a familiar expedient in later disasters (see Ormonde Brown's recollections below).

A 1928 *Scroll* provides an in-joke clipping purportedly from a 1938 *Bangor Daily News*. It records the deaths of 150,000 people from the sudden outpouring of an underground river. I quote a representative paragraph:

> At 9:10 A.M. today a large volume of water started gushing from Charleston hill, sweeping farms, cattle, and trees along with it. Few people were aware of the danger until they were swept away. All the village washed away before the powerful water except the H.C.I. gym, a cement steel structure which was begun in 1928.

One imagines that the humor rests on the difficulty of getting anything like enough water out of that hill.

A note in the 1939 *Scroll* says that from October 18 to October 20 "The water pipes take a vacation and there is a drought in the dormitories and Institute." Again, in the mid forties, according to Ormonde Brown ('47), there was a drought occasioned by the breaking of the pump in the pond, a period during which "one didn't get too close to his fellow students."

> Water was hauled in by trucks in ten gallon cans. Students brushed their teeth at the pump on Mr. Higgins' lawn. You flushed the toilet by pouring down a bucket of water. The pump was hard to replace because we were just coming out of war time conditions. We had a long wait for a replacement pump to be delivered. I remember when it came. We loaded it on to a toboggan and pulled it to the pond. We helped the plumber put it in. We came back to the dorm all but frozen. Ma Hillman made us cocoa and sandwiches. From there we headed for the showers. A shower never felt better.

All this talk of tight budgets and tricky sanitation doesn't mean that Higgins students were eating poorhouse rations and dying of typhoid. Quite the contrary, though Higgins wasn't raising any sissies. The only lack that dismays me in retrospect is the absence of an infirmary, and even then I am dismayed more for the faculty than for the students. Coburn didn't have one either; schools like Higgins and Coburn couldn't. Nurses (unless some teacher had had the foresight to marry one) and infirmaries were too much for the budget to bear. Anyway, the school was designed for the healthy; sickness was an aberration not to be encouraged.

Lack of on-the-spot professional medical care would not have unnerved most students or their parents, for it's a deprivation all too familiar to rural Maine. During much of my own childhood in Charleston there was no doctor nearer than Dover, fifteen miles away (nor is there now, I think). Serious cases were likely to be backtracked out of Dover to Bangor, twenty-five miles on the other side of Charleston. We did have a retired veterinarian who was now and then consulted for a simple case; one of my childhood friends assured me that the evil black ointment he supplied for her poison ivy was meant for cats. The school, however, did not employ the vet, and tried to be scrupulous about diagnosing ailments that might be dangerous. Beryl Segre ('61) assures us that sick students were "taken into Bangor regardless as to day or night."

Very early in the century Charleston seems to have had its own doctor; I find a reference to him in a 1902 *Scroll* advertisement. For a number of years Corinth, the next town south, had a doctor or two who came up and treated Higgins students, and in my student days and later, Linus Stitham from Dover was the school doctor. Earlier, in the twenties, Hugh Smith tells me, Dr. MacDougal from Dover, whose son Albert attended Higgins, would come down for ball games and drop by the dorm afterward to do a little free doctoring: "Trot out your cripples, Smith," he'd say.

Nursing was done by the faculty. Of course, all boarding school faculty have to cope with the first symptoms before transferring the student to the infirmary, but Higgins faculty had no place to send their invalids. I remember my mother, as the principal's wife, reluctantly going to paint the sore throat of some girl whom she considered particularly unappealing; a faculty friend of mine in the sixties holding down an unmedicated epileptic for most of one weekend; a boy getting as far as Hugh Smith's room, collapsing on his couch, and deciding to ride out his illness there. Other stories are too loathsome to recount.

Of course none of this was great fun for the patients either. Frances Ward ('38) writes, "I hated to be ill. Miss Mitchell made us drink a big bowl of hot ginger tea. I never wanted my mother so much! Fortunately I was not ill too often." Ginger tea was gone by my time, but "Chicken soup for everything!" Barbara Abbott ('58) recalls. Martha Bragger ('35) writes, "Many in the dorm got boils one winter. The local doctor put a poultice of some black, smelly stuff on my boil. It didn't help. I went home on weekend and my father put on a poultice of honey and egg-white. It drew out the poison right away and it soon healed." (The black poultice sounds suspiciously like the poison-ivy "cat medicine," but surely not?) "No one got sick or injured," says Franklin Dufour ('41). "Couldn't afford it!"

A few memories are more pleasant. Jake Bishop ('55) has written to tell me how dorm boys would take their illnesses to Margaret Matheson, whose husband was coach and Dean of Boys. "I don't know how the school got the stuff but she had bandages, potions and pills that wouldn't quit. You'd go to see her and tell her all your intimate symptoms, she'd take your temperature, feel your head, look down your throat, mother you, dole out medicine, and somehow you would live." The hand on the head may have been particularly potent; Margaret Matheson was a highly decorative, elegantly dressed woman who cultivated an air of feminine fragility otherwise unknown at practical Higgins. It is hard to imagine her coping with enormous, rashy young men, but it is easy to imagine their getting well out of sheer gallantry.

The school tried, understandably, to send its seriously ill—and especially its contagious—students home, unless the trip seemed likely to kill them; there was some prejudice against sending Swans Island measles cases home on ferries in January, for instance. Liz Chase ('46) recalls that she went home to have her mumps, but stayed at school for flu "and was cared for well. I remember a teacher coming in and rubbing my chest with something for a cough." A 1926 graduate who prefers to be quoted anonymously provides a detailed account of the course of a contagious disease.

> In December of 1923 my roommate B— and I came down with what Dr. Weymouth called scarlet fever. We had high fever, sore throats, etc. The health officer from Bangor was called to confirm his diagnosis. Immediately Higgins was closed for the Christmas recess (four days early) and the children were dispersed to their homes. B— and I had to stay in our room for a few days. Miss Clark stayed too; she passed us

our food, but no one entered the room to care for us. When we were able my father came for us in our high old Reo car. There wasn't much snow so he could get through from Atkinson. B—'s folks (in Medford) didn't want her to come home as they ran the post office. Of course, we were quarantined. My folks put us in the living room in single beds but no one came into the room. They also passed our meals through the door. I believe we were a week late getting back to Higgins after Christmas vacation. No one else caught the disease and we often wondered how we got it in the first place!

The isolation of contagious students in their rooms was typical. So was closing the school early. Betty Roundy ('30) says that they got measles every spring and I guess that's not much of an exaggeration in certain periods. A 1946 letter to Ricky Shamwell's mother in Washington says that, "due to measles and mumps in the school," spring vacation will be seventeen days instead of the ten originally planned, but that "Ricardo may live in his room in the dormitory and I will find a place for him to take his meals if he stays over the vacation."

In short, the school was not obsessed with health care. Everybody, student and faculty, had a full schedule, with no time for illness. Nobody had time to hover, nobody had time to malinger. Merrill Clement ('43) says, "Most injuries didn't receive much treatment. Broken bones were cast. I think a few injuries got care in Dover-Foxcroft. Many injuries were taped and time cured." And Alden Mitchell ('41) remembers, "I had a second degree sunburn on my back and finally hitched a ride to East Corinth around 5:00 a.m. to see a Doctor to get some relief from the pain."

Food, on the other hand, gets very good reviews for the most part. One graduate, unable either to forget or to reproduce Cora McLean's Indian Pudding, wrote to my father for the recipe, and the McLeans, contacted in Aroostook County, supplied it. Nettie Hillman ('42) admits that she has always tried without success to duplicate Reggie Lunt's meatloaf, and her husband—Willis Parker ('39)—writes, "I would drive miles for another slab of his meatloaf between two slabs of his yeast bread. Mrs. Hillman's pies were superior, especially the custard. Sometimes I got to lick the bowl when she made peanut butter frosting." Martha Bragger ('35) says that she is still bowling over her relatives with the Higgins grapenut pudding recipe.

As one might expect, there were fluctuations of one sort or another over the years. For instance, Ellis Holt '27, who was a teenage vegetarian, remarks in passing that the nutritional supplements arranged by his mother annoyed the other students, for they only sometimes had milk and never had peanut butter. In later years the big aluminum pitchers of milk were a given. Earlier Ellis Holt would have starved, for Hugh Smith tells me that when he came to Higgins in 1920 there were no vegetables, only meat and potatoes, until the faculty protested. Pastry hit a peak in Ruby Hillman's years—late thirties, forties. Food during World War II was poor, says one alumnus, and "somewhat rationed," adds another, though the muffins are said to have been good. Frank Mace ('44) says that he was always hungry then, though food sounds fairly plentiful on paper: a compulsory report to the Office of Price Administration says that in December of 1942 the school used 800 pounds of flour, having bought none of its baked goods; 982 pounds of beef, 228 pounds of sugar, 262 pounds of butter, 100 pounds of dried beans, 206 gallons of fresh milk, 45 pounds of condensed milk, 375 pounds of canned fruits and vegetables, 108 pounds of sausage or luncheon meat, and so on with veal, lamb, pork, fish, soup, and other commodities, including eight gallons of fresh cream.

Here are some of the Higgins foods that graduates recalled with pleasure: red flannel hash, baked beans and brown bread; strawberry shortcake; stew beef and gravy; pancakes with real maple syrup; eggs poached or soft-fried, "two or three dozen on a platter"; fried ham; Bobbie McLean's Sunday night potato salad; salmon loaf with egg sauce; homemade ice cream on Sunday; corn on the cob; Sunday chicken; fish; hot donuts; homemade bread, rolls, biscuits, and muffins; roast pork; vegetable soup; pies, especially Ma Hillman's pineapple pie; salmon salad formed in an ice cream scoop; steaks; roasts; grapenut ice cream; steamed hot dogs; Ma Hillman's apple upside-down cake; spaghetti; chicken and gravy; oyster stew; chowder. Here are some foods not remembered with pleasure: gristle and gravy; liver; muffins with sawdust in for April Fool's day; "old mackerel, been dead a couple of weeks, eyes sunk in"; too-frequent boiled dinners; cold meat and baked potatoes twice a week (which chef Reggie Lunt candidly called "the easiest thing I can think of").

Because, perhaps especially for adolescents who have left their mothers, the personalities of the cooks help to flavor the food, we should not leave the chapter without a nod to them. Some meals were personal indeed. The out-of-season partridge that Robert Bearman ('46) impulsively shot one day was cooked up in the Higgins kitchen for him, and Ernie Ross ('51) says that "The cook would bake me a blueberry pie each time I hit a home run, and I loved her for it."

Some Higgins cooks passed through quickly—the cook who drank, the cook who was caught running around the dining room with a female student flung over his shoulder. Others stayed long enough to be institutions: Bobbie and Cora McLean; the Foggs; Ruby Hillman; Reggie Lunt; Mabel and Ed; Liz, Lil, and Hilma. Kitchen help had vivid memories of the cooks. Neal Brown ('56) writes:

> The food was excellent. I waited tables, and I ate like a horse. Ed and Mabel, a married couple, were the cooks during all my years at H.C.I. Mabel was a portly, no-nonsense, Maine country woman who called the shots in the kitchen with little protest from Ed. My favorite dish was Mabel's baked beans and brown bread, washed down with that fresh raw milk supplied by the Higgins cows.

Perhaps the cook who most delighted the faculty for his idiosyncracies if not his meals was Reginald Lunt. I was so small a child during his tenure that I believed his name really to be Wedgie—it made as much sense as a lot of other names—but in fact he had a speech impediment. He had also an eccentricity of vocabulary that went beyond spoonerisms or malapropisms and left his hearers drop-jawed. Examples survive. Yes, he said, he was prepared to make supper for the visiting team; he was having chop suey and had the credentials out already. On another occasion, when the boys were thought to be up to something nefarious—stealing food, perhaps?—he offered to "slotter up through the dorm" and find out. It is such things that give an institution, in the long run, a private vocabulary.

The scramble to provide necessities for a family of up to two hundred hungry, contagious, shower-loving adolescents in the face of a low budget, defaulting parents, iffy services, and dry wells, tells us something about why principals burn out. Only for its first eleven years, until 1910, did the school have its founder there with his checkbook out, ready to make up any year-end shortfall in his benevolent enterprise, and it is to the credit of the school that it continued to put student welfare first and trust that finances would work out. The plant was sound, the food good, the education solid, but there was never much margin for emergencies. Like the man in Stevie Smith's famous poem, "Not Waving But Drowning," Higgins was "much too far out all [its] life" for safety, but it gave up and went under only when its reserves were at last so tiny that the smallest of mishaps would have destroyed it in midyear.

VI

COURSES OF STUDY

It was many years after I had graduated that I met
[Mr. Tracy] on the street and we were going over the
old days. He began to laugh and asked me if I would
like to hear the incident that still stood out in his
mind about me. It seems someone asked me if it
were true that he was the outstanding math teacher
he was reputed to be. I agreed enthusiastically but
added that I was in absolute awe of his ability to tie
a necktie. That, after he had struggled four long
years to teach me Algebra—I might add, with only a
fair degree of success! I can still see the knots in those
ties.

—ANON. ('35)

he mission of Higgins, and of schools like Higgins, was
complicated by the diversity of its clientele. First of all, it
was, by origin, an academy, and therefore designed for the
intellectually elite. Charleston Academy, its earlier coun-
terpart, was part of a system that had supplied a relatively sophisticated education, even preparation for college, in a time when Maine
education beyond the grammar school level was sparse and iffy. Even
after the Free High School Act of 1873, private academies were set
apart as superior. State Superintendent of Schools Mr. Luce, in his
City Report, Bangor 1883, is blunt about the high schools: "They are
for the masses, not for the few, and they should be held firmly to the
work required to fit the masses for the common business of life." In

his opinion, high school graduates should be decently literate, able to speak coherently and do simple accounts, knowledgeable enough to vote, "fairly intelligent" about geography and history (especially of their own country), and informed enough about health not to destroy themselves by self-neglect. High schools were not expected to pay much if any attention to college preparation.

Private schools were another matter. They were, for instance, expected to offer Greek, a late nineteenth-century requirement for entrance to Colby, Bowdoin, and Bates, among other colleges, as well as Latin and other languages. They were also expected to offer a passable science program at a time when science was rather a new subject for schools (though at Bangor, chemical apparatus was in use at the girls' high school as early as 1859, before the boys had it). This was a formidable curriculum for a school operating with only four or five teachers. Keith's thesis has preserved the poignant tale of a Mr. Bartlett from Castine Normal School, who came to Patten Academy in the 1870s. He found "the idea of the academy, with Latin, Greek, French, and German . . . too much for him" and left after one day.

But Higgins's obligations were more complicated even than that: having embraced its mission of making education available to all Maine students who might otherwise be deprived of it, Higgins found itself bound to educate a substantial number of students for whom college was not a prospect. Some vocational offerings, therefore, seemed obligatory. Through most of its history we see something like three strata of course offerings, though no sort of "tracking" into levels of ability. First, there is the program for college prep; second, a similar but marginally less demanding program meant to produce liberally educated farmers, housewives, businessmen, and so on; third, programs designed to inculcate specific skills—nursing, teaching, office work. I shall follow the development of these strata one at a time.

The College Preparatory program, as it appears in the 1891 catalogue, is demanding but, by even slightly later standards, quaintly limited—in the fall term of one's junior year, for instance, the curriculum is Latin, Greek, Rhetoric, Elocution, and Vocal Music. In all, the program involves four years of Latin, including composition in that language; two of Greek, including composition; Ancient History, Ancient Geography, Mythology; three years of Math; much less

English than one expects now (and the first year of it is called "Reading and Spelling"!); Physiology, Physics, Geography, U.S. History and U.S. Constitution, World History, Elocution, Drawing, and Music. A student successfully completing this course was admitted to Colby without further examination.

Shortly after the incorporation of Higgins, its first principal, C. C. Richardson, set about the acquisition of scientific equipment—a telescope, a microscope, and so on—and in the 1902–03 catalogue the sciences have so multiplied that College Preparatory has split into two components, one with Greek and one a "Latin Scientific" course in which Sciences or Modern Languages may be substituted for Greek, though what the program in fact shows is French as a fourth-year substitute for Virgil. Physics has been joined by Botany, Chemistry, Geology, and Astronomy. This course is designed especially for those who are to enter "Technical Schools." By 1902 the College Preparatory (Classical) course also has assumed more modern lineaments—four years of English (rhetoric, composition, and literature), three of math, four of Latin, three of Greek (they are reading *Anabasis* and *The Iliad*), a year of science (part physics, part botany), and a year of French. History and geography appear to have gone by the board. Perhaps one is expected to know them, like spelling and reading, already, for a preparatory year (which one can take at Higgins or elsewhere) includes U.S. History and Advanced Geography. Three years later the two college prep courses have recombined, with some options of election, and by 1917 we have much the same program I knew in the fifties, though all along the way it has spells of dividing and reuniting the science/classics streams: four years of English, four of math, two of history, two or three of a modern language, and, according to taste, three or four of Latin or four of science, with dabbling back and forth encouraged. In its rigor this is not, with some variation of detail, unlike the new, tough curriculum currently being instituted by New York State.

Clyde Russell ('18), in an article that he sent back to the 1922 *Scroll*, says that "Like any business, high school must be measured by its product. The product of Higgins is its alumni." And he goes on to report what he knows of Higgins students currently at college. There are fourteen (seven of each sex) at Colby, prominent in literary matters, elocution, sports. There are four students at the University of

The Institute building.

Tibbetts Hall.

Tracy Hall.

The girls' dormitory.

The athletic field.

The gym.

Charleston's main street, October 1940. The building on the right
is the Post Office. Photograph courtesy of Alden Mitchell ('41).

The 1922 girls' basketball team. I admire the piratical headgear.
In 1922 they were not yet resenting the bloomers that made their
younger sisters curse Principal Tracy's conservative bias.

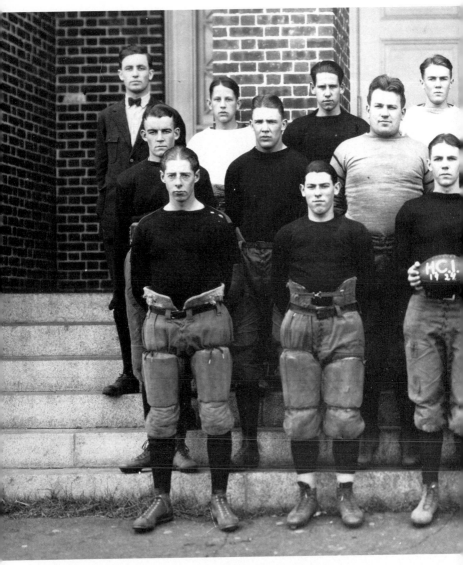

In 1924, football uniforms were still somewhat impromptu.
One man in the middle row is wearing a Hebron Academy jersey
inside-out; he is probably a postgraduate. Among the players,
I can identify with confidence only Leon Thorsen ('26), front

row left, who was later a most generous and valuable trustee.
I think that few, if any, of these men are still alive, for Hugh
Smith, whose photo this was, liked to walk me through it, saying,
"He's dead and he's dead and he's dead and he's dead."

Judging by costume, this orchestra is from the late 1920s.
This must be one of the last photos taken in the old Institute,
which burned in 1930. The portrait on the left is the founder's.

The one on the right represents Principal Foss and was later much borrowed as a prop for school plays. The one in the middle may be the founder's friend Charlie Tibbetts.

Gymnastics on the front campus. This is probably Joe
Roderick's spectacular team from the late thirties. We seem
to be using a length of clothesline in lieu of a high jump.

Academic regalia and the school trailer, 1938. This photograph
captures nicely the mixture of formal and informal that, in
retrospect, I find particularly characteristic of Higgins.

A piece of no-occasion Higgins snow sculpture in progress. This was taken sometime in the early forties, so perhaps it's a hostile gesture. At any rate, the cannon is pointing roughly in the direction of Europe.

These are the fondly remembered benches by the athletic field. Students here are not lined up for the camera; they really sat in a row like that all the time.

Sophomore Prize Speaking, spring of 1956. Because
I can, and because several of them are named elsewhere
in this book, I shall identify the participants. Back row,
left to right: David Jewett, Warren Hall, Erroll Page, Ronald
Perent, David Gray. Front row: Doris LaFlamme, Roberta
Simpson, Darthea Palmer, Ann Tracy, Sandra Rankin.

"Students are taught to provide their own amusements." The bottom man on the right is John Keith ('48).

Joannie

Skating at Amphitheater Pond.
The nymph in the mackinaw
is Joan Johnson ('47).

Fall Picnic at
Amphitheater Pond, mid 1940s.

"After classes are over," my mother labeled this shot in
her album. The Institute steps are just out of sight on the left.

Maine and two at Brown. People in college prep were not segregated; everyone took classes together. Intelligence was appreciated, and most of the students acted college bound, even if practical considerations would prevent some of them from going.

The second-stratum program, therefore, was in many respects identical to the college prep course. If it seems slightly more practical, it is not necessarily easier; the 1905 offerings, for instance, insert Physiology, Civics, Bookkeeping, and Psychology into a program that still includes Greek and Roman History. This program is at first, in 1891, simply called "Academic." Catalogues from the thirties and forties, when students were listed with their programs as well as home towns, confirm my suspicions that the middle stratum was much the largest, a good three-quarters of the school, with about one-eighth of the student body diverging to college prep and another eighth to vocational. I find no difference in that respect between the Depression and postwar prosperity. As the 1917 catalogue suggested, the second stratum kept the possibility of a B.S. open, though it was intended, as the 1891 catalogue says, "for a broad finishing course and a part of its branches are elective so that it may be made to serve the purpose of a complete education for the student, whatever be his calling in life." English, math, and science were stressed. In the postwar, college-conscious fifties, the catalogue description is optimistic, leaning toward the likelihood of either a B.S. or a technical school. The course is then called "Scientific" as opposed to "Classical"; the latter prepares one for a B.A. but not, evidently, for life. We are told, still, that the Scientific course is suitable for those who plan to "complete their formal studies with graduation from secondary school." By the mid sixties, expectations seem to be down. The middle way is now called "The General Course," and, unlike College Preparatory, Commercial, and Home Economics, it has no specific requirements in the catalogue, which says merely,

> There are in any school which accepts students of the full range of abilities those boys and girls who do not wish to follow any designated pattern but wish instead a program within their abilities in order to prepare for everyday living. These students should, with the help of the guidance department, select the subjects from the entire curriculum that will force them to work to the limits of their abilities and at the same

time give them materials they will find useful in their homes, their vocations, and their hobbies. No general course is listed in this catalog for it should be formed to meet the needs of the individual.

The 1972–73 catalogue lists no requirements, just courses available and "Areas of Study," which still include college prep, business ed, general, and home ec.

Higgins had, at one time and another, four vocational programs, though never more than two simultaneously. The earliest of these was the Normal Course, or Teachers' Training, first offered in the fall of 1902. Until 1932, when state law required all elementary school teachers to have at least a year of college-level Normal School, the Normal Course of a good secondary school was considered sufficient for the training of elementary school teachers, who were badly needed for rural classrooms. Some academies rather specialized in teacher training. Lee Academy, for instance, the majority of whose students were in that program, even called itself Lee Normal Academy until 1913, when the state legislature asked it to drop "Normal."

The Teachers' Training curriculum at Higgins was identical in its first two years to the program designed to produce well-educated citizens. In its last two years it added School Management, School Law, History of Education, Methods of Teaching, Psychology, and what was clearly, though it goes by various names over the years, classroom observation and practice teaching. For this last, remember, Higgins was equipped with a "model school" in its very own basement, two rooms with three grades each (in the years I went there) of elementary school children who were no doubt ravenous for the novelty of practice teachers. In compensation for the specialized courses, Normal students were let off some subjects more advanced than their teaching would require—Solid Geometry, for instance. The 1917 Teachers' Training Course gives a choice in the last year of Physics, Chemistry, or German, whereas the fourth-year "English Scientific" students were required to take both Physics and German and had already been required to take Chemistry the year previous, when the prospective teachers had been learning School Management and School Law. The 1917 catalogue assures us that "Graduates from this course have obtained State teachers' certificates without examination and have been uniformly successful as teachers." The state, not incidentally, gave some financial aid to schools training teachers.

In 1934, the gaps left by the withdrawal of the Normal course and its concomitant state aid were filled by the installation of another state-approved program, Home Economics. An essay in the 1938 *Scroll* sings the praises of this innovation. Homemaking, Marion Bartlett ('38) asserts, has become a science rather than a drudgery. Further, mothers "in this machine age" are neglecting to teach their daughters the fundamentals of homemaking. Since a girl still has to eat, dress, and associate with others, "she should know how to make herself desirable." It is a good, practical essay studded with bits of straightforwardness ("We can oftentimes make up for nature's lack of kindness by our style of dress"), and it suggests that the course has met with enthusiastic approval. The 1945 *Scroll* describes a tough, action-packed program. The girls spent their first nine weeks canning everything in sight—3,867 cans of corn, shell beans, tomatoes, pumpkins, cauliflower, string beans, pears, apples, applesauce, chicken, and chicken soup. They also made it possible for local women to assemble and send to the boys overseas five hundred cans of cookies, candy, puddings, baked beans, brown bread, pickles, nuts, and so on. Besides that, they learned to care for the sick, gave luncheons for the faculty, made coats, dresses, and suits, and took care of a live baby. These things were happening under the energetic supervision of Carlene Hillman ('38). Catalogues from this period assert that the course prepares one not only for life but for college and for hospital training in nursing.

State aid, as anybody knows who's gotten it, carries a price—bureaucrats feel free to huff down your neck. On December 19, 1947, a Mrs. Louise Fettinger ("Itinerant Teacher Trainer") wrote a snippy letter about home ec at Higgins, especially because the school was not offering Science of Living for freshmen. It is obscurely comforting to know that courses with silly names and fluffy content go back at least forty years, though you would think that in 1947 everyone would have been aware that life takes a lot of turns for which no science can prepare one. Mrs. Fettinger calls it "an excellent fundamental course in general living" and suggests that it will lure more students into home ec courses, a point of more interest to her than to my father, who replies, "I believe that at Higgins we have always tried to cooperate with the Home Economics Department. Since, however, from a graduating class of 62 last year, 45 were accepted by colleges—one of these M.I.T.—I can hardly see Higgins as an annex to the Home Economics Department." The home ec program, with a brief hiatus under Stub Foss, survived until the end of the school. In my own time, home ec courses enjoyed some popularity as electives for college-bound girls who were caught up in the domestic hype of the great fifties nesting urge. I still have a photograph of a freshman home ec class; nearest the camera, knitting industriously, is a friend who now teaches science in a community college.

Briefly, around the time of World War II, there was a Nurses' Training Course. The program appears in the 1937–38 catalogue, but not in the 1935–36 edition; I do not have the year between. It is listed in the 1946–47 catalogue but not in the 1950–51; again, the intervening years are not available. The 1937–38 listing is explicit about intentions, and I think that I hear the voice of my father, who liked to draw conclusions about success and failure:

> This course is offered to Seniors of unusual ability or to Post-graduates, who wish to train for nursing. The principal causes of student failures in hospital training are: Lack of knowledge of Chemistry and Home Economics, and inability to master Anatomy when physically tired from the general routine of training.
>
> This is a one year course and includes: English, Anatomy, Chemistry, and one or two years of Home Economics.

The Commercial course may have started in 1948–49—a surviving letter recommending the Thomas Natural Shorthand system suggests that it is to do so—but at any rate it was in place by 1950–51. It is clear from correspondence that my father hoped to offer the amount and sort of typing and shorthand that would give people an edge in college paper-writing and note-taking, as well as prepare them for office work. In the end, though, Gregg two-year shorthand won the day, and the course was clearly vocational despite incursions from the college-bound who wished to type. Bookkeeping and Business Math were added to the shorthand and typing, as well as something called General Business and, at last, a senior course called Office Practice. Straight business or commercial courses were of course nothing new; Bangor High, for instance, had had one since 1898. Perry Wortman in the sixties took over what had been the model classrooms in the basement and assigned them to commercial courses that had hitherto made do in the library and elsewhere. The 1966–67 catalogue encourages the commercial student to take a maximum of college prep courses and a minimum of commercial subjects if he or she plans to go to a business college.

You can see how homogeneity of the student body is attained—*all* students are encouraged to take as many and as tough college prep courses as they can bear, and for most of the school's history they are all taking them together; college-bound students dipping into vocational pursuits are taking the real thing, too. You may only want to type papers at a leisurely pace, but for a while you count your words-per-minute as closely as if you'd be paid for it some day, and you type all the better for it.

I have discussed briefly in Chapter IV such academic appendages as Bible and Music. Like these, Physical Education was something that Higgins usually, but not quite invariably, had. I was thankful that in my own time this advantage was available for only a year or two, but that is not to speak harshly of phys ed in general. It was probably not badly needed, though, in a school like Higgins. In the first place, a lot of the students played sports, a much higher percentage, I should think, than in a larger school or a public school. Of those who did not play, some were prevented by heavy chores at home. Those prevented by their own ineptitude got exercise by fighting their way to classes through snowdrifts, carrying trays of dishes, scrubbing floors, mowing lawns, and so on. Muscle tone was not a problem at Higgins.

A few, perhaps a half dozen of my two hundred respondents, expressed some dismay, in retrospect, about the quality of their education at Higgins, especially when compared to what their children and grandchildren are being taught. Educational content is more sophisticated everywhere now, I think, but at the same time I must admit that in some ways Higgins was unsophisticated for its own time. Ormonde Brown ('47) confesses that other students at college had been "exposed to a lot more than [he] had experienced." I went to Colby in the fall of 1958 largely unacquainted with post-Victorian fiction and uncertain how to pronounce half the words I knew. I was surprised, too, to find my professor alluding right out loud to Old Testament material as mythical. On the other hand, I already knew the whole first semester of college math and I tested out of the foreign language requirement and freshman comp. Mary Jane Keith ('52) said she had learned so much English literature that she was halfway through college before she saw anything new. Mary Day ('40) said that her Higgins anatomy class was better than the one she took at Eastern Maine General Hospital.

And I do remember learning some fine things in high school. For instance, I found out who was in those Indian suits at the Boston Tea Party; I read *Les Miserables* in French and quite a lot of *The Aeneid* in Latin; I was introduced to Gerard Manley Hopkins, still my favorite poet; I learned to type; I read a most eye-opening biography of Byron (the Maurois *Byron*, I think); and I found out there was a whole world of drama between Shakespeare and trash.

When I asked alumni what they remembered learning, they alluded particularly to languages, math, and ancient history (which they hadn't liked). Many graduates spoke more generally. "Learned more there in two years than anywhere else," says William Niehoff ('43). "Too much to list!" says a 1940 grad. "It would take reams of paper," says Harvey Davis ('29). "Everything," says Carlene Hillman ('38), and "Everything," says Erwin Kent ('52); "The foundations of the heavens and the verities of nature," says Albion Farnham ('29). Some intellectual episodes are so monumentally instructive—the first trip to Europe, for instance—that afterward you can't even remember what it was you used not to know. For a lot of students, maybe in some periods most students, Higgins was one of those episodes.

About half of my respondents took question number 22—"What do you remember learning?"—as a moral rather than an intellectual question. How to Study, they would tell me, or Cooperation, or Respect. Those answers, I think, are a comment neither on the vagueness of the question nor on the unintellectual orientation of the respondent, but on the educational impetus of the school itself. Higgins education was strong in two directions: it supplied a solid basis of fact and formula upon which to build further and more sophisticated knowledge, and it developed certain sorts of mental muscles. Almost four hundred years ago, Francis Bacon recommended specific studies to strengthen corresponding mental weaknesses, which "Like as Diseases of the Body, may have appropriate Exercises," advice we too seldom take in our desire to go on doing what we do well. For instance, he says, "if a Mans Wit be Wandring, let him Study the Mathematicks; For in Demonstrations, if his Wit be called away never so little, he must begin again. . . . " The wits of most Higgins students got a good dose of math, languages, English, science, and so on, and one imagines that they were enabled thereby to exercise logic, concentration, clarity, subtlety, and a host of other virtues. That, at any rate, was the school's intention.

We can see in classroom anecdotes and in *Scroll* collections of famous classroom stupidities that the faculty were trying to teach their students to think. That both the following examples are my father's efforts should not be taken to suggest that he was engaged in the struggle alone; far from it. Raymond Olmsted ('44) remembers "a story Mr. Tracy told in math class, in pointing out the importance of observation or paying attention, of a teacher he had once dipping a finger in some bad tasting liquid, then apparently putting it in his mouth to taste it." The upshot, of course, is that the whole class tasted the evil liquid themselves, not having noticed that the teacher had dipped one finger but tasted another. The *Scroll*, in a time when the jokes really happened and were not yet prefab with local names inserted, preserved many a classroom comeuppance for woolly thinking. The 1926 *Scroll*, in an anecdote entitled "Some Dog!" records the efforts of a too-hasty sophomore to solve an Algebra II problem about how long it would take a certain dog to catch a certain rabbit:

> Bright Soph (after working diligently for at least three seconds): "I find that the rabbit would take minus three jumps before he could be caught."
>
> Mr. Tracy: "Then according to that, the dog started so quickly that the rabbit backed into him."

Harvey Davis ('29) quotes my father as saying, "I do not expect you to remember all you have learned; just learn to apply yourself in life." If that is not the most academically sophisticated of educations, at any rate it is a durable one. I think of the medical school graduation speaker who said, "Half of what we've taught you is wrong, but unfortunately we don't know which half," and of a charming woman in her nineties, a retired English teacher, who told me with a wry grin, "Of course now we know that nothing I used to teach was true." Theories, even facts, go out of date; intellectual skills are more adaptable. Several graduates found out when they went to college that there were things they didn't know, but they did know how to work.

Arthur J. Roberts, President of Colby College 1908–1927, was beyond doubt the man my father most admired. He was quoted in our house a good deal at one time and another by my father and Hugh Smith both, and it is with some bemusement that I find myself quoting him for the first time; it makes me feel old. His views on education, however, make a suitable end to this chapter, for not only my father but his predecessor, Howard McLellan, and his successor, Philip Keith, graduated from Colby under Roberts's strongly individual hand. President Roberts always asserted that Education was the Enrichment of Life. And then he would round on those who had been arguing that it was possible to have too many educated people, and ask triumphantly, "How can you have too much enrichment of life?"

VII

CRIME AND
PUNISHMENT

One lovely, warm, moonlight night, I awoke after midnight, in a state of insomnia, and decided to tiptoe out-of-doors and wander about. Stealthily I descended the creaky hardwood corridor to the stairs and down to ground level. As I reached ever so quietly for the latch, a flashlight suddenly lighted the front door—Mr. Keith asked where I was going. In a gruff, cracked voice I replied, outside to find a couple of dimes I'd lost while rough-housing on the lawn that day. I further claimed that they'd reflect in the brilliant moonlight. Suffice it to say, he didn't buy my story. Instead, he suggested I sweep and wash the north and south reception rooms, after which I could peel the next day's potato quota—he was quite a sport—while he checked on my progress.

—BRAD BROWN ('47)

T he first Higgins catalogue (1891–92) contents itself with counseling students to maintain "a gentle and orderly manner" in and about the school, to attend classes and exercises, not to leave town without permission from the principal, and to attend church on Sunday. They are liable to expulsion for profanity, intemperance, or "any other kind of immorality."

By 1917, perhaps earlier, these general regulations have evolved into the form and substance they were to keep through 1958. They are in no way remarkable, but I set them down for readers unfamiliar with such promulgations.

REGULATIONS

1. Each student in the Dormitory is responsible for his room and a charge of one dollar will be made for each defacement of room or furniture.

2. Damage done in the halls or bath rooms of the Dormitory will be assessed on all students of the Dormitory.

3. Students are to keep their rooms neat and clean, and in the care of their rooms as well as in their conduct they are to conform to the requirements of those in charge.

4. Study hours are as follows: 8.30 A.M. to 11.15 A.M.; 1.00 P.M. to 3.15 P.M.; 7.30 P.M. to 9.30 P.M. The time from 3.15 to 7.30 P.M. is designated as recreation period. Every student is required to spend the first two hours of the evening study period in the study halls of the Institute Building under the supervision of instructors. The student is required to be in his own room for the remainder of the study period. Friday evenings are for social events. During the study hours the students must be in their rooms or recitation rooms. Ten o'clock is the retiring hour and must be faithfully adhered to.

5. Permission to leave town during any part of the term must be obtained from the Principal after the consent of the parents or guardians has been received, except in case of sickness or trips with the athletic team.

6. Students are required to attend regularly and punctually the exercises of the school; to be orderly and attentive during all public exercises, to be diligent in their studies, and in general, to observe such conduct in the schoolhouse and in the towns as shall tend to the good appearance, reputation, and advancement of the school.

7. Any immoral conduct, card playing, profane or indecent language, intoxicating liquors, or other practices detrimental to the good morals and interests of the school, shall subject the offender to reprimand or punishment by the Principal, or to dismissal by the Executive Committee.

8. It is the aim in discipline to inspire in the student correct and helpful habits and to inculcate a regard for that

which is manly and womanly in character. The number and character of the so-called "rules" are determined by the conduct of the students.

9. No student who persistently disregards any of the rules of the school, or whose influence is in any way pernicious, will be allowed to remain in the school. Moreover, *any boy or girl who cannot willingly and cheerfully comply with the school management, is requested not to apply for admission.*

10. Parties of boys and girls may go on hikes or picnics outside the village limits provided they have the consent of the principal and one of the teachers as chaperone.

Regulation number 7 is obviously the peg whereon the most dramatic tales of crime and punishment hang, but the perspicacious reader will notice hidden possibilities in numbers 3 and 9.

In 1959 Perry Wortman added official clauses about smoking (allowed for boys over sixteen, with parental permission) and possession of firearms for hunting (permission from parents, a hunting license, and a course in rifle safety required). By 1966 he had been driven to add a clause on personal appearance: "appearance is often an indication of attitude and . . . dress or hair that is far away from that normally expected and accepted is merely an attempt to flout authority." In the same year the regulations contain, once again, a notice that church attendance is required for Catholics and Protestants. Students of other faiths need not attend, he notes, but usually do. By then Higgins had foreign students, and the "other faiths" were sometimes too exotic to be accommodated in central Maine.

So much for the regulations as printed. We all understand that they omit mention of crimes that for propriety's sake we must assume Higgins students would never consider—larceny, fornication, arson—and they do not and cannot mention all the misdemeanors open to creative adolescence, except by a general allusion to "practices detrimental." Here are a few of the peccadillos that graduates admit to: whistling in study hall, going to the pond at night, stealing apples, playing strip poker in the library, picking the lock and dancing in the chapel at noon, kicking Coke bottles downstairs in the middle of the night, bringing a snake to class, stealing biscuits from the oven, hiding during bed check, locking the janitor in the coal bin, having a master key made, breaking streetlights, burning a hole in the headmaster's car upholstery with a cigar, locking a teacher in the music room, getting caught naked on the first floor, paddling freshmen, hanging long underwear in place of the flag, wearing pajamas to study hall, and dropping a water bomb on the principal's head. Notice that I said *graduates*—these pranksters survived.

Smoking (except as specified) and drinking, as activities especially anathematized in boarding schools, deserve a little elaboration. It's not clear to me precisely when smoking became permissible for boys at Higgins; apparently it was not allowed in the late twenties when Hugh Smith first taught there. Carl Hamlin ('39) says that they could smoke in the boiler room in his time. Since nobody knew then quite how bad it was for the body (though I remember the notion that it would stunt one's growth), other issues were involved in its prohibition. Baptists, of course, don't go for it; it's a vice. Probably even more important is the fact that, done in the wrong place, it's a terrific fire hazard. "Most dormitories are burned by smokers. If a dorm burns in the night students usually burn to death," my father writes to the parents of an expelled smoker in the early forties. There may have been some feeling, as well, that it was not quite gentlemanly, and I can guarantee that in my father's view it was something no lady, indeed no "nice girl," would ever do.

I wrote to ask Hugh Smith about smoking rules at Ricker and Coburn and include his reply in full.

> Secondary school boys weren't supposed to smoke. Of course, smoking wasn't as prevalent as it is now until after 1920 and World War I. I never saw a woman smoke until I went to a summer resort to work in 1923. So all or most prep school catalogues said smoking was not allowed.
>
> I never thought it was fair to take a seventeen or eighteen year old boy into the school who had been smoking probably since he was fourteen years old and tell him he could not smoke or force him to pretend that he wasn't.
>
> I was of the personal opinion that we were using the rule at Higgins to get rid of obnoxious boys, which I didn't think was fair either.
>
> At Ricker they were allowed to smoke outside the building on the back campus. At Coburn they were allowed to smoke in back of the buildings and not inside any building, for fire protection. They were not allowed to be standing on the porticoes or doorways so that the only things visitors saw was a boy posted outside with a cigarette in his hand.

> At Coburn when I found a veteran smoking inside a bathroom I fined him a dollar and collected the dollar before he had any more permissions. I told one boy whom I knew pretty well that if you had fun you had to pay for it, and he said that it wasn't that much fun.

Drinking is understood by both Baptists and schools to be bad for any number of reasons, ranging from the metaphysical (drink is an instrument of Satan) to the practical (drunken teenagers are worse than sober ones). The strength of the prohibition necessarily makes the acquisition and smuggling in of alcohol, if not the drinking of it, a tempting ritual demonstration of adulthood, so there's perpetual skirmishing between the rum runners and the border patrol. (Respondents tell me that during Prohibition the students fell back on hard cider. Beer was the sin of choice in other periods.) But readers not familiar with the social context should understand further that in towns like Charleston there was no tradition of cocktail partying or genteel social drinking. Of course one surmised that there was a little private beer drinking and backslapping going on here and there in Charleston's racier circles, but I literally never saw an adult take a drink until I was away at college, and my mother in her sixties still felt furtive about buying brandy for her fruitcake. If a town chanced not to have its own Town Drunk (some good man brought to ruin and prized as an example), there would likely be one within the next town or two. Our exemplum, who lived about half-way to Bangor, was college-educated and had been an unusually promising youth—a poet and a classicist. We often saw him shambling along beside the road, prematurely old. "That man knew Greek and Latin," my father would say as he slowed the car to offer him a ride.

Alumni through my own time may be surprised not to find dancing mentioned as a third cardinal sin, for it was always rather an issue. The Reverend John Higgins had been (says the *Portland Sunday Telegram and Sunday Press Herald* on the occasion of Higgins's hundredth anniversary) "a bitter foe of dancing," and his daughter, Ethel Beck, long a trustee of the school, felt the same way. My father, as a matter of fact, hadn't a thing in the world against dancing, though I imagine he was glad enough to avoid, by his deference to the founder's prejudices, one more distraction from the school's proper business. The Portland paper quotes him as saying, "We believe in school friendships, allow the boys and girls to mingle and all that, but dancing is prohibited. It is one of the school's regulations and must be enforced." I hope that it will not outrage alumni at this late date if I admit that he sent me to ballroom dancing lessons before I went to college, and that I have found a letter written to a boy's mother in the spring of 1940, saying that he understands that her situation "might be embarrassing" if her son isn't able to attend a certain dance, but that he wants him back on Friday.

The unrest and agitation caused by dance deprivation held steady over the decades. The December 1922 *Scroll* contains an editorial that fantasizes about the chapel floor with a good coat of wax on it and argues in oddly undemocratic fashion that the "evils in modern dancing" can be set right by having "the better class of people" (i.e., Higgins students?) take them up. There's a funnier and more covert swipe at the rule in one of those "Senior A-B-C" poems, same issue: "T is for Tewksbury from Bradford, you know, / Where dances are held, but they won't let us go." One perceives, through alumni memories, brief terpsichorean outbreaks over the years, sudden flashes of Corybantic feet, but nothing lasting. Merrill Clement ('43) said that in his last two years the teachers tried to have dancing in the chapel on Friday nights, "but only a few couples danced." Dennis Blodgett ('54) says that in his time, students danced in the gym for the first time in Higgins history. In my own years Nick Hashey, the football coach, sneaked in a little dancing in the guise of physical education, gym classes temporarily coed and fully clothed. A graduate as late as 1961 reminded me of an expression in vogue among Higgins students when she was there—"Might's well, can't dance." I don't think that my father's successors had anything against dancing either, but to break a prohibition so longstanding requires either a passionate conviction in favor of dancing, which no principal had, or a passionate determination to run one's own school in one's own way, which Perry Wortman had, so he at last instituted dances at Higgins. I don't know whether the founder flipped with disapproval in his grave, but I do know that a number of students were made very happy.

Dress code, another classic species of restriction, though it was more demanding than that of the public schools, was never very stringent. By my time, and for some period before that, boys were obliged to wear a tie to class and a tie and jacket to meals. In earlier and poorer days they were required merely to be "clean, neat, and well dressed," as Marguerite Smith ('28) says—a gesture of deference to clothing budgets. Regulations for girls varied more widely over the years as new moral pitfalls emerged with each new fashion, and we can see the school shifting its battle for modesty and warmth round and round the female body as it decrees long skirts, high necks, no skirts shorter than X, no transparent shirtwaists, long stockings, no slacks except with special dispensation for blizzards, and so on. Even the capitulation to jeans in 1969–70 ("as long as they were clean and not full of holes") may have represented an effort to cover the almost totally exposed leg of the miniskirt era.

In 1919–20 there was a short-lived effort to get the girls into uniform, a move almost certainly designed to blur economic differences. The June 1919 *Scroll* reports that the girls have voted to begin fall term wearing the "well-known Peter Thompson suit of dark blue serge." Now no longer well known, it was a kind of sailor dress with a middy blouse and a red tie. In the 1920 school photo only about half the girls are wearing it, and the movement seems to have worn itself out. Maine individualism runs deep.

Whatever the costume, it is as natural as breathing for students to chew away at the edges of the dress code. A 1927 graduate reports that her contemporaries used elastic waistbands so that they might roll their skirts shorter after the morning measurement. In the fifties girls created illusory stockings by drawing eyeliner seams up their legs, and boys pushed authority by wearing four-in-hands instead of traditional ties, and bolo ties instead of four-in-hands, and now and then brown shoelaces instead of bolos. Jake Bishop ('55) tells me that once all the boys tried wearing tie, jacket, and pajama tops to breakfast. But these were not important infractions.

By now the general reader will doubtless be slavering after tales of caning, flogging—all the traditional boarding school torments that lead to perversion later in life—and no wonder if the faculty *had* gone in for them, given the thousand annoyances that even kindly disposed adolescents *en masse* will daily, nay hourly, provide. In fact, although no official punishments involved corporal chastisement, there seems always to have been a good bit of spontaneous, impulsive violence on the part of the male faculty—wise off, get slammed against the wall. I have no evidence pre-1917, but since educational development has been in the direction of less, rather than more, violence, I think that we are safe in presuming its earlier existence.

Philip Keith, for instance, not at all a violent seeming man, was legendary for possessing not only the fastest but the most powerful feet in the east. Bill Oliver ('39) recalls a truant being kicked all the way upstairs to study hall, while Buddy Meader ('59) remembers two boys who had been cracking their knuckles during the sermon being kicked downstairs from church. (I am impressed at his kicking more than one boy at a time: did he get two at one blow, or were they docile enough to wait their turns?) A 1935 graduate writes:

> My roommate and I skipped school to go to Bangor to a Rogers Astaire movie. It was nearly 10 below and after receiving a ride on a truck loaded with baled hay we made it to Bangor. Study hall was nearly over when we reached the door entering the Institute—and were met by Mr. Keith. What followed still makes strong men cry. If you have ever heard stories of the size and dexterity of Mr. Keith's feet, believe it.

Gerald Osgood ('38) remembers Keith threatening some noisy students in a class with "Be quiet or I'll throw you out, and I won't bother to open the door." My father, too, is on record as offering a milder version of this threat: "I haven't thrown a boy out of a class for some time, but I can still do it." Another teacher did really throw a boy out of study hall, by his hair and the seat of his pants.

All this show of muscle was apparently not simple faculty self-indulgence, though it must have been a relief at the time. It had theory to justify it. Dad writes (3/26/43) to a student's mother, "You understand, Mrs. B—, that we do not believe in manhandling boys. However, this may be the exact thing that W— needs. There is a certain period in a boy's life when he has to have either a mental or a physical shake-up."

My own classmate, David Jewett, whose wit was the delight of our student lives but a dreadful temptation to faculty wrath, complained one spring that there were imprints of his body all along the upstairs Institute corridor. He took it gracefully, as boys generally seemed to. One day, I remember, he was being wigged around the corridor by

Roger Wing, the coach. "What kind of a dance do you call that?" someone teased him as he was putting himself back together. "Fling with Wing," he said. Later yet, Stub Foss, the penultimate principal, who was himself a product of the Higgins system, enjoyed for a while an especially good reputation for being able to roust boys without stirring resentment, though there is some alumni feeling that now and then he outdid himself. And even Peter Chase, who ran the school in its final year, reports that, pushed too far, he mashed a pie into the face of a food-stealing boy. It is nice to see traditions hang on.

Girls were not involved in anything of the sort. They were a protected species and therein lay their own hardships. Nor do I remember female teachers batting boys around, though I think that they could have gotten away with it; still, perhaps it would not have looked ladylike.

Official punishments ranged from a reprimand (which administered by my father was so formidable that perhaps it ought not to be put at the lower end of the scale after all), through loss of privileges, loss of work, and compulsory work (e.g., splitting wood, shoveling coal, polishing floors), through degrees of incarceration (confined to campus, to dorm, to room) to suspension, probation, and finally, expulsion. "Our discipline problems here are almost nil," said my father in the centenary newspaper article. "Most of our students come from rural communities, and, in many cases, the parents are making real sacrifices that they may attend school. The boys and girls realize this and they give us little trouble. We have few cases of suspension or expulsion. It might interest you to know that in my 20 years as principal, I have never had a strike or revolt amongst the pupils."

Of course, all principals have their own styles of discipline. Hugh Smith tells me that he, for instance, preferred to head off impending blowups, whereas Dad preferred to let them blow and regard the aftermath as educational. I don't think, though, that any of the Higgins principals were eager expellers. "Expulsion" from public school is a major gesture, but in the end the taxpayer's child has to be taken back and educated; expulsion from a private school is final, total, an authentic banishment from that particular society. Perry Wortman says that he sent home a higher percentage than any other principal, but one must take into account that he was dealing with a different type of student during the turbulent sixties. Howard McLellan, Philip Keith, Charles O'Connor, and Leon Meader seem to have been about as far from vindictive as men can get. Charles O'Connor tells me that he expelled three students during his year at Higgins: one for smoking in the attic, one for pregnancy, and one for indecent conduct. During Leon Meader's (and my) time at Higgins I remember four expulsions, though there were likely more. Two of the expelled had demonstrated bad attitudes so often that they passed through probation on their way to expulsion; the third master-minded a purely recreational riot of staggering proportions; and the fourth wrote his name in shit all over the men's room. I suppose that a fifth student, a sweet-faced sophomore boy whose room proved to be a cache of expensive stolen goods, must have been expelled as well, but all I remember is some men coming to take him away.

Early in my exploration of this topic a friend asked me what my father had most often expelled people for. "For pissing him off," I said, and although my answer was impulsive and somewhat unjust (alumni on every hand volunteer testimonies to his fairness) it holds some tincture of truth. Bad Attitude, that elusive catchall, was the quickest road to trouble on any level. How else can we account for the two-week campusing in the 1920s of a girl who, sent from English class to get her required coat from the dorm, came back wearing as well her hat, gloves, scarf, and overshoes? I suppose that bad attitude is regarded in schools as a kind of communicable disease, and there-fore any suspicion of it calls for strenuous action. Two of my father's favorite observations were pertinent to the hazards of defiance: he used to say that the only reason the boys didn't rise up in chapel and throw him out the window was that it didn't occur to them as a thing possible to do; and the time to expel, he believed, was when a student was about to do the school more harm than the school could do him good. A few deeds were either so dangerous (smoking in the old wooden dorms) or so flagrant a violation of clear rules (drinking), as to warrant almost automatic expulsion. Almost. There was always some leeway to consider individual circumstances.

Looking for patterns, I see that his treatment of student misbe-havior was very like his treatment of my own. That makes sense, for he had put in about twenty-five years of Higgins parenting before he got a chance at me. So I shall assert with confidence that he was sharp-tongued with folly, punitive with defiance, but often unexpectedly sweet about actual misdeeds; and that the mere thought of his displeasure was quite a check on the last two categories, maybe even on all three.

Romantic folly irked him particularly. Perhaps he would have thought "romantic folly" a redundancy. Elizabeth Chase ('46) recalls the embarrassment of his saying to her future husband, who was cozying up to her in a study hall seat forty years ago, that he thought Miss Chase could sit in her seat without any help. More than one graduate reported his saying that he didn't want his girls looking at their boyfriends "like a calf looks at a pail of warm milk." Wholesomeness was a cardinal virtue in his book, and soppiness wasn't wholesome. That is not to say that he was without sensibility. Leone Dakin ('21), later a trustee, tells me that one lovely, full-mooned fall evening he called her out of study hall and gave her secret permission to go with her boyfriend while he returned a neighbor's car and walk back with him; sixty-plus years don't seem to have taken the shine off that gift. But that was early. Another twenty years of watching adolescent romance may have soured him a little.

Looking over draft correspondence from about 1938 to 1944, the period for which secretarial notebooks have arbitrarily survived, I find perhaps fifteen expulsions, near expulsions, or less dramatic but nonetheless definitive actions, like refusing to have a student back the following year. Of the students involved, one had smoked, one had smoked and perhaps stolen as well, and two were runaways. One of the runaways had taken along a thirteen-year-old companion (who was not expelled) and thereby marked himself as a bad influence; the other had gone to Bangor for two days, though behind in his schoolwork, and "fooled away his money" at the movies. All the others were in trouble for insolence and bad attitude. The particulars vary but the principle seems consistent.

> I am very sorry to inform you that I have sent G— home for the balance of the school year. This morning G— was over to school, then left without permission and spent the forenoon in the dormitory. His excuse was that his stomach troubled him. G— is not sent home for this one act. He has been continuously out of place. Only this week, I had a talk with him

and tried to straighten him out, but I didn't accomplish anything. (5/17/43)

I am sending J— home for this reason. I put the boys on probation and specified that they should not enter the kitchen. . . . This morning J— deliberately went through the kitchen when he went into the dining hall to breakfast. That is a clear-cut case of deliberate insubordination. I am very sorry for you and Mrs. M— but I am not sorry for J—. He was hunting for trouble. (Undated)

I went to his seat and told him pleasantly to turn around again and study. I was working at the blackboard. A moment later I looked back and he was turning around fooling with the students behind him. If I had not been keeping him for discipline I would have handled the case much more leniently. As conditions were, I couldn't be lenient. Either J— was running the school or I was. (Undated)

Faculty are not as eager to get rid of troublemakers as one might suppose. Disruptive students are often popular with their peers, not just because they enliven routine but because troublemaking is as often the effect of initiative, intelligence, creativity, sensitivity, or excess of humor as it is of moral decadence or cussedness. Faculty like these virtues, too.

Today the faculty voted to send P— home. I am very sorry and the rest of the faculty feel the same. He had simply crowded me to a place where it was necessary to let him run the school or have the faculty run it. (6/1/41)

"Crowded" is a good word. Anybody who has taught in a private school knows the distress of being backed into irreversible action by some promising and personable student with a bent for self-destruction. (Or at least, any person of taste and decency does; there are always a few teachers who prefer the bland and cooperative.)

A kindred dilemma is catching a good student in a trap designed for a bad one. Teachers and administrators would do well to remember Jephthah's tragic vow, for as soon as they threaten "the next student who— ," ten to one, some innocent will barge into the situation and have to be punished. A letter too long to quote sets forth the case of J—, who *would* keep talking across the aisle at detention when told to be quiet, and this not forty-eight hours after a major edict that "some of the boys would lose work if their conduct and attitude did not improve." J— had not been on the mental list of prospects, but some self-destructive impulse urged him to test it. "So far as I am concerned," my father writes, "the latter part of the punishment [i.e., loss of work] was completely unnecessary. If he could just have sat down quietly after he had been disciplined. . . . " He adds, of J—'s defiant and recurrent conversations, "I could fail to see the first time, but I could hardly stand and permit J— to talk all afternoon." Once may be an impulse, a moment of mad indiscretion, while more than once suggests problems in attitude. Faculty who really do not wish evil on their students sometimes find voluntary blindness or deafness convenient. Myrtle Crocker ('46) sent the following story about discreet deafness. I need to explain first that my father was called "Black Bill" from the ominous darkening of his face when he was angry.

> One day a group of us town girls were [fooling] around in the girls' coat room. One of the girls said to my girl friend, "Here comes Black Bill," and my girl friend, thinking she was joking, stuck her head out the door and said, "Hello, Black Bill" just as your father walked in the other door. We were all holding our breaths, thinking your father would say something, but he walked by as though he never even heard her.

Some punishments, too, were allowed to take care of themselves. One graduate knows that he was clearly identifiable as a neighborhood apple thief by his inability to sit with any illusion of naturalness on his rocksalt-peppered bottom. How can a responsible principal follow an act like that? Nothing was said. At least once (and I suspect many times) my father set up the students' own anxiety to destroy them: he told four basketball players caught smoking that he'd talk to them later, and "later" dragged on and on until the end of term.

As I've said, my father could be tolerant about actual misdeeds, especially isolated and quirky ones. He was remarkably nice to me when he discovered that I had pleased my friends by hiding little pictures of bottles in my *Scroll* illustrations, for instance. I do not think he found that situation amusing, but certainly his sense of humor sometimes precluded punishment. Leone Dakin ('21) told me about a trick window in her dorm room that could be thrown off its rollers if opened with sufficient violence. It was her custom to do this whenever she had food from home that she wanted to share with her boyfriend, who was the student handyman. One night, unjustly exiled from a dorm party, she and her roommate laid out their food, painted their faces, rigged themselves up, flung up the window, and sent an SOS for repairs.

> To our amazement who should come up but Mr. Tracy himself. He took one look at us fixed up like two Harridans and went over to fix the window. Imagine our chagrin when he easily put it down with one finger! Evidently we'd not put it up with the usual bang. He had some of our refreshments and went out of the room with his mouth buttoned up so he wouldn't laugh.

Sabra Lee ('18) wrote about one mad spring afternoon when my father was out of town and the student body bamboozled a local substitute principal into letting them get up a party during school hours, with a Santa Claus, a Christmas tree, and herself banging out popular tunes on a resurrected reed organ. With the fearsome unpredictability that was to win him a reputation for omnipotence, my father suddenly appeared. Sabra offered her vindications the next day: the fellow students who had asked her to play the organ were both ministers' sons; further, she had expected to play "Love's Old Sweet Song" and "Mammy's Little Baby Loves Shortnin' Bread," but *not* "Alexander's Ragtime Band" or "Darktown Strutters' Ball." At first she assumed that his face, as he turned his back and stared out the window, was red with anger. Later she discovered that he had been struggling with laughter.

But to get back to impulsive crime in general, we should not leave the topic without some attention to theft and vandalism, the latter not only impulsive but irrational. Dad grouses in a letter to a parent in May of 1941, "P— and four other girls broke a lot of glass in the Charleston Grange Hall last Sunday afternoon. There is no reason, cause, or common sense to the act so far as I can see." He goes on to say that the bill for repairs will be forwarded and the girl should earn the money herself. Ellis Holt ('27) recalls sawing and splitting wood with a gang of friends to pay for their having broken a streetlight on the way home from Sunday School. That punishment has a corollary—upperclassmen who jeered and threw water at the woodsawyers were sent to finish the job in their places. The angriest letter about vandalism dates from some time in the winter of 1943. One presumes that wartime conditions made the crime more infuriating; perhaps, too, vandalism, like young love, becomes more annoying as the years go by.

> Six boys intentionally broke the glass from a window in the heating plant. If we had not discovered this in time, the automatic pump would have frozen. There is no excuse for boys of high school age committing an act of this kind. . . . If this money is not earned by the boy or deducted from his spending money I do not care to have the boy back in school.

Restitution seems to have been the principal penalty for minor, spontaneous thefts:

> I am very sorry to report that your son and another boy visited the grammar school rooms and picked up a collection of pencils and pens. I investigated the situation and the boys returned the pens and pencils to me. I think the boys were equally at fault. I charged the boys $2.50 each to settle any claims for pens and pencils destroyed and also to punish them for their offense." (3/27/43)

In another case, when a boy stole basketball shoes and a basketball suit from the coach's room, the faculty ruled that he should buy the items, but gave him 20 percent off on the suit because he had stolen a used one!

"The strength of discipline depends on the respect which those who are subject to this discipline have for its fairness and justice," my father wrote on October 15, 1940. That makes sense, and it worked for him. "Fair" is an adjective used over and over when alumni respondents talk about him as headmaster, and God knows his discipline was strong. And yet I am surprised that students perceived the fairness of his intentions when one boy would be expelled for smoking, say, and another not. (Of a boy who within a short period has smoked in the basement of the Institute, quarreled with a teacher, and had his social privileges revoked, he writes merely, "W—'s conduct seems to be perfectly all right now. I believe that W—, as boys sometimes will, got rather unruly for a few days. . . . ") Adults understand the theory that real fairness in private parenting lies in considering the needs of the individual child rather than dispensing across-the-board uniformity of treatment, but children do not naturally take to that system.

Further, he was capable of impulsive expulsion, as far as I can tell. Ronald Bishop ('49) told me about the night that twelve or fifteen boys were caught swimming up at the pond and presented in the small hours to the principal, who woke up and expelled them all on the spot. But the next day he reinstated them, so perhaps the willingness to reverse himself if he overreacted was part of the fairness his students perceived. I saw one instance of this myself when I was very young, and it made an impression. A girl came to the door of the kitchen, wanting to go home but having no written permission to do so, and I think she may have been already on the warpath when she came. I can see her standing there redfaced on the threshold, crying and chewing gum, announcing that she didn't intend to bother with a permission every time she wanted to go home. In that case, he snapped, she might as well go home and stay there. In a bit it seemed to occur to him either that he had expelled her accidentally or that she might perceive him as having done so. He asked at the porch window where Miss So-and-so was; packing, his informant told him rather icily. That's the last I remember of the incident, but he was clearly on his way to unexpel her.

In the end, his students must have perceived him as fair on the basis of his personality and intentions rather than on the consistency of the evidence: he was a fair man, therefore he must have committed a fair action, rather than the converse, that he committed fair actions and was therefore a fair man. Certainly he could be trusted to care about students, even students he'd gotten rid of, as the next letter will show. It is written to a boy who has been asked not to come back the following year, for not only has he smoked but there is strong circumstantial evidence that he has subsequently stolen a watch. He appears to have been trying to argue his way back in, but we do not have his letter. The response to it is long, detailed, thoughtful, and patient, but I've excerpted only the part that strikes me as funny as well.

> There is no connection that I can see and I certainly didn't mean to imply that there was any connection between smoking and stealing a watch. Many people smoke who don't steal,

and I have no doubt many people steal who don't smoke. However, your smoking in the dorm had placed you in a serious disciplinary position. . . . When you did get in further difficulties then the smoking incident was reviewed as well as the leniency that had been shown you. This is a very natural method of procedure either in school or after one has completed his education.

One type of punishment we have not yet discussed is the discipline wreaked upon offensive students by their peers, who, given a chance, can get straight to the point with devices off-limits to the faculty. A faculty member, for instance, cannot enforce hygiene by putting a dead woodchuck into the bed of a smelly boy, as John Bradeen ('28) recalls being done, much less drive him to the showers by pouring Absorbine Jr. on the crotch of his pajamas, a remedy that Pete Minott ('38) remembers a friend of his applying.

The faculty can, of course, manage to be looking in the other direction while these things are done. My father told a story wherein a scrupulous student asked his permission to beat up a boy who needed it for reasons that now escape me. Certainly not, said my father, but he thought it likely that he and Mr. Smith would both be away from the dorm at around nine o'clock.

With that story in mind, I asked alumni what they would have done about a loathsome peer. Most of them claimed that they had no loathsome peers, which is a testimony to something, but whether to the quality of the student body or to the deceptiveness of memory I'm not sure. Of those who admitted the possibility, some thought they'd ignore him and some thought they'd try to reform him. I gather that interstudent relationships were fairly peaceful over the years. I have only a few stories of retribution. In the late twenties there was a priggish boy who got a fellow student expelled for a vice in which he also indulged; he was subsequently "hounded across country," says Ellis Holt, under a barrage of rocks and apples. A 1934 graduate reveals that when the town girls' lunches were being stolen, one ingenious mother made sandwiches with Ipecac and the thief fell into the trap. Bill Oliver ('39) remembers a kleptomaniac who was caught in the act, ducked into a tub of water, and paddled dry. A 1970 graduate tells me of a boy who hit his girlfriend, a girl very much more popular than he was, and had to flee the wrath of the other boys.

I have been struck, writing this, by the good cheer with which the boys in particular seem to have taken their punishments and battings around. For years I listened to my father and Hugh Smith talk of students who came back twenty years later and thanked them for one of those "mental or physical jolts" to which I earlier alluded. The Student Who Came Back had a certain mythic status in my mind, but I felt, all the same, incredulous, for I could not conceive of being anything but still furious twenty or forty or sixty years after such a blow to the pride. Lately I have remembered that the Student Who Came Back was always male. Many more female than male students were still cross about particular punishments that they considered excessive; in fact, the handful of male respondents who resented anything at all were likelier to resent an omission than a commission—for instance, the school's failure to replace the alarm clock of Walter Elden ('27), which was stolen by visiting basketball players who used his room.

Perhaps this difference in reactions is gender-related. (My brother, in sixth grade or so, had a tough teacher whom the boys adored and the girls hated. "I sure do like that Mrs. Eaton," one boy told my mother, "but gorry, don't it hurt when she hits you with the bell." Once a boy locked her in the girls' toilet; when she burst free, he ran for the outside door, but she heaved the bell after him and knocked him cold. It was all considered fair play.) Or perhaps because the girls were not cuffed around, their punishments seemed more serious, formal, humiliating. It is not possible to conclude from the existing evidence whether grudge-holding or acceptance of cuffing are indeed sex-biased characteristics, but a poem that appeared in the 1922 *Scroll* seems a fair summation of what has emerged as a dominantly male attitude.

When you're only simply fooling,
And it's only playful fun
And you hear Hugh's footsteps coming
And you don't have time to run
And you just step into the closet
And you shut the door with the prayer
That though he may suspect you're in it
He won't think to look in there.
But you hear the footsteps nearing

And he opens wide the door
And you wish that you were sinking
About ten feet right through the floor
And his voice rings out on the balmy air,
"What in the deuce are you doing in there?"
And you mumble and stutter, "Nothing, Sir,"
And you feel just like a yellow cur
He says, "Two weeks on the campus, Son,"
Then, oh boy! ain't we got fun.

VIII

CALENDAR

I think the worst season for me was the late spring—graduation. Saying good-bye to the grads that I'd never see again. . . . the upperclassmen that wouldn't be back.

—BARBARA ABBOT ('58)

A ll sensible boarding schools stud their calendars with occasion and ceremony. Self-preservation, if no higher motive, mandates that they do so, for students crave incident and will invent it themselves if not otherwise accommodated; years are longer, too, for adolescents than they are for us, and so require mileposts. Some recurrent events are supplied by school authorities, some by nature, some by happenstance, but each phenomenon rolling by—the senior play or the first ice storm or the day all the snow slides off the Institute roof at once with a roar like Niagara—offers some hope that the world is an ordered and regular place, even an entertaining one. Nothing short of a high church calendar offers such a lovely recurrent shape as the calendar of a well-regulated boarding school.

By the early 1920s, and perhaps earlier, the Higgins year had taken on a pattern that would hold, with only minor variations, until the 1960s, when it was altered not by the revolutionary spirit of that decade but by Perry Wortman, a strong and perhaps unsentimental principal who overrode Higgins customs in ways that seemed to him sensible. My brother, who graduated in 1968, recognized nothing in this chapter until Senior Essay Day in April. Many of the changes—the introduction of proms, for instance—must have made the students happy, but the more like a public high school Higgins became, and the less (in the neutral sense of the word) peculiar, the less point there is in writing about it, so we shall stick to the shape of Higgins's middle years. The events that follow seemed, in their time, as immutable as the Charleston hills.

Autumn, in a boarding school, is a season of reunion and the renewal of hope. Friends and roommates meet again; they construct fresh nests and assess new faces for romantic possibility. And in a small town like Charleston, even those too old or too young for high school feel a quickening of the spirits, for the likelihood of human drama—delinquency, fainting, public hysteria, expulsion—is increased a hundredfold. Therefore, the first major occasion is the day of arrival itself. Not more than a year ago I dreamed that it was the day the students came back, and there I was, sixteen again, walking up the gravel drive by the girls' dorm with my two dearest friends. On the steps of the boys' dorm our allies and comrades, Gray, Jewett, and Eaton, were leaping to their feet, trying in vain to look offhand, though in fact all six of us were too buoyant to keep our feet on the ground, so intoxicated were we by the joy of the annual return.

As far back as the school's infancy in the 1890s, autumns were marked by the onset of hikes and picnics. Many a graduate from the 1920s cited as a favorite memory the "welcome back" steak fry at a brook down behind the school, when my father, then principal, is said to have cooked the steaks himself. A 1926 *Scroll* describes "a supper of potatoes, beefsteak, bread, cake, and coffee" after which the students "gathered round the dying fire and gave cheers and sang songs." That cheerful and imbalanced menu is clearly one of my father's own devising; it captures perfectly his "potato is a vegetable" school of nutrition. Steak fries persisted through the penniless thirties, but were presumably done in by wartime rationing. When I was a child in the forties we were still having picnics, usually at Amphitheater Pond (another of the founder's improvements), from which the school derived much of its water and on which students skated in season. Merrill Clement ('43) wrote, "I remember the old car that the cook used to take the old wooden trailer up to the pond for a picnic. Everything was served from pots in the trailer." Indeed, a snapshot survives of faculty members dipping up beans and glasses of milk for a line of boys with their pants turned up to the proper height for 1946. The menu had declined from steak to beans, but food was not the point. The sharp air and the leaves on the still surface of the pond were more important. "Beautiful beautiful falls," Leroy Kennedy ('57) remembers, "the smell of autumn leaves." It was the smell of real life, school life, beginning again.

Freshman Reception, a more formal celebration of the new academic year, came ten days or so into the new term. Although the 1926 *Scroll* describes it as "the one big social event of the school year," I can't recall that it impressed me and my peers quite that way. Still, even in the fifties it possessed a certain ceremonial weight. If you had a new dress for "good" that year, you wore it even though it was wool and too hot: Freshman Reception was that important. A 1916 *Scroll* describes the occasion in "A Letter Written in the Fall Term":

> Last Friday night a reception was given the Freshmen by the upper classmen. We were escorted the whole length of the chapel by the Seniors and introduced to the Faculty, who looked on us with reassuring smiles which seemed to say, "Some day you will be wiser than you are now." Then somebody shouted "Tucker!" and with "Heskey" at the piano we all joined in the games until about 10:30 when refreshments were served. Then a Senior announced the last game, after which we returned to our rooms.

In the 1926 account, games were down and entertainment was up. "Myrtle Paine and Leon Williams gave readings. Mrs. E. E. Herrick sang two solos. Ruth Ramsdell and Katherine King played two piano duets. Only one game of Hello and Good-Bye was played. Refreshments of punch and cookies were served." Games were mercifully gone before my time, but the rest of it looks familiar—the introductions, the readings, the solos, the punch and cookies.

After the last of summer weather wore away, as it does early in Maine, picnics gave way to football rallies and campfires grew to bonfires. The climax of the season (by 1937) and object of the most bloodthirsty rally was the annual Armistice Day game with our ancient enemy MCI—Maine Central Institute. No ironic contrast between date and attitude occurred to us, for in armistice we heard only the "arm." This was a school rivalry so fearsome that even now I find myself quite unable to consider subscribing to the long-distance alternative to AT&T. Scraps of memorabilia testify to the importance of that game—a large, glossy, printed program taped in Marilyn White's 1949–50 scrapbook, quite an unusual extravagance; a letter from my father to Principal Purinton, saying that the game should take place on Armistice Day "regardless of the day of the week." Mary Jane Keith ('52) remembers in particular one wartime Armistice game rally when the school was honoring a student who was leaving for the army. "We sang all the old World War I songs and had a grand patriotic evening," she says.

I have been dismayed to find that the original highlight of the fall term, perhaps the most popular annual event in Higgins history, had disappeared before my time. The Athletic Association Fair was instituted by Principal Linwood Workman in 1908 on Washington's Birthday, but later moved to November. It had booths, handicrafts and food for sale, and in the evening a much-loved student/faculty/town play, in which the principal or submaster seems often to have played the lead. The magnificence of this affair must have escalated yearly, to judge by random *Scroll* descriptions. In 1909 there were three booths for fancy articles, ice cream, candy, a grab bag, and *Out of His Sphere*, a play about a restless farmer who is drugged and carried off to be a rich man but in the end prefers his old life. By 1910 the grabs were drawn up out of a well in a bucket, there was a Japanese tea booth and a double ice cream parlor with tête-a-tête tables, and an orchestra played throughout. The production that year was *The Valley Farm*. In 1915 there was a "large tree full of oranges which brought to the purchaser a package from a nearby booth." Nineteen twenty-one turned the whole chapel into a Japanese street, with cherry trees, butterflies, and a tea garden. An oyster supper was followed by a play called *Wives to Burn*. Though subsequent students went on adding fortune tellers, teepees, African Dodgers, and musical programs, some kind of orgiastic peak seems to have been reached in the fall of 1923, when seven booths were decorated to represent different holidays. Picture it: the freshmen's Christmas tree, the juniors' Independence Day flags, the Y.W.C.A.'s Halloween cats and owls and witches, not to mention the signs of May Day, Thanksgiving, Easter, and Saint Patrick's Day, all jostling for place; the hawking of punch, cookies, hot dogs, ice cream, homemade candy, fancy work, Higgins banners, grabs.

In the fall of 1929 the AA Fair was "postponed" and apparently never rescheduled—cancelled, I imagine, in deference to Depression-stricken students who could not have taken part in all that consumption. Perhaps, too, my father felt that such a mad extravaganza distracted too much from studies, for I note that he did not revive it when the Depression was over. I find one reference to a pale version of it in the fall of 1930, and then no more mention. My brother reports, however, that a ghost of it appeared in the winter of 1965, when the Varsity Club gave a fair with homemade ice cream, bowling, and gambling.

The seniors had been doing an annual play since 1922, maybe earlier. The juniors seem to have taken up the custom at about the same time the AA Fair and its play disappeared. By my time, those two classes produced all the theater there was at Higgins. Their play-giving was both honorific and obligatory. The freshmen and sophomores were obliged to participate in Prize Speaking, a more solitary and harrowing species of entertainment (see below); juniors and seniors, having lived through that and demonstrated that they could memorize, were accorded the pleasure of working in groups—and a great pleasure it was, with meetings at ordinarily unauthorized hours, backstage huddles of wonderful complicity, and the excitement of joint creation. The seniors usually gave their play in November, the juniors in April. Higgins plays were well attended by school and town, and as the only drama in Charleston they were valued by us all considerably above any possible literary merit. In fact, our efforts ran the gamut from comedy (*Patty Makes Things Hum*, *Judy Pulls the Curtain*) to mystery-comedy (*Great Caesar's Ghost*, *Finders Creepers*), and there they stopped. The agonizing struggle to "get inside" Juliet or Anne Frank, so often depicted in modern adolescent literature, was unknown to us, whose stage personae rarely required two dimensions, let alone three.

After Thanksgiving, the onset of serious winter was marked for the girls by the imposition of a subruling in the dress code: they were obliged to wear stockings until Easter, not for formality's sake, but for warmth. I think that knee socks were a permissible alternative for classes when I was there, but mostly we wore nylons with white bobby socks over them, perhaps an unconscious attempt to look normal and pretend that winter wasn't happening. You can see the unnaturally shiny legs above the socks in group photos. I imagine that for the picture-taking the nylons were authentic; however, stockingless girls sometimes improvised with eye-liner seams, and the artistic added olive oil for gloss.

Exams came before Christmas, something of a curb on holiday merriment, but (depending on the vigor of the music program) there was sometimes a Christmas concert, and I find in old yearbooks the occasional mention of a Christmas operetta. Not only Higgins but the local grade schools took part in Christmas concerts. In 1951, for instance, the West Charleston children sang "My Radio Doll" and "Santa Claus Is Coming to Town," the Glee Club tackled "Jeanette Isabella," and the band banged out "March of the Three Kings"; this just for starters. The dorm girls usually had a party, and once or twice in my childhood the home ec classes found themselves in a child-rearing (or perhaps a party-giving?) segment of study and devised a Christmas treat for faculty children. We knew quite well that our innocent gambols were being studied, but we were so used to being HCI's token children that we took scrutiny for granted; we were happy, in short, to play their games, trip the levers, and make off with the cheese.

January is to the year what three A.M. is to the day: dark and cold have lasted a long time already and will last a long time more. The month was redeemed only by the prospect of midweek snowstorms so violent as to disrupt routine. Indeed, any degree of disruption was welcome—the north wind that sent us to the coatrooms to get our jackets for classroom wear, drifts deep enough that the girls were issued permission to wear slacks, and, once in five years, a storm so bad that school was closed for the day. Even snow, that monotonous superfluity, could grow interesting again by its sheer excess. If you could say, "We had to tunnel . . . snowshoe out the back door . . . call a bulldozer, because the plow was too light," then winter justified itself. And while all this snowing went on, the basketball season had been getting into full stride, pounding down the weeks toward tournament. When the details of clever plays and close games have faded, the smell of sweaty uniforms persists, and the peculiar fat spank of a dribbled ball, the vibration of a rim shot, still echo in the mind as winter sounds.

Sometime in February there occurred a phenomenon called Religious Emphasis Week. Not a promising title, you say? Ah, but you never knew the Reverend Bill Turkington, who came to us for close to twenty years, from the mid forties to the mid sixties. Actually I remember him best from grade school, when we needed him even more, not for our sins but for our delight. I don't imagine that he had the slightest obligation to come down to our basement classrooms and entertain us, but he did it, and there were no more welcome words in the language than "Mr. Turkington is coming." For us little Baptists every week was religious emphasis week, but only one day in the year was circus and concert and celebration, and that was Mr. Turkington's day. And what did this magical, curly-headed Irishman do that so enraptured us? Well, he could play hymns on his trumpet mouthpiece *without the trumpet*—that was always a big hit—not to mention what he could do with the trumpet attached. He sang us comic songs, which we begged for year after year: "Sing the one about the preacher and the bear! Sing about the gooseberry tree!" Every year we howled with joy, as if we'd never heard them before. They were, essentially, ethnic jokes set to music, and it gives me a bit of a turn to think about them now, but what did any of us know in the forties and fifties? All I can plead in our defense is that at least all the butts of the jokes were seen as extraordinarily crafty, not extraordinarily stupid, as in today's one-liners.

Old school papers tell me that upstairs with his Higgins clientele he was singing Irish songs as well, speaking on free will and self-control, answering questions at forums, speaking on the five crowns of Jesus, playing the accordion and the piano in addition to the trumpet, telling jokes, and making himself available for counseling. Higgins adored him and entertained him right back tooth and nail—teas, banquets, amateur shows, the Girls' Glee Club singing "Irish Lullaby." I don't know how students before or after his years managed to hang on until March and the relief of Tournament.

"Tournament time": Queen Guinevere in Camelot never uttered

that phrase with half the longing for glamour and incident that we did. By March our lives were reruns in black and white and we all suffered from cumulative claustrophobia, for when it snowed in rural Maine all entertainments beyond walking distance were perforce given up, sometimes with weeping. But in March also the snow was collapsing into gritty piles, brown patches were showing, the first whiff of rotted vegetation hung on the air: it was an unaesthetic period, but vaguely hopeful. And then there was the annual prep school basketball tournament at the University of Maine.

I am indebted to Ronald Bishop ('49) for making a connection that I had felt rather than understood. After remarking that he was "greatly inspired by the magnificence of that whole spectacle," he adds, "Also, that, in my mind, was always the beginning of spring. I can remember being impressed that the snow was melting at basketball tournament time. Nowadays even, the first day that I see the snow melting after a long winter and there's that certain touch in the air, my mind immediately goes back to the time of those basketball tournaments in Orono when we were at Higgins." It is no exaggeration to say that Tournament held for us the hope of the winter solstice and the release of Carnival.

That is not to say that we behaved riotously; quite the contrary. But we went to Orono, to the University of Maine field house, for a Friday and a Saturday. The field house was huge, immense, with electric scoreboards (at Higgins you perched on a rafter and shoved cardboard numbers into slots), and you bought real tickets and got, for ten cents, official programs printed on slick pink ticket stock. I can feel myself here slipping back past even my adolescent admiration to my childhood awe of the place, though there probably isn't much difference. Still, understand that I may not be speaking for the more sophisticated Higgins student when I tell you that I was excited by my annual sight of dry ice, in which the vendors packed their Eskimo Pies and Dixie Cups, or remark upon the giddy height of the upper balconies, where the Meader boys and I were allowed to unkink ourselves when we were very young and had sat still for too long. A yet more poignant pleasure for all ages was the reunion with Higgins graduates attending the university, whom loyalty often drew back to watch the basketball contest. I remember feeling quite breathless with suspense—*would* one see dear so-and-so, otherwise lost forever? The keenness of my pleasure when, in my freshman year at Higgins, Mary Jane Keith (then a junior at U. Maine) came and sat with me at tournament has remained with me for thirty years.

The pink programs bore on their backs records of earlier tournaments. The two in my possession (for which I am grateful to Erma Joy ['50], who unlike me had the sense not to throw out her scrapbook) list no tournament earlier than 1922, but the first official prep school tournament is said to have taken place in 1921, when it snowed so hard that the Higgins players had to go part of the way with a double team of horses. There were no tournaments in 1944 or 1945, for in those war years there was a shortage not only of gas but of experienced basketball players.

The four prep school teams with the best records would be invited to Orono and pitted against each other in pairs on the Friday. On Saturday, before the championship game, the two losers would play a consolation match; this meant that nobody had to slink home for good on Friday night, and the fun went on. I'm copying names of winners and runners-up from the back of the program: Higgins, Hebron, Bridgton, Coburn, Kents Hill, MCI. Surely Fryeburg used to play too? Perhaps they were eliminated in the semifinals. These were our familiar tournament companions. I say companions rather than opponents, for I recall a comfortable feeling that we were with our real peers, whom we saw here annually. All season we, and they, had been playing not only each other but large public high schools and the freshman teams of colleges, but those outsiders were never in at the finale. Besides that, for a number of years my father's closest cousin, Hugh Smith, was head of Coburn, a school with which we enjoyed cordial relations. Even in my vicious and highly partisan childhood I used to think that there would be some consolation in Uncle Hugh's team winning if ours couldn't. And our arch-rivals, MCI, though on this occasion we especially wished to beat them into jelly, in the camaraderie of the moment seemed more than usually entitled to exist.

Around 1931 the school began competing for five-year trophies—impressive, urnlike objects whose bases were aswarm with tiny foul shooters. Kents Hill retired the first of these, Coburn the second, and Higgins the third, in March of 1948. John Mooney, Lester Stevens, and John Keith, the submaster's son, emerged with particular renown and the distinction of all-tourney honors; Roland Fotter, who had coached the 1948 team, would be dead within the month. My old friend Keith Stanley ('59) wrote to say that he had seen that tournament and remembered it as his first taste of the excitement and school spirit of Higgins. He must, like me, have been about seven. I remember it, too—the exaltation of riding home in the back seat with two enormous trophies jostling me for space, the five-year one we'd retired and the new one we'd started.

One post-tournament ritual deserves mention. Riding home in the dark through Bangor, we'd stop at the Coffee Pot, a flat-roofed, one-story building on State Street. Its name in neon, with a blue neon coffee pot between the two words, lit up the front. There one acquired for thirty cents a long sandwich of unusual potency, itself called a Coffee Pot, wrapped in waxy white paper with a black diamond-shaped logo. Coffee Pots were a run-amok version of what in Maine is known as an Italian sandwich (a remote and superior relative of subs, hoagies, grinders, and such lesser fry); they contained salami, cheese, tomato, onions, green peppers, pickles, oil, sometimes black olives, and, at the Coffee Pot, to the best of my belief, cayenne pepper. Coffee Pot sandwiches were the only food in my plain-eating Maine upbringing honestly beyond most juvenile palates, though I think perhaps the Meader boys could eat them. They could eat chokecherries. I can remember poking doubtfully at the edge of my mother's Coffee Pot, at the damp and red-freckled edge of the roll, and feeling my finger turn hot. But they were a part of the tournament ritual; one craved them then as pregnant women are said to crave pickles and ice cream or the malnourished to crave laundry starch, and I have no doubt that if I had brought my adult palate back and taught at Higgins, sooner or later I would have been eating them, too.

After Tournament the year picked up speed. In March there was usually a second event of some, if lesser, importance: Sophomore Prize Speaking. Dates for the sophomore and freshman speaking contests were not graven in stone, but the elder class, as with the plays, tended to go first, while the freshmen followed in May.

Public speaking had been all the rage in public and private schools for at least half the nineteenth century and into the twentieth, and in Higgins's compulsory speaking contests we may discern the residue of that mania. Earlier in the school's history, in the 1890s or so, speaking contests were called exhibitions—"Junior Exhibition" and "Prize Exhibition for the Lower Classes" (the latter title intended to designate freshmen and sophomores, not to make invidious social distinctions). These exhibitions occurred in May, on consecutive nights, and seem to have been part of Commencement Week. The Rich family collection of Higgins memorabilia includes some exhibition programs, lovely embossed pieces of late Victoriana the size of dance programs, one of which displays amidst its flowers an all too suggestive sickle. They reveal that the "lower classes" have memorized pieces from Dickens, Scott, and so on, while the juniors, who already have their class motto on their programs, have written their own pieces. Probably this show of sophistication marked their change into seniors, but it looks as though Junior Exhibition may have been dreary listening. Titles include "Memory," "Home," "True Success and How to Attain It," "Pluck," and "Words of Cheer." Two others, "Women for Business" and "Cremation vs. Earth Burial" may have held possibilities.

In my own time, these displays of histrionic effort were called simply "Freshman Prize Speaking" and "Sophomore Prize Speaking," except when some program maker remembered to call one or both of them "Humphrey Prize Speaking" after D. S. Humphrey, the first trustee treasurer, whose two-hundred-dollar gift still generated the prize money.

The rules and customs were thus: all freshmen and sophomores were obliged to try out for their class speaking contests; that is, each student was to choose and memorize a piece roughly five minutes long, prose or poetry, comic or solemn, and stand on the chapel platform to recite it before the whole school without fainting or getting sick. The tryouts for each class, a pleasant diversion for those not involved, could be counted on to fill at least a couple of chapel sessions with unusual interest. No one was excused, however speech-impeded, halt, or mentally incapable. Perry Wortman recalls rushing off to the boys' dorm upon being warned that one of his less stable students seemed to be coming apart under the stress of memorizing his piece; Perry urged him to satisfy honor with something shorter and easier, a sonnet, say—there was, you'll note, no mention of excusing him altogether—but the boy persisted and indeed, against all odds, made the finals. I remember watching one of my own class-mates on the platform and thinking that although I'd often heard about people's knees knocking together, I had never before actually seen it. But somehow ten of us from each class, five boys and five girls, would survive our awful battle with stage fright and go on to become finalists. I do not think that this provoked much envy: pieces for the finals had to be fifteen minutes long.

There, in a photograph, we pose on the platform, girls sitting, boys standing behind. The wall is decorated with twisted crepe-paper streamers in our class colors (red and white) and our class numerals (1958) in crepe-paper-wrapped cardboard, and we ourselves are no less decorated. For this harrowing occasion was not without its delights, and the delights, for the girls at any rate, had to do with costume. As I've said, Higgins, in deference to the biases of its founder, did not permit dances, but two occasions, Prize Speaking and Senior Banquet, offered us female students half the joy of a prom: the acquisition of one's first evening dress. Preoccupation with costume was not so irrelevant to the recitation of "A Soldier of France" as one might think: Prize Speaking was in fact the one time when every adolescent girl's delusion that the eyes of the world are on her and her clothes was absolutely true, and no doubt it was equally true for the boys.

A literary piece in the 1905 *Scroll* suggests that the importance of costume for speaking has been consistent over the years. The heroine of the story, a hitherto unpopular sophomore, wins the speaking exhibition for her class with Whittier's "The Witch's Daughter" ("Poor Mabel from her mother's grave / Crept to her desolate hearth-stone, / And wrestled with her fate alone"), at which the audience weeps unrestrainedly. The telling detail is that the win-ner's mother has sent her a "little white mousseline dress," while a more popular speaker is attired in white silk but disgraces herself by fainting before her turn comes.

Contemporary costume does not offer many rites of passage, and what there are seem mostly to involve underpinnings—first bra, first nylons, first jockstrap—so that the fine publicity of being breeched or getting out of knee pants or letting one's hemline down is unavail-able to us. But the first evening gown is still a public event. Myrtle

Paine ('27) captures the feeling of it in her recollection of one ceremonious occasion at Higgins: "My mother had made me a beautiful ashes-of-roses satin dress and I felt good. Ruth Sargeant cut my hair—a bob. I hadn't asked my parents. I felt grown up."

My own Prize Speaking dress—how can a fond heart omit it here?—was a ruffly fifties number in yellow net and stiff white lace, and I admired every frill of it. The second year we wore our dresses, three friends and I unwisely decided to embellish our glory with hoops. (This was the period, if you remember, when skirts looked like lampshades and the reckless among us stiffened our crinolines with sugar and water.) The antebellum effect was good until we sat down, when we discovered that the pressure of the chair legs against the hoop backs sent our skirt fronts flying to our eyebrows, an exhibition indeed. This adventure shed some light on the uses of multiple Victorian petticoats. We solved our difficulty by instructing the boys on either side of us—we were alternated by sexes—to catch our hoops and steady them whenever we sat down. That they did this kindly, competently, and without jeering, is a testimony to the friendship between the sexes at Higgins in my time.

Of course to some degree the wearing of new and complicated apparel added to the tension of the occasion, as well as giving one the confidence of new status. Girls with no appreciable breasts upon which to hang their strapless formals were in particular trouble. I can still see one willowy, boyish girl a couple of years older than I, emoting through "The Soul of the Violin" while she hitched compulsively at the front of her green net dress. Then there were boutonnieres and corsages to be arranged, and those were not familiar matters either. In my sophomore photo, two of us girls have put our corsages on our shoulders, two between our breasts, and one at her waist.

The selections were in some ways the most remarkable part of the whole performance. I don't know how they were generally come by; indeed, I can scarcely recall how my own were acquired. To be sure, pieces were to be had from books—the little sister scenes from Booth Tarkington's *Seventeen* were popular, and I once did "The Tell-Tale Heart," but that may have been for tryouts. One year I recall buying something embarrassing called "A Sleep of Prisoners" from an elocution teacher in Bangor, but that was about all I got from her, for although I could memorize, brave it out, and keep my dress up, no elocution teacher could have rescued my declamatory style from indifference. Perhaps Higgins itself had some stash of speaking pieces; certainly over the years we heard the same ones, as well as the same sorts, over and over. And I mean years, decades, generations. "The Soul of the Violin" was done as early as 1910.

The most awful moldy old tear-jerkers kept showing up to set us all blubbering again—"Mickey's Marker" is a case in point. I haven't heard it for years and I hope I never hear it again, but the memory of it is vivid and I assure you that the death of Little Nell is a dry business beside it. Its short-lived hero is a penniless, crippled child who spends most of the piece limping through the snow in pursuit of a gravestone for his dead mother. Other titles in the old programs call up unpleasant suspicions of tears, too, though I can no longer guarantee the content of the pieces: "Daddy Doc," "Danny's Little Tin Soldier," "Crimson Rambler," "The Last Mile," "Angel Unaware," "Apple Blossoms." There were comic pieces, too, like family jokes that always get a laugh: "Dorothy Dumb at the Musicale" (none of us had ever been within earshot of a musicale, but no matter), "Sis Hopkins and Her Beau," "The Flea Gang's First Cigars," "Taking Sadie on the Bus," "Tobias at the Millionaire's."

Higgins's most striking and best-remembered speaking contest took place in May of 1925. Ben Williams (whom you saw in Chapter II selling hot dogs out of his footlocker and whom you will meet again in Chapter XV, as Chairman of the Board of Trustees) received, on that occasion, the most sustained applause ever given to a Higgins speaker and won first prize as well. He was reciting a comic piece about horses and early automobiles, and in those days the faculty sat across the stage, as in chapel. "You see that horse's tail," he said, making a well-rehearsed gesture with his thumb—and pointed straight at my father, a complication that nobody had foreseen. It was a full ten minutes before the screams of rapture died down enough to let him finish; every time he opened his mouth, his audience howled anew. Boys dragged themselves into the corridor, where they lay wheezing and weeping on the floor, gasping to passers-by, "Ben just called Tracy a horse's tail!" We do not know by what triumph of stage presence my father sat out those ten minutes, but he is said to have counseled forethought when next he spoke to Ben's coach.

The 1925 speaking contest reminds me of another, but unofficial, seasonal phenomenon that always occurred a few weeks before graduation: the arrival of the June bugs. They are part of all my late-spring memories, whirring and dive-bombing through the open Institute windows at night, creating a jolly stir at evening activities. In the morning, drifts of June bugs would lie dead on the study hall floor, their feet turned up in a last gesture of buffoonery. A round, sticky-footed beetle roughly the size and color of a preserved date is bound to make an impression on adolescent sensibilities one way or another, and it must be confessed that not everyone appreciated June bugs as much as I did. One of the other speakers in May of 1925 was, if I recall the story correctly, a boy who particularly disliked them. He was just declaiming, "Thunder and lightning and rain! And rain and lightning and thunder," when a June bug flew, or fell, into his wide-open mouth. Unable to think of any more decorous solution, he swallowed it. He won second prize.

But we're getting ahead of ourselves, taking March and May at a swoop. We have forgotten April. Like October, April does not re-quire much administrative help. Junior Play was almost superfluous, though it was an idyllic interlude for the juniors who were doing it. They could flaunt their newer, lighter clothes at rehearsal, linger in the later twilights, and fall in love with each other, especially if their characters were required to embrace, an activity otherwise dis-couraged. For freshmen, sophomores, seniors, and juniors not en-gaged in the production, the play was merely a brief, pleasant incident immersed, like Easter, in the midst of their own flaunting, lingering, and loving. For a little longer the portents of May could be ignored.

Besides the June bugs, at least three ceremonies hinted at the ap-proach of graduation. I am guessing at the sequence, which probably varied. The first of these, Senior Essay Day, was an odd and not altogether pleasant ritual and may have happened in April itself. Senior Essay Day was a good idea in principle, for it theoretically obliged every senior to write a documented paper. One of its peculiar features must have guaranteed the honesty of the products, for the seniors were herded into the main study hall with their index cards and pens, issued paper, and required to produce an essay of some considerable length, with footnotes. Could this odd custom have memorialized some early outbreak of plagiarism? The flaw in the system, as I knew it, was that students with class parts were permitted to write their graduation speeches rather than an essay. This was kindly intended, but it meant that the people most likely to have further brushes with research were the least prepared to do it.

Induction into the National Honor Society was a second portent. It marked the first appearance of senior caps and gowns, if only a few, and so constituted a milestone. New members—juniors, additional seniors, postgraduates—were inducted in their ordinary spring finery. Scholarship, character, leadership, and service were the qualities that got one into National Honor. Scholarship was a simple matter of grades; as for service, most people in a school of two hundred have done enough to get by. Leadership was not examined too closely, but now and then some teacher would turn feisty about character. I can think of at least two cases where otherwise sterling candidates were excluded for known sexual congress, no matter how honorably they had behaved in the context of it. I read now in the paper that some woman years out of school has gotten her faculty's decision reversed, has become at last a member of National Honor Society, and cares about it. Teachers inflict these wounds too lightly. At the candlelight induction ceremony (first performed at Higgins on May 1, 1951), four seniors personified the requisite qualities and recited the traditional speeches. We had too little candlelight in our lives, so this was solemn. The prose was good, too, and sticks in the mind. "I had rather have honor than honors," Character begins, and Scholarship promises that "A learned man hath always wealth within himself."

The tradition of Senior Banquet, the third portent, was begun by Mrs. Ellen McCulley Higgins, widow of the school's founder. Each spring the senior class was invited to her house (later to become the girls' dorm), where she presided over the festivities, a stout, stately, white-haired lady dressed in black with a white lace jabot. I am indebted for these details to Sabra Lee. She went to Senior Banquet in the spring of 1918 with the irrepressible Jack Nicholson, whose student witticisms reverberated down fifty years of my father's anecdotes. (Mrs. Higgins's banquet, though, seems to have sobered even him into propriety.) There were four courses, Sabra Lee says, served by local women hired as waitresses. The girls wore ankle-length dresses, then called reception dresses, and the occasion was formal with a capital Old English F. After Mrs. Higgins remarried and left town, the formality of the banquet was evidently weighed and considered worth retaining. The juniors had theretofore given the school a gift during Commencement festivities, e.g.:

> June 13. Junior Day we presented a handsome card cabinet for the library to the school as our class gift, that is, we would have presented it if the plaguey thing had got here in time. Mr. Workman said it was a munificent gift. That sounds pretty well, anyhow. (1910 *Scroll*)

Later, they assumed instead the expenses of the banquet, making it a last act of vassalage to their elders.

Before I go into Commencement Weekend itself, as I knew it, let me quote Sabra Lee again for a picture of earlier arrangements. Class Day Exercises, she says, were held on the football field, to which the school piano had been moved. (I like the thought of that piano on the football field.) Graduation, with the aid of a grand piano and a Bangor orchestra, was held in the church. "The girls wore white street length dresses," she writes, "white gloves and shoes and the boys three piece suits. The faculty sat up by the pulpit with the speaker of the day, usually the President of Colby College." Students mounted the steps, bowed to the faculty, received their diplomas, and went down the other side of the platform. "It was really an impressive affair," she concludes, and it sounds so. Then the graduates went off to alumni dinner to try out their new status.

In my memory, Commencement is a four-part affair: operetta on Friday night, Class Day (which at Higgins was called Last Chapel) on Saturday night, Baccalaureate on Sunday morning, and Graduation on Monday morning. The operetta, of course, depended upon our having a music teacher, but we usually did. Though for years I thought of the operettas as having been Gilbert and Sullivan, I can find only *The Pirates of Penzance* as evidence. Rather, records show that we did, for instance, *The Tea House of Sing Lo* (1937), *The Gypsy Rover* (1938 and 1952), *The Belle of Barcelona* (1949), and *The Golden Trail* (1951). The operettas were a more glamorous undertaking than the plays, the costumes gaudier, the make-up heavier, the casts larger. The music had a distinctive, once-a-year-only lilt. And the characters—gypsy kings, evil stepmothers, dwarves, pirates—colored the known personalities of the student performers in a way slightly dizzying to my infant mind; some scandal of malfeasance hung round them for me forever after.

Last Chapel, in my time held not on the football field but in the gym, was probably everyone's favorite bit of Commencement. The tears of graduation were still two days away but the revels had begun. On this night we heard the first four class parts, less exalted but more fun than those saved for Graduation. The History, the Will, the Prophecy, and the Gifts could all be counted on for laughs. Even quite a small child could understand some of the allusions in the Will and the Prophecy, and I remember the most delicious suspense, as good as Christmas, when the class gifts with their fluttering shipping-tag labels were fetched out of their box one by one. The humor didn't vary much over the years. In 1927 Ellis Holt, who had never to that point produced any whiskers worth shaving off, was given a razor, and Walter Elden, who was expected not to marry, was given a box of bachelor buttons. These were good, reliable jokes. My own gift, thirty-one years later, was a little white china figure that came with the rhyme, "Here's a man / About time, Ann."

It was at Last Chapel, too, that athletic letters were awarded, and the little medals for expertise in various disciplines (provided by Balfour, I think, who sold us class rings). Then there was the more serious business of scholarships, serious not only because everyone needed money, but because some scholarships memorialized the Higgins (or Higgins-related) dead: the parents of Wendell Dogherty ('29), a good and generous friend of the school; my father's first wife, a Higgins teacher, who died suddenly in the fall of 1938; and most of all, Michael Surtees, an English refugee who was killed on campus in his junior year (1944), by a falling coal pile, and won a place in the Higgins pantheon by saving his companion. All the scholarships were based on character as well as need, but there was a kind of understanding that the Surtees scholarship, awarded by the junior class, would be given to a junior boy as much like Michael as possible, even when nobody remembered him any more. I believe that very late in the school's history girls sometimes got the scholarship—a possibility that had always existed, for I find in the school catalogues no mention of gender.

For me, the most solemn and most dreaded part of the program was the singing of the school hymn. Nobody has known until this moment how "Faith of Our Fathers" harrowed me when I was a child. "Our fathers chained in prisons dark"—I could hardly get through it without breaking down. For of course I didn't visualize *fore*fathers in those prisons, but *our* fathers: Mary Jane Keith's, Buddy Meader's, and mine, oh especially mine. It still seems to me a dismal hymn, but I believe that it was the third Mrs. Higgins's favorite.

Baccalaureate Sunday was not memorable (though no doubt our distinguished speakers would be sorry to hear me say so) but it was restful, a kind of Sabbath lull. Seniors attended in a body, and the United Baptist Church, attractive in the best, though not quite the starkest, New England tradition, wore more flowers than was its custom. Only Virginia Rozelle ('41) has remembered her Baccalaureate text: "For other foundation can no man lay than that is laid, which is Jesus Christ" (I Corinthians 3:11).

Several ceremonial particulars of graduation require notice. Ours was an ordered universe in as many respects as possible, and class colors are a case in point. They came in four combinations—purple and white, green and white, blue and white, and red and white—and rotated in that order, inexorable as the seasons. Not even my own prickly, prideful class thought of tampering with the red and white that fate had laid down for it. I am therefore shocked to see in the last days of the school—class of '73 please take note—the admission of such inappropriate and decadent combinations as light blue and royal blue. The fall of Rome is nothing to it. "Class colors" meant that for four years red and white crepe-paper streamers had embellished official class occasions, that our Commencement program was printed in red, and, most important, that our marshall's baton was wound with our own distinctive hues. Delivered to the principal's sunporch in a white pasteboard florist's box, that baton was the single most glamorous totem known to the school year. Satin ribbons, woven like the ribbons on a maypole, wrapped its shaft until on either end they burgeoned into rosettes and fell away in streamers. Flashing in the marshall's hands, it would look as pure as a waterfall.

Class mottoes, unlike colors, were open to choice, but until 1959 they were traditionally in Latin, fine inspiriting sentiments that made even those who couldn't read them feel a cut above public education: *Certum Pete Finem,* Aim at a Certain End; *Esse Quam Videri,* To Be Rather Than to Seem; *Praemonitus Praemunitus,* Forewarned Is Forearmed; *Non Nobis Solem,* Not for Ourselves Alone. My own class aptly chose *Possumus Quia Posse Videmur,* which we rather loosely translated as "We can because we think we can," and there has fallen into my hands a winsome snapshot of the school dining room tricked up for Senior Banquet, with the motto *Nil Desperandum* worked in crepe paper amidst the streamers.

Yet another traditional matter was the Class Ode. Some person or persons in the senior class were obliged to write one. Or to write the words, at any rate; it was unusual to have anyone able to compose the music, though the class of 1928's Ruth Ramsdell managed it, as did Priscilla Jones in 1940. Usually some familiar tune was chosen, and a list of those might provide an index to popular music through the decades. The class of 1901 sang its ode to the tune of "My Old New Hampshire Home"; 1910 chose "Where the Roses Twine the Trellis by the Door"; 1911, "Down in the Old Meadow Lane"; 1912, "There Are Strangers in the Old Home Now"; 1916, "Annie Laurie"; while 1919 went for "Soldier's Farewell." Postwar fashion seems to have abandoned melancholy for a different sort of romanticism: "Stars of the Summer Night" (1922), "One Fleeting Hour" (1924), "Let Me Call You Sweetheart" (1930), "Drink to Me Only with Thine Eyes" (1934), and "Drifting and Dreaming" (1936). They sang to "The Bells of St. Mary's" in 1941, and in 1948 chose "Now Is the Hour" in deference to the taste of their late coach; I was old enough to remember and be impressed by the gloom of that rendition. My own class took "Graduation Day," an irresistably appropriate, trumpery little tune that came along at just the right moment.

Mostly the accompanying lyrics are not memorable, though now and then a phrase emerges to catch a little at the heart—"Don't forget the good old class of 1909"; "We shall always be true to the Orange and Black / And the friends whom we used to know"; 1939 sang, all too prophetically, "Near the trench line of life we are standing." Alas, I find nothing quotable in the 1958 ode, but I must admit that I have found endlessly useful one couplet from the throwaway lyrics that we wrote first to get the mischief out of our systems. "As we change our tassels from left to right / We think of the party we'll have tonight" has helped me in many an academic procession to place my tassel correctly, for I mutter our lines and go on to calculate, "and then back from right to left for the B.A." and so on.

We graduated in gowns and mortarboards, white for girls and black for boys, and we felt superior and dignified on account of it. But my mother said that when she first arrived at Higgins in the late thirties, both sexes wore gray. This being considered appropriate for prep schools, there were some objections about bad taste when Higgins went to black and white like colleges. And I suppose that those graduates who had worn white dresses or three-piece suits did not favor the adoption of caps and gowns at all.

The gym stage was transformed for the ceremony by the erection of tall chicken-wire flats woven full of fresh cedar greenery. Ormonde Brown ('47) tells me that he still can't smell cedar without thinking of graduation. The class motto, letters wrapped in white crepe paper, marched across the cedar background as well as it could with the lumps, and I see that my own class worked a giant 58 in lilacs as well, but I don't know whether this was customary. Graduation time was lilac time in Maine, and baskets of them at the edge of the stage added to the smell of Commencement, along with polish, dust from outdoors, and the perfume of mothers.

We always hired a violin or two to accompany the piano, and their unfamiliar half-tempo keening of the march from *Aida* seemed grief itself. At public school graduations the happy participants expect, however wrongly, to go on seeing one another. At private schools the tone is far more ambivalent. The Wortmans, formerly at public schools, told me that they'd never seen anything like the weeping that went on at their first Higgins graduation.

Seniors were lined up in double rows, shortest in front, paired by sexes as long as the girls lasted, but there were always half a dozen pairs of flapping black-robed giants at the end. They marched in from the tennis court in time to the music, with an odd hitching step that caused the line to sway from side to side. (Or at any rate they did except in 1952, Mary Jane's year, when the string trio from the music conservatory had not been told about half tempo and the graduates came in at a gallop.) The president of the junior class was obliged to lead in, hitching backward and sweeping the wonderful baton in a sharp diagonal to mark the beat. At my own graduation, Harold

Stearns proved unable to do this. He tried, he tried hard and often, but he could not march backward. We were unprepared for this emergency; who would have supposed that Stearns had no reverse? At last Buddy Meader, who was in the same class and could march in any direction you wanted him to, was swathed in Stearns's robes and told to do it. This was a first-class solution, for we liked Buddy very much, and as the principal's son he carried prestige sufficient to feed our pride; besides, he was doomed to move out of state and have no Higgins graduation of his own, for his father was leaving. A similar calamity threatened the class of 1926, but Shorty Davis, a senior saxophone player who was marching at the head of the line, beat time with his finger for marshal Harry Nason and thus saved the day.

After speeches of the usual sorts, diplomas were given, hands were shaken, the class ode was sung, and we moved into a portion of the program peculiar to Higgins: officially "The Reverend John H. Higgins Memorial Service," it was called, with no disrespect, and by everyone from the trustees on down, "The Graveyard Speech." For the Graveyard Speech the graduating class trooped off in formation but without music to the cemetery just south of campus. It was a friendly cemetery, a pretty spot with lilies of the valley thick along the front of the iron fence and lots of big trees; there local children played games and rolled down the sides of the central mound that bore the Higgins family obelisk. A great iron door in the side of the mound opened to the tomb (useful in initiating freshmen), where the winter dead were stored until spring thaw. To the right of the tomb were the graves of the Higginses, perhaps three dozen identical, modest, white marble stones set out in rows, among which was the Reverend John's. There the procession would halt to listen to a eulogy and lay a wreath.

The Graveyard Speaker was a rather special boy whose grades had not decreed a class part but who cut something of a figure, a boy especially virtuous or lovable or responsible, and no fool, a boy who clearly should be doing something at Graduation. His election (in the Calvinistic sense, I mean; I don't recall how he really was chosen), like the Surtees Scholarship recipient's, was a delicate matter, but somehow the lot always fell to the right person, and all the Higgins sages would say, "Ah yes, of course, just the boy for it."

When Robert Houghton ('37) wrote, of his graduation, "It was pouring rain. No one would take the flowers and put them on Mr. Higgins' grave. Mr. Thomas asked me and Gee Machen to do it. We did," I hoped that I had discovered the origins of the Graveyard Speech, a clever ploy of my father's to get the wreath delivered come sleet or rain or dark of night. In the end, though, I found an earlier allusion to that speech in a letter from Martha Bragger ('35). All the same, it is safe to say that the typical Graveyard Speaker was somebody who *would* take flowers to the grave no matter how hard it was raining.

I shall not speak of the summer Alumni Day, though it was once a daylong round of ballgames and revelry (I remember it chiefly as a chapel full of people singing "Down by the Old Mill Stream"), for that is outside the shape of the school year. When the graduates straggled back to the gym to reunite with those parents who had not followed them to the cemetery, when they began to shuck off their robes and rejoin their blood families and wander up the little rise to the boys' dorm and dinner for those who wanted it, then it really was the end, the year at Higgins was over.

IX

SPORTS

Played a little football but had to quit to pick potatoes.

—LLOYD ROZELLE ('47)

I may as well admit right away that nobody could be less qualified to write about sports than I. I am a standing joke among my athletic friends for my innocence of sports terminology and even motives. Indeed, I am obliged to approach these rites as though I were a sort of tourist—friendly and interested, but wondering what the dickens those natives are up to.

Sports, I would say, were important at Higgins, even very important, but important for slightly deviant reasons. That is, I do not take them to have mattered in the same way that they would have in a school noted for sports or catering to athletes or putting particular emphasis on physical fitness. They mattered, rather, because they were *something to do*. For the teams, sports meant—as well as the usual suspense, camaraderie, and what not—trips out of town. (If you've never lived in rural Maine, the significance of that may escape you.) They meant for the fans a reason to gather and shout and work up adrenalin. They meant rallies, and trips to Orono for the basketball tournament, and hand-holding in the bleachers. They stood in for movie theaters, arcades, pool parlors, and so on, as well as offering their own innate attractions.

Also, even as late as the forties, sports were a considerable novelty to some of the students. A number of alumni wrote in to admit that they had never seen a football game until they came to Higgins. "Although half the team had never seen a football before . . . " say some of the early write-ups, and they are not necessarily kidding. It was said that my father could tell from watching a boy walk across a farmyard what kind of ballplayer he'd make—a useful knack, for sometimes there was no other evidence.

The novelty of sports may account for some peculiarities in the attitudes of Higgins's athletes over the years. If you grow up without a lot of mainstream jock assumptions, maybe a game really is just a game. Alumni who wrote of their sports careers at Higgins remembered them with pleasure, but they told me funny stories instead of wallowing in past glory or giving me score-by-score accounts of great moments. Apparently they appreciated sports because playing was fun, suspenseful, challenging, even glamorous, and because playing well sometimes helped them to get into colleges, but not because they mistook sports for sacraments. I have a friend who called to her teenage son as he ran onto the field in his brand new uniform, "You look just like a football player, honey!" and this articulates for me an attitude that I suspect lurked in the mind of many a Higgins athlete—hey, I look just like a football player. And then they all scrambled onto the field and *acted* like football players, too, despite intimidating odds.

Sports served, further, as some outlet for the almost hysterical school loyalty that I have described elsewhere; they fused the whole school into one white-hot unity of intention. My brother remembers hearing about a cook (but we do not know which cook) who used to go on all the out-of-town trips, bearing sandwiches for the boys, and who would go away and weep bitterly by himself if they lost, recovering in time to be supportive and jolly when the boys came out of the showers. Losing and winning, in fact, mattered very much. As for how we played the game, my brother and Mary Jane Keith, both of whom know far more about sports than I, agree on the principal Higgins philosophy of athletics: It doesn't matter how little you are, if you can be tricky. You can't cheat, but within the boundaries of the rules—well, the cagier the better.

Although there were, from time to time and as opportunity permitted, some fine track and cross-country teams, the three principal sports during most of Higgins history were, predictably, football, basketball, and baseball. One, you see, for each season. Of these, baseball was much the least gripping. It had the sort of disadvantage that, say, Pentecost has among church festivals—no frills. Football and basketball, like Christmas and Easter, had the drama of rising action: they marked the turn of seasons into a new school year, or (with Tournament) into spring. There were related rituals, foods, traditions. Baseball came when the year was falling into summer, a semi-sad time at boarding schools, where it means separation, sometimes permanent. Baseball watchers were lazy, drugged with spring fever. And when have you seen cheerleaders at a baseball game?

Football, according to Keith's history, "was first played at the school in the fall of 1901 and the *Scroll* of that year made the comment that it was the 'first and probably the last time that the game would be played at Higgins Classical Institute.' " What could have gone wrong? Perhaps exposure to quite an ordinary (i.e., violent, bloodthirsty, filthy) early football game put the school off it. In any case, they got over the prejudice. The first regular schedule of basketball games with visiting teams also took place in 1901. Baseball was being played by 1898 and probably a good bit earlier, for it had already been a popular sport for some decades. Girls' basketball was established at Higgins by the 1920s, but softball not until thirty years later.

School publications make it clear that early sports were informal, quirky, and ill-equipped, coached briefly by outsiders hired for a couple of weeks. The accounts in the *Scrolls*, my friend Graeme Francis points out, are obviously written by students for whom sports are an innovation. They have a jocular, so-what air very much in contrast to the play-by-play jargon-laced accounts that begin in the 1930s. They fall into verse—"We went to Corinna the other day, / To show those fellows how to play, / And as you see, we did right fine, / Trimming them easy, 24 to 9" (1918), and private jokes— "Smith got mad because Humphrey was kicking him on the shins" (1926). Of a 1910 football game, the sportswriter announces, "On Wednesday, October 12th, we met the enemy and we were theirs." "The less said about the game the better," quips a 1927–28 basketball write-up. The tone of these accounts was simply a continuation of the tone in which student writers had been accustomed to comment on individual athletic outbursts such as walking, bicycling, boxing, with which students had been diverting themselves before team sports took over school life. For example, about the gym at the

Trustee House in 1898, someone wrote, "Regularly night and morning could be heard the blows of boxing gloves, the irregular thumps of the dumb-bells and occasionally a shriek from the wounded. . . . " When students insist on doing things in clumps instead of privately, the accounts switch to the plural. By the early seventies they are back to an unprofessional stance—no scores with the photos, just captions and quotations about why they enjoy playing.

One peculiar joy of sports at Higgins, according to William Chase, Jr., ('35), was having as postgraduate teammates boys you'd played against when you and they were at competing high schools. It was the postgraduates who made it possible for us to risk playing (and occasionally to beat) the freshman teams at Maine colleges and who made us ineligible to join high school leagues, though we sometimes had single games with the larger high schools. That extra year of growth and experience makes a big difference in the late teens.

But there were, in the end, some strategic problems in football. Perry Wortman, on principle, did not solicit athletes as athletes. The consequent diminishing of Higgins brawn in the sixties made it dangerous to play college freshmen, while the presence of any postgraduates at all made high schools our size reluctant to play us. So we scheduled games with big high schools like Brewer, which would field fifty men in uniform to our twenty, and there we were, in trouble again. As my father always said, if you lose a basketball game only your feelings get hurt, but you'd better have a good strong football team if you're going to play at all. The Wortman solution, to use the PGs as assistant coaches but keep them off the field, permitted Higgins to join the Little Ten Conference of local high schools. As his scheme further intended, undergraduates who might not otherwise have had a chance to play varsity were members of the team. In fact, in my brother's time Higgins had a football player with an artificial leg. (It had a cross-country man with no toes, as well; when we lost, it wasn't for lack of spunk.) This new arrangement worked for a while, but by 1969 the football team was losing all its games and a third of the team was injured and out. At that point Stub Foss reincorporated postgraduates into the team and rejoined the prep school league.

Before we go into separate sports, one more common thread deserves a mention. A 1908 *Scroll* already refers to MCI—Maine

Central Institute, in Pittsfield—as our "old rivals." When and where that rivalry started and how it got so hot is now beyond living memory, but hot it was, especially in football and basketball. The Armistice Day football game, for instance, was a traditional HCI-MCI showdown, and we'd rather have beaten them in an ordinary game of basketball than won the tournament from somebody else. The MCI teams were big and tough and frequently, though by no means invariably, beat us. Perhaps it was my World War II childhood that made me regard them not just as the opposition but as the enemy; I was born into a world where Germany, Japan, and MCI threatened on every hand. I always thought of them as an instance of the wicked prospering and flourishing like the green bay tree; indeed, if I had known when I was a child that today Higgins would be gone and MCI alive and well, I would have dropped out of Sunday School on the spot. In high school my best friends pointed out to me that I was a fool, that MCI was attended by ordinary, even perfectly nice people, not fiends from hell, so I tried to revise my thinking. But the mystique lingers, for only the other day I was standing at the sink and trying to remember what tune popular in my high school days was coincidentally the tune for the MCI school song. My instant conviction that it was the sinister, slinking music to "Hernando's Hideaway," when in fact, as I remembered later, it was "The Happy Wanderer," suggests that my friends were too late to effect a thorough cure.

So why am I admitting this craziness? Because the whole school (except maybe for my best friends) felt more or less the same way, only not quite so acutely as I—for maximum intensity you had to start young. Still, Rena Gray has told me that when the boys were living in hideous makeshift after the dorm burned in 1956 and she offered her two sons a chance to go live at MCI in real dormitories, they were shocked at the impropriety of her suggestion. Neal Brown ('56) also reports having refused the generosity of an uncle who would have paid his way for him if he'd gone to Pittsfield instead of Charleston. Jake Bishop ('55) wouldn't go there for a week's summer course in First Aid. And Rena Gray, again, told me that when she herself was at Coburn as a student, they had felt exactly the same way about MCI, so perhaps there was something in it after all.

FOOTBALL

John Pullen (a Ricker graduate and author of *The Twentieth Maine*) has written to me,

> My most vivid memories of Higgins have to do with the football games against Ricker, in a couple of which I participated, although I was not that much of a player. I remember that from one end of the football field at Higgins, right in the playing area, part of a large boulder projected. I remember thinking, the first time I saw it, "These must be tough men, to play with a rock in their field." Also, I think at the same end of the field, any points after touchdown that were kicked sent the ball into a chicken pen and caused great excitement among the hens.

They *were* pretty tough men, though I suppose that knowing where the rock was helped a little. Robert Reny ('51) mentioned another occasionally helpful anomaly of the Higgins field: the south end was lower than the north, and the east end lower than the west, so if you knew in what direction to run, you were hard to stop. In the 1930s the field was improved through the WPA program, the town having been unable to devise a project of its own. A plea for alumni contributions of ten dollars each for further improvement—sent out, I should judge, in the early forties—seems not to have yielded enough money to do much good. In the sixties Perry Wortman thought of keeping the field mowed all summer so that it wouldn't be so stubbly in September.

Sometimes human error made for further complications in those casual days. Ellis Holt ('27) told me that, as manager of the team, he had been assigned to replace the goal posts, which had been pulled up and left leaning against Bunker's barn during baseball season, and to line the field with wet lime. Examination discovered not one but two possible sets of goal-post holes, both plugged with two-by-fours, so he unplugged the newer-looking set and dropped in the posts, which fitted perfectly. Lining from that end, he realized only as he approached the other set of goals that he had chosen the wrong holes, that he had two surplus yards of football field. Anxious to be off for his weekend in Atkinson, he compromised by setting the last two lines at eleven-yard intervals; he figured that as the teams changed goals the handicap would be fairly distributed. The officials, who felt otherwise, were obliged in mid game to improvise new ground rules for playing on a 102-yard field.

Early equipment was no better than the early field. My father used to say that when he went to Higgins all they had for shoulder pads were horse collars. I think that this was just his way of putting things, but my brother isn't so sure. Certainly the men look horribly defenseless in early football photographs, frail, unpadded, unnumbered. In this they were probably no more deprived than their peers in other schools, but it is true, too, that my father had some disdain for equipment fetishes. In fact, he once devised a famous play, a psychological fake-out. Some of it I am unable to reconstruct, but the gist of it was that a player would look as though he were coming out of the game, would throw his helmet to the purported sub (they were short of equipment), and then the *boy without the helmet* would get the ball and go for a touchdown. The play (once fairly standard, I'm told) where a light player runs up a lineman's back and jumps over the opposition was also popular; "He could land just like a squirrel," my father would reminisce fondly. But could this have been good for the lineman's back?

Protection, as I was saying, looks meager, and furthermore the teams were not large. In the fall of 1922 so many Higgins men were injured that the school wanted to cancel a game with Coburn. Coburn suggested that, instead of canceling, they fill the vacancies with local alumni. Los Higgins ('14), Stan Higgins ('17), and Wash Baker ('18) were dragooned out of real life and suited up, along with a few more recent graduates. The *Scroll* sportswriter reports that "The old timers were all right as long as their enthusiasm lasted, but it did not last very long." Coburn beat them 32 to 0.

A last note on informality of equipment: Ellis Holt also told me that when he was manager they played a game in a wet snowstorm that made the ball hard to handle, so he craftily went up to Hollis Soule's General Store and bought the entire stock of work gloves. To his dismay, he was ordered to render up his surplus gloves to the opposition. Higgins was tricky but chivalrous.

Coaching, too, was at first a somewhat informal business. Coaches were hired for a couple of weeks, often apparently taken away from the midst of their own undergraduate studies. After being instructed in the rudiments of the game, the teams were, evidently, left to their own subsequent devices. Later, permanent faculty did the coaching, or coaches were put on the permanent faculty and taught; these are not quite the same in effect. Now and then luck provided an athlete of renown who was a fine teacher as well, e.g., Punk Keith (whom I have elsewhere scrupulously and unnaturally called Philip, but that really will not do for this chapter). Alumni report a variety of coaching techniques—for instance, Punk Keith's psychological prepping; Jess DeLois's scientific strategies; Nick Hashey's reliance on brute strength, of which there was never quite enough.

Sometimes real athletes could be overspecialized. Once my father hired a crackerjack college lineman who came to him later for advice in coaching. Dad pointed out that he, the lineman, was the football specialist. That was all very well, said the lineman, but all he knew was how to block a particular hole; he'd never gotten into the broader strategies.

Accounts of football seasons in the extant *Scrolls* are interesting from time to time. The 1910 team, for instance, won only one game (against Brewer), to celebrate which the girls were allowed to take the six o'clock electric car to East Corinth and meet the returning heroes—"Happy was the meeting and joyous the return," says the writer. The next year, Mr. Arthur Taylor of the class of 1900 promised that the alumni would give every varsity football man an HCI jersey if they were undefeated; given that incentive and a lot of trick plays, they were. The December 1911 *Scroll* alludes to a game played on an entirely unlined field at Orono:

> It seemed however that Orono expected to fight instead of play foot ball and consequently got together a team of mill men and pugilists. While Orono was fighting, Higgins ran up a score of sixteen, holding her opponents to zero. The field was poor and without lines, and arguments were plenty.

In 1913, when they won four, lost three, they accomplished a good deal by the then unusual strategy of passing; a look at the outsized football in the photograph will explain why people didn't do it much. "Lots of fumbling and mixing of signals," says a cheerful report of a 1914 game, and in 1921 a game with Brewer was "close but slow because of the many disputes." Through the twenties success fluctuates; the 1929 team was called "the best in years," though it had the lightest set of backs in all the state prep schools, for nobody crossed its home goal line the whole season.

In 1931 the teams begin a long and rambling search for a name. "Highlanders," they're calling themselves in the 1931 *Scroll*. In 1941 they try "Witches," in 1950 "Preppers," in 1952 "Hilltoppers," and in 1954 they decide on, and stick with, "Knights." By and large, in the thirties they seem to be losing slightly more than they win. In 1932 a small team whose "first practice was certainly discouraging to the on-looker" so revved itself up that "the vicious tackling of the Higgins team was a pleasure to watch."

Now and then the accounts avoid details, as in 1936 when the writer merely comments that there were a lot of injuries, but mostly someone finds something positive to say—"Higgins showed power except in the scoring zone" (1930). Often only the big game with MCI is written up in detail. One writer embellishes with weather— "with brown leaves swirling in the fall winds . . . ," etc.

After the war, things pick up. The coaches are candidly surprised in the 1946 *Scroll* that the football team has won six out of seven games. For several years in the late forties and early fifties they managed to beat MCI, whatever else they lost. Indeed, in 1952 they are said to have lost a two-year state championship.

They were on rather a losing streak in the mid and late fifties, when I was a student; in a 1956 *Scrawl* Coach Nick Hashey says that they've tried their hardest, even though nobody would ever call the team great. Not that they lacked spunk in the fifties, or initiative. In the fall of 1953, says Jake Bishop ('55), the team discovered that the uniforms had not been cleaned after the 1952 season, neither be-tween games nor at the end. There was no money for cleaning, so the boys bought Woolite, repaired to the only bathtub available (in the girls' dorm) and with the help of the female teachers hand-washed their wool uniform shirts and black twill pants. The manager painted the helmets, the boys painted the shoes with black dope and changed the cleats, and I am assured that they fielded an unusually good-looking team, to the pride of Coach Donald Matheson. This was the same team that, reduced by injuries to ten men in the midst of a game against the Bowdoin freshmen, refused to forfeit, so that the referee took a man off the opposing team to make it even. Bowdoin's president, impressed by Higgins spirit, asked the team to his house after the game.

But it took an unusual visitation of blood-lust in those years to make the football team rise above its handicaps and actually win— kind of like the old joke about getting the cat to haul a piano upstairs by using a whip. Keith Stanley ('59) has sent a fine account of one such game:

> The game was at Kents Hill; we had gone there by car because the school couldn't afford a bus. We were a pretty rag tag bunch compared to the sleek and well outfitted Kents Hill team. While we were in the visitors' dressing room before the game, the opposing coach came in to "welcome" us. As he was about to leave he said, "Oh, by the way—we will be serving cider and cookies in (such and such) a hall after the game. If you feel *able*, you're invited to join us." Believe me, when he left, you could have heard a pin drop—nobody said a word. It didn't take a genius, however, to be able to look about the room and those sullen eyes and *know* that we had been challenged and insulted. We did our perfunctory warm-ups in sort of an eerie quietness. As the game progressed all hell broke loose. There is a term in football called the fore-arm-shiver (a little dirty but effective). I remember busting the nose of the guy across from me with it (he weighed about 245 and I perhaps 175). That sort of thing created a situation where they were more interested in killing us than beating us. Overall they outweighed us about 30 pounds a man in the line and about 20 in the backfield. Most of us played both defense and offence with very few subs. We proceeded to beat them soundly. . . . By the way, we all went for cider and cookies after the game.

In the sixties things look bleaker yet. In 1964 the team didn't make a single point, let alone win a game. From 1966 only photos, no write-ups, survive, and in 1969, after another no-win season, Stub Foss pulled Higgins out of the Little Ten Conference and tried the prep school league again. In 1970 they won one out of four, but in 1971 I find no account of football in the *Scroll*, nor do I ever again except for an announcement in 1972 that school energies will be devoted to building up the younger students for a later team, rather than playing a real schedule. From 1973 to 1975 soccer replaced football as the fall sport.

BASKETBALL

Basketball was the most important of the Higgins sports, perhaps because of tournament, perhaps because the season was so long and the recreational alternatives in winter so few. It seems to have been from the start somehow less subject to confusion and controversy than football, but perhaps that is not true. Certainly there were difficulties about facilities. I have already described the makeshift court at what was formerly the Free Temple Baptist Church, with its hoops in diagonal corners, its spectators huddled behind chicken-wire barriers. The earlier gym, a superannuated lodge hall donated by the Oak Hill Lodge of Good Templars, was memorably described by Punk Keith, who would have used it as a student:

> Its heating system was a huge box stove which, though inadequate to heat the huge barnlike interior of the building which consisted of a single room, did serve as a sort of an oasis of warmth to which, on occasion, one might flee. At remote distances from the stove the temperature was like that of out doors. The lighting was poor, emanating from kerosene lamps placed at intervals. Much of what happened on the basketball floor in those days happened in a semi-darkness which would not be pierced by the eyes of either spectator or players.

Mind you, basketball players in those days were used to some odd courts; it wasn't uncommon to have gymnasiums upstairs over grange halls and such, with special rules to accommodate the chance of basketballs bouncing out the door and down the stairs (just as, at Brownville Junction, there were special rules regarding baseballs that rolled under boxcars).

The new gym in 1928 must have seemed like the Taj Mahal, though in fact it was smaller than regulation. The foul-shooting circles and the center circle touched at their edges, while red lines intersected the black at intervals to mark theoretical distances, such as where half of a full-sized court would be if one needed to know. Still, it was well lighted and warm enough, spectators could get out of the way, and the floor took a good polish, for Robert Reny ('51), once waxed it so zealously that the players could hardly stay on their feet.

The only other problem with basketball sprang from the season in which it was played. All through Higgins history, visiting basketball teams were amazed and disheartened to learn that they had to change into shorts in the dorm and then run through the snow to the gym. Perhaps this at any rate gave us some psychological edge for home games, like the rock in the football field. Our players struggled through the snow to away games, sometimes arriving stiff and cold and going onto the floor at a disadvantage. "The trip was made from Charleston to Pittsfield [a matter of forty-five or fifty miles] in sleighs and the team went on the floor immediately after reaching Pittsfield," says a 1928 account of a game lost to MCI. By tournament time the blizzards had usually let up, but I have heard more than one account of the ingenious bypassing of floods to get the team to Orono. Then, too, people are sick in the winter. I find several notes of games canceled on account of flu, mumps, or measles.

In 1901, the first year of a full basketball schedule, the team was coached for a week by Ralph Good, "the well known athlete of Colby College." Higgins students were already taking pride in playing clean (cleaner than Monson, they suggest, having lost a game to them under what they feel were dubious circumstances), an attitude that persists over the years side-by-side with a delight in trickiness. The team had a good year in 1912—only one loss as far as we have statistics—but three games were canceled "because of the unhealthful conditions of the gymnasium." That would be the Oak Hill Lodge, described above; perhaps the unhealthfulness had to do with cold. Higgins beat MCI both times. The first time, says the *Scroll*, MCI came to Charleston with a heavy team but "couldn't keep the pace that was set and undertook to play a little football on the side, but their knowledge of football did not avail them much in shooting goals." Some sort of championship playoffs were going on at Orono that year too, but all authorities seem to agree that what we called Tournament didn't happen until 1921.

The team for the first "real" tournament was coached by my father and captained by Punk Keith, who also shot the first Higgins basket. Evidently we did not win. Not much information about basketball in the twenties has survived, but by 1932 things were picking up. Twenty-five men went out for the team, and "a shortage of complete suits was noticeable," says the *Scroll*. My father was still coaching in 1936 (or, as the case may be, coaching again), and "Coach Tracy's crack outfit" lost only two games and won the tournament—a fine year. This was followed by a bit of a slump in 1938, when we won only four out of thirteen; "The H.C.I. boys were playing a better brand of basketball than usual and seemed to be hitting the basket," says the *Scroll* of one winning game.

The peak years for Higgins basketball, I should judge, were 1936 to 1950; those are the dates of the first and last Higgins prep school championships, with two more in between. At the 1941 MCI–Higgins game, which we won, the Higgins gym was so full that fans sat on the rafters and looked down at the game. We won the tournament in 1943, the last one before a two-year recess for the war; we were runners-up to MCI in 1946 and in the finals with Coburn in 1947, when perhaps we won (I have no data), for we retired the five-year trophy the next year.

John Keith, son of the 1921 tournament captain, was captain of the Higgins team in 1948, another big tournament year (the Keiths, with some justification, always called the five-year trophy retired that year "the Keith trophy"), and Roland Fotter coached. Mary Jane Keith tells me that Fotter's techniques were ahead of his time, that he taught the sort of hard, quick passing and long shots that pro teams use now. Indeed, his players passed so hard that one uncaught pass splintered a good-sized piece of wood off the Higgins backboard. We were runners-up again in 1949 and back in first place in 1950.

After 1950 things went downhill except for a patch in the sixties. In 1951, 1952, 1953, and 1955 we lost the tournament to MCI, and the bitterness of that was not sweetened even by the consideration that we had to be fairly good to get there. In 1958 we lost every game, in 1959 every game but one. In the early sixties we moved into a different league. In 1965 we were obliged to forfeit a number of wins in what had promised to be a championship season, for we had inadvertently harbored an ineligible player on our team, a man who had done just a bit of a senior year elsewhere at an earlier date and neglected to make this clear. My brother, who was there, says that of course the man in question was distraught at what he'd done, but that the other students behaved admirably, were kind and comforting and never gave him a hard word. Nineteen sixty-seven and 1969 were both good years, too. After that, suddenly, there are no scores given in the yearbooks, just pictures and captions ("What goes up must come down"), so I presume that they didn't want to talk about it. There was some spirit at the end, though, for Michael Gallant ('71) told me a story about a moment in a slaughter of the Higgins team by Washburn: "Al Lord and I were on a fast break. He fell in front of me and I started to fall. The crowd was laughing. As I fell I shot and it went in. We both got up and stuck our tongues out—real sports, but we felt better."

TRACK AND CROSS-COUNTRY

Track and cross-country were on-and-off sports at Higgins. No teams existed, as far as I can tell, in the twenties or forties or part of the fifties, but there were teams very early and very late in school history, and for all of the thirties. I imagine that these sports depended upon Higgins's having some faculty member with the talent or inclination to coach them. When we had such teams, they seem to have been pretty good, sometimes even spectacular, for I suppose that nobody felt obliged to have them come hell or high water or amateur coaching, as they would have basketball, say. Eleanor Mills, who taught music at Higgins in the late thirties, has passed on an endearing story about track:

> You probably don't remember old Mr. Perley, who was a character in Charleston. He used to sit on the Post Office porch and make remarks about the "modern" schools in general. When our track team would run in the spring he had a fit about their lack of clothing, he couldn't stand shorts and bare arms. Your father laughed one day when he said, "Professor—for godsake learn 'em and feed 'em, but can't you clothe 'em?"

Old Mr. Perley, by the way, was father of the Reverend John Higgins's first two wives.

In 1908 Higgins sent a track team to the University of Maine meet for the first time, and in 1909 a Higgins team seems to have won at least one meet. A team was fielded in 1910 as well, for its photograph appears in the *Scroll*, misleadingly labeled "Basketball Team" (the young man in the center is holding a discus, unless his basketball has had an accident), and we know that it was coached by submaster Harron. After that, track seems to have subsided for a while, though in 1914 a field day was held with three nearby schools. In 1929 a track team was "re-organized" and looked promising, and in 1931 "the first real attempt to have a track team" was made—how short is memory. In 1933 a cross-country team, of which only one member had ever run before, became the Prep School Champs, and in 1934 the track team had such good dash men that at Milo "a rare scene took place during the meet when six Higgins men ran, hand in hand, to tie for first place in the half mile." Paul Snow was coaching that year. After 1940 I find no further reference to track or cross country until a letter from Stanwood King ('50), who built the track pit for the long jump, and says modestly that he "sort of formed" a track team, admitting that he made about half of the team points himself for each meet—a clear case of a star who had to provide his own firmament.

The 1960s brought track and cross-country back with a flourish. In 1964, cross-country was Higgins's most successful team—faint praise, perhaps, in a season when the football team lost all its games, varsity basketball had to forfeit its wins due to an ineligible player, and the girls' basketball team lost twelve, won four. I think that it is safe to say that, on the whole, track and cross-country were Higgins's best sports from then until the school closed, though I do not have a full run of scores to support my supposition. What records we have tell us that the 1965 cross-country team was undefeated in its regular season and held the Central Maine League Championship, and that the 1966 track team was undefeated. Both the 1967 and 1968 track teams held the Penquis League Championship. In fact, the 1968 team was so good (reckoned to be one of the top two or three in the state) that when the boys were forbidden to attend the state meet because it conflicted with their graduation, one junior went alone and finished as third team all by himself.

But the great, stupendous, dramatic Higgins cross-country team of all time (though it came to a bad end) was the 1973 Indian team coached by Derwin Emerson in the days when the school was

151

recruiting students, principally Passamaquoddies, for whom the Bureau of Indian Affairs would pay tuition. Mike Francis, Sam Neptune, Bob Lewey, Brian Altvater, Frank Sabbatus—they outran everyone they went up against. Mike Francis kept breaking his own records and everyone else's for the 2.5- to 3-mile routes. He so consistently outran even his own swift teammates, I'm told, that once when he had a bad day, they automatically stayed behind him because they assumed that they couldn't pass him. The team went off with confidence to the state meet, having already beaten Bangor Christian, their closest competitors, by a wide margin in an earlier contest. Alas, they celebrated a night too early and a good bit too hard; the next day they lost, but even so it was a great season for Higgins morale.

BASEBALL

No Higgins sport was so long-lived or so underdocumented as baseball. The earliest recorded team sport at the school, it persists to the very end: the 1975, or last, *Scroll* has a photograph of the toughest-looking baseball team you've ever seen—broad-shouldered, menacing, ununiformed. It's a resilient sport. But yearbooks go to press when a baseball season is all or mostly still unplayed, and by the next spring, who cares how the old season turned out? In 1953, for instance, all ten of the games were played in May. In Maine it takes a while for the field to thaw and dry out. I feel abashed at not knowing more about Higgins baseball, for I am told that I myself, in the first spring of my life, operated as a kind of baseball talisman, that the team used to line up and shake my four-month-old hand before they went off to play. I presume that by the next spring it was already clear that my magical powers, if any, were not sports-oriented.

Like the other sports write-ups, baseball's early ones are a fine combination of the ingenuous and flippant. "We would like to offer some excuses for losing this game," says the June 1910 *Scroll*, "but cannot as we were surpassed in every phase of the game." "Good batting and decidedly poor fielding were features of the game," it says frankly of another. My favorite comment in that issue suggests an early attitude that baseball is just one of a number of possible occupations: "On May 13, instead of planting trees, Higgins played Old Town High at Charleston." Of course they are making a deliberate Arbor Day joke, but what ballplayer now would think of saying that baseball is "instead" of anything?

A few notes survive. The 1922 *Scroll* records a team that won every game; it would have been the 1921 team, for Punk Keith was catcher (as he was later at Colby) and he graduated in 1921. Later in the twenties, too, the team should have had at least one good season, for my father enrolled Harry Ashmore ('26), who had pitched professionally, without realizing who he was. Raymond Farnham ('31) informs me that his senior year's baseball team was "great"; by that time, Punk Keith was back and coaching it. The 1934 team lost only to Hebron, and beat MCI, which "expected to shellac us nicely and send us home in disgrace." After that we get mostly forecasts in the *Scroll*—a baseball team has been formed and it looks very promising / pretty promising / passable / utterly hopeless. In my own graduating year, 1958, the *Scroll* reports that forty-two are out for the sport, Higgins has a new indoor batting cage (the only one outside of collegiate circles in Maine), and "this could be the year." I have not the slightest recollection of whether it was.

Barring late thaws, baseball seems not to have had the difficulties with environment that beset football and basketball. It is, after all, the game that kids can play with a bat and a ball in a vacant lot. But Charles Dunham ('38) recalls some inconveniences peculiar to the sport:

> I was manager of the baseball team one year; I had to chase foul balls down back of Stan Higgins' barn or wherever they were struck. I had three or four baseballs for the game. I had to account for each bat and the catcher equipment. It was like pulling teeth to get any equipment out of H.C.I.

It is not hard to imagine that this was so: it's the end of the year, parents haven't paid up, ready cash is depleted, and you've got this improvident, prodigal damned sport, the point of which is to knock its own equipment as far away from recovery as possible. It might have done better in the fall.

GIRLS' SPORTS

Girls' basketball began at Higgins, and in the east generally, I gather, very much earlier than it did in other parts of the country, the midwest for instance. The earliest reference I have found to a girls' basketball team at Higgins is 1912, but there is no news thereof. In 1915 a team was organized by two teachers, Miss Wiswall and Miss Fowler, and it won its only real game. Certainly teams existed from then all through the twenties, for photographs survive, though reports do not. The photographs and costumes seem charming to us now, though I believe that for years the girls were boiling with rage about the latter, being obliged by my conservative father to wear black stockings and bloomers long after other schools had given them up. The 1917 team, all five of them, sit on high stools and look serious; they are wearing low white sneakers very like the Keds of the 1950s and 1960s. In 1919, in contrast, the team members lie on their bellies facing the camera, their feet up and crossed behind them; they are wearing heavy sweaters and headbands, grinning at the camera—rather a racy photo, and delightful. (The 1959 cheerleaders pose in an unconscious echo of that photograph, but they can't take it seriously—you can see that they're giggling.) In 1922 they have kerchiefs pulled tight around the tops of their heads and tied in back; their arms are crossed in front of their middy blouses in a posture that was perhaps meant to look aggressive.

In 1924 the girls are being coached by Florence Preble. According to the *Scroll* report, they are practicing two nights a week and expect to win a lot. We do not know whether they did. In 1928 the team is already being called the Lassies, a fairly obvious name, and one that stuck till the end of the school. They play only about half a dozen games a season, far fewer than the boys, but whether the arrangement betokens frailty, inferior status, or a paucity of opposing teams, we do not know.

Some attempt to treat the girls decently (though not equitably) is evident, for in 1936 anxiety arises over how few opportunities girls have, with only one sport, to win themselves varsity letters. An elaborate and desperate system of points is assigned to all sorts of vaguely athletic activity, with a concomitant system of rewards ranging from a fifty-point class numeral through the regular letter (one hundred points) to a five-hundred-point "symbolic pin" given only to seniors of the highest all-around excellence. Point-earning activities range from basketball (ten points) down to the acquisition of a dental certificate (five points), hitting folk-dancing, horseshoes, first-aid, paddle tennis, and a myriad of other things on the way. By the next year somebody has pointed out an injustice and the system has been changed to permit a regular letter for basketball alone.

The girls' basketball record is spotty, long losing streaks punctuated by sudden bursts of glory. In 1938, for instance, the team was undefeated, though it had only four experienced players, and it looks to have been the best team in the school that year. So was it in 1939, coached by Leola Mitchell, despite a Keystone Kops episode: due to a scheduling mix-up, the Higgins team traveled to LaGrange for a game, while at the same time the LaGrange team was on its way to Higgins. The '39 team's efforts were rewarded by the alumni association, which gave them a trip to Colby to watch the boys' game, and by my father and his mother-in-law, who gave them a "marvelous supper" in the library.

After that, for a while, the record is bleak. "There was a great deal of sickness and the season wasn't very successful," says the 1946 *Scroll*; in fact, they lost every game. "This team maintained an unbroken record of two years' standing; that is, no wins," says the 1952 *Scroll*, and in 1953 they extended their record one more year. Then, after years of mediocrity (one alumna told me that she got pretty good at foul shooting but never got the hang of shooting with someone jumping up and down in front of her), in 1966 they were Central Maine champs. We have no figures after 1969, but a 1970 graduate told me that in her junior year, "we changed from six players on the court to five players. We all ran full court; that was quite an adjustment—we pooped out easy at first." That does not sound promising.

Higgins softball first appears on paper in the mid forties. For the same reason that we don't know much about how the baseball seasons turned out, we have little information on softball. The years when Anita Boyer ('61) was pitching are said to have been resoundingly triumphant, and in 1966, a great year for girls' sports, the softball team as well as the basketball team were League Champions.

There was also, briefly, in 1972, a girls' cross-country team. I couldn't locate any data on them, but a slightly earlier girls' relay team has left an anecdote passed on to me by my brother: they were undone by their good manners, for one girl paused to help up an opponent who had tripped. It pleases me to have gone to a school where compassion goes deeper than competition.

POSTSCRIPT

Other sports surfaced from time to time, but I have not examined these because they were so short-lived. Joe Roderick coached a wonderful gymnastics team in the late thirties, for instance, the first of its kind in Maine, which traveled all over the state with exhibitions— "good advertisement for the school, as your father well knew," says Roderick now. And I have taken for granted junior varsity sports, as people so often do.

I asked alumni what they had learned from sports—in my case an authentic question. Lots of them said that they had learned to be good losers. Paul Goss ('50) said that the determination he learned in his sports experience had helped him finish his doctorate. I liked that very much and think about it from time to time. It makes sense, of course—the long season, the apparent futility of it all, the grit and self-discipline, the pushing of oneself beyond endurance. It's the only thing anybody ever said that convinced me of the hypothetical connection between Sports and Life. But my favorite answer came from Jake Bishop ('55), and, given the conditions for Higgins sports, it makes me smile a little, although it was not at all intended to be funny: he says that athletics at Higgins helped him survive Parris Island's deadly military training.

Sports buffs offended by any undue lightness of tone should bear in mind that it's in the best, if earliest, Higgins tradition. Sports were important to school life at Higgins and were a great source of diversion, even of joy from time to time, but except in the heat of the moment nobody thought they were the most important thing. Character and academics were the most important things. Sports were just the most important activity.

X

PUBLICATIONS

"Holy Jeez! The Torch!"

—TENNESSEE WILLIAMS

THE SCROLL

T he status of yearbooks as sacred objects has perhaps received too little attention. In thousands of quiet schools such as Higgins, the annual arrival of the yearbook is a momentous event. We open its covers with awe, knowing that inside lurks a kind of arbitrary mandate about memory—some day, if our private memories fade, we will remember our friends' faces by *these* pictures; from the hypothetically best years of our lives, these are the fragments that we may be certain of keeping. Alumni had preserved, and graciously loaned to me, *Scrolls* from all decades. Leroy Kennedy ('57) told me, "When I get a little bit down in the dumps I always dig 'em out."

An exploration of the Higgins *Scrolls* will probably tell us something about Higgins but even more about the evolution of the modern high school yearbook, its changes in size, content, format, and intention, from a literary magazine with a June issue to a major hardbound souvenir of the school year. All the more reason to explore them, perhaps. Though fashions in high school yearbooks may have come to Maine a little more slowly than to metropolitan spots, the purposeful logic of their evolution suggests that they will have come in something like the same sequence.

Scrolls also, of course, reflect the taste and originality of the students who put them out and the tone of the school in a particular year. The June 1910 edition still stands out as elegant among seventy-eight years of *Scrolls*. It is tall and slim (six and three-quarter inches by ten and a half inches), and chaste in cover design. A sheet of satin-striped tissue protects its frontispiece of the founder. Enterprising students have sold a two-line ad at the bottom of every page to Andrew's Music Store in Bangor (e.g., "You ought to hear the angelus piano player at Andrew's, 98 Maine Street, Bangor"). The June 1909 *Scroll*, on the other hand, although it's a rather fancy edition with three colors of ink (red, blue, and black), reflects a dreary term. Not many socials or basketball games, the editors note. Lots of bad weather. The sudden death of the girl who was to be valedictorian. In 1974, the nervous year when the school almost closed, a remarkable number of the students in photographs seem to be standing on roofs or hanging from trees.

The first *Scroll* appeared in the winter of 1897. A thin volume in a soft paper cover, it sold for fourteen cents a copy. It included departments called News, Personals, Alumni, and Locals, but it was to be principally a literary magazine. "Although we may not produce anything of value," its editor says, "still, 'As the twig is bent, the tree's inclined,' and some good may come of it in the future." Literary pieces include three articles and a poem about bubonic plague; it appears that someone is making the senior English class read Defoe's *Journal of the Plague Year*.

Early literary performances often show considerable technical proficiency and wit, especially when they are playing with in-jokes and local allusions. In the May 1898 issue, for instance, there's a long comic poem about an unruly horse named Mary Jane. I quote briefly to suggest the level of competence:

> He sent to Dexter, to Corinth, at home;
> He scoured through Dover and Atkinson;
> At length, from the last selected few,
> He picked out the one he thought would do.
> Do! I tell you, I rather guess;
> She was a wonder and nothing less!

Some poems preserve the authentic sounds of speech sufficiently that we may guess the origins of the writer (though we cannot iden-tify the individual, for the fashion in early days was to use initials only, sometimes absurd initials like XYZ, or no signature at all). In the 1912 water-pump poem quoted in Chapter V—"Men come from Bangor; / It stirs our anger"—it is fairly clear that unless Bangor/ anger is understood to be a slant rhyme, the poet is from out of state. "Ban-ger" is an out-of-state pronunciation; natives say something more like "Bang-gaw." Conversely I have an undated copy of a poem written by Mabel Bunker for her Charleston Academy class, con-taining the indigenous rhyme, "And now we bring the letter F, which stands for Walter Foss, / He boards at home as you will see and drives a smart red horse."

To return briefly to *Scrolls* as physical objects, earlier editions are smaller than modern yearbooks, not only in number of pages (June 1910's is the first one with enough pages to permit a square spine, and that doesn't happen again until 1928, as far as I can tell) but in length and width. Six and three-quarters by nine and a half inches is a typical, though not invariable, size. The 1897 cover design consists of "The Scroll" written diagonally across the center, a tangle of owl and torch and books and Higgins initials in the upper left corner, and a scroll with laurel wreath and inkpot in the lower right. This cover design will be used through 1906, and the owl with his appur-tenances will make one more appearance in 1914. This is the first of four designs to recur with any persistence. It was followed by a straightforward drawing of a parchment scroll, a design that hung on, with interruptions and in various color combinations, until about 1915 and was occasionally revived thereafter; 1952 saw its last appearance, this time with Higgins spelled acronymically down the side ("Honor, Illumination, Geniality," etc.).

The third and most impressive design was new in 1938, used for 1939 and 1940 as well, and revived in 1951. Drawn by Mal Clark, the goddess of scholarship sits enthroned in front of an enormous Higgins seal, at her right a student, at her left a football player. The fourth cover, I am still pleased to say, is my own design, not madly original but serviceable from 1957 through 1968: "The Scroll" is written diagonally in script across the upper left half, while class numerals and a large embossed gold school seal occupy the lower right.

Long before senior photographs or summaries of activities make their appearance in *Scrolls*, we find word games and jokes that we might have supposed to be more modern. The May 1898 *Scroll*, for instance, contains an alphabet poem involving the names of Higgins students and a section called "Locals" that treasures up especially ludicrous classroom errors. This latter item, a cross between joke page and gossip column, will in the end be replaced by conventional jokes with Higgins names attached, but at first the exchanges are largely authentic. If they do not now seem to me very funny, my own advancing years and not theirs are the problem, for a fifteen-year-old friend stopped by, read some, and found them uproarious. E.g., from the November 1914 *Scroll*,

—In General Science. Prof. Shorey: "Miss Hamm, what is the
heat of fusion?"
Miss Hamm: "O Centigrade is the heat
of confusion."

Although we cannot altogether trust developments to arrange themselves neatly by decade, it will be convenient to talk as though they do. Toward the end of the 1900 decade we find several innovations of note. The June editions are becoming rather more important than the other two, a step on the way to proper yearbooks. For instance, in June 1908 we find the class parts printed, the speeches in full. In 1909 we find for the first time a photograph of the senior class, though it is a group photo and no names identify the sitters. June 1910 has not only a photo of the senior class but photos of the track and baseball teams as well. In the March issue of 1910, Senior Statistics, the earliest of yearbook standbys, appears in very much its modern form. Infinite variations will be struck over the years, but 1910 uses Disposition, Natural Expression, Favorite Study, Future Vocation, and By-Word.

From 1910 to about 1920, content takes a number of interesting and not altogether congruent directions. Stories incline to the soppy. The December 1910 issue alone includes a newsboy who dies saving a golden-haired female child from runaway horses but is glad to leave this life and join his crippled sister in Heaven, a writer's mother as queen of the fairies, a dog forgiving the cruelty of its master, and a heroic adolescent girl who saves eight victims of shipwreck and dies of pneumonia. On the other hand, class parts are getting funnier, for they now include Prophecy, Gifts, and so on. (In 1914 Lawrence Higgins, who will later contribute fifteen vigorous, likeable, intelligent HCI students of his own, is advised with his gift to "be careful what kind of seed you get, for, 'You reap whatever you sow.' ") Doggerel flourishes. The February 1912 issue indulges in such prophecies about seniors as, "Irving Rich will be a merchant / And sell us everything nice, / Molasses, codfish and crackers, / Flour, sugar, and all kinds of spice." The codfish is a great relief beside the heroic children, and the advertisements too are nicely unpretentious: "If you don't live in Bangor, we can sell you coal just the same." There are, as well, some pieces of literary criticism and a phenomenon that dies out sometime in the twenties, letters from travelers, missionaries, etc. The most alarming of these appears as late as 1922 and tells us how much our attitudes have changed. Dr. Emmett Russell, a missionary to China, writes home that the Chinese "filth without is only a sign of the filth within." Of General Wang's funeral he observes, "Weird was the music, barbaric the sight—and somehow the Devil seemed very, very close by."

To return to the decade in general, a couple of other developments deserve note—names now identify the men in a football photo, and rather more student art work is included than formerly. The November 1914 editorial page is headed with a delightful sketch of (we presume) Editor Leah Colbath at nearly midnight, in her nightgown and cap and a heavy sweater, trying to beat the deadline at a fine, angular old typewriter, her copy of Emerson at the ready. And we might note that the February 1917 *Scroll* is creeping on toward modern size—it is eight and one half by eleven inches.

The *Scrolls* of the 1920s are interesting in several ways: first, for the flavor of the decade, which is just as it ought to be; second, for their increased level of intellectual sophistication, a good reflection on the school; third, late in the decade, for some major advances in yearbook evolution. The tone throughout the twenties is cheeky, restless, pleased with its own flaming youth and wit. The class historian for 1923, for instance, dances just on the edge of overstepping with a description of their first day at school, when "Mr. Tracy gravely informed us that straw hats and chewing gum went out of style about September 1st." This, says the historian, was the first of a series of "timely lessons" to which most students listened; those who did not, who had to be shown, "have been shown so promptly and efficiently that today there is not a doubtful member among us." The next December's *Scroll* contains an editorial that assumes, not argues, a general dissatisfaction with Higgins social life. (This even though, according to another article, the Girl Reserves have given a Halloween party that included "a Pigmy dance by four of the girls." How could anyone complain after that?) The December 1924 issue has six pages of witticisms with headings like "We Wonder," "Can You Imagine," and so on, and nicknames are flourishing—Shrimp, Gramp, Mooch; you can fairly hear heels being kicked up. Editorials are optimistic, though they warn against too many moving pictures and dime novels. We may note also in 1929 the only appearance of a school mascot, which seems, like Colby's, to be a mule.

Literature has abandoned sentimentality in favor of local color, a great improvement. The April 1923 issue has a plotless but anecdote-studded account of an old tinker, just such a narrative of eccentricity as we all grew up on, as well as a river-driving story, an article on blue herons, and a comic tale full of regional dialect. On a different level, the 1928 *Scroll* contains John Bradeen's poem on gossip, after Virgil (which, he tells me, teacher Eva Alley caused to be printed and pasted into the Latin texts), plus the story of Dido and Aeneas rendered into a splendid imitation of Biblical language by RR, who I think must be Ruth Ramsdell. I note in the 1929 *Scroll* easy allusions to More's *Utopia*, to Sir Galahad and St. Paul and Ovid. Classroom errors are more and more the kind that teachers ordinarily share with one another ("She did not shrive in that climate"), and the student body is finding them funny.

You will note that I said "the 1928 *Scroll*" without specifying any month. No one has sent me a 1927 *Scroll*, so I may be wrong in asserting that 1928's is the first modern yearbook, but it would have been like that class to pioneer. Modern, first of all, because it is the only issue of the year. It's roughly the right size for a modern yearbook (eight by ten and three-quarter inches), it has a square spine, and the crackle-patterned orange cover stock is decorated with a very professional sketch of the Old Institute by M.D. ('28), whom I take to be Maurice Dennison. This is the first *Scroll* I've seen with individual photos of the seniors (three to a page) and those familiar little paragraphs of activities, quotations, and comments. It seems to be, as well, the first yearbook with snapshots of school life.

The economic reverses of the 1930s are reflected in yearbook reverses. From 1933 to 1937, senior photos disappear, except for a group photo in 1934. The books are smaller and thinner again in the early part of the decade. Quite a few group photos still appear, however, these being no expense to the individual student, and economical entertainments like Senior Statistics are expanded, in 1933, to include juniors, though consistent attention to underclassmen will not flourish until the 1950s. In 1936, when the seniors are, as in early years, represented only by a page of statistics—Name, Commonly Called, Favorite Pastime, Song Hit, Facial Expression, Fitting Occupation—we may note a couple of familiar figures: Jess DeLois, who is thought well suited to be a fisherman, will be back at Higgins coaching in the forties, and Phillip Hamm, for whom a career as deacon is predicted, will be a professor of mathematics and last secretary of the Board of Trustees.

Essays in the thirties are serious: How does one select one's life work? What qualities are needed for jobs? There are discussions of the future of aviation and the blight of billboards, and a lot of opinions expressed—for conservation, popularity, and pacifism; against parole boards, capitalism, communism, and reckless driving. The 1939 *Scroll* has two articles on Jews: one on Hitler's mistreatment of them, another on their laudable tenacity to their faith. One cheerful note brightens the thirties, however: in 1937 the girls' basketball team appears for the first time with bare legs.

In the forties, seniors had weightier subjects than yearbook improvement on their minds. Indeed, the 1945 *Scroll* (as may have been the custom of the times) is dedicated not to some favorite teacher but to "Those who have made the Supreme Sacrifice in the great struggle for Right and a Better World and to those who are daily stepping forward to fill their places in the ranks." Stories and essays both during and after the war are predictable but fascinating. The 1944 *Scroll* has essays called "Military Training for the High School Boy" (against it), "What Shall We Do With Japan?" (give her to China), and "What Shall We Do With Germany?" (sit on her good and hard). Even nonmilitary stories flirt with horror. In the twenty pages of literature in 1945 I find such titles as "Alone," "The Scream," "Murder in the

Night," "The Scare of my Life," and "A Horrible Night." By 1946 the topics are distinctly postwar: starvation in France, the scarcity of stockings, the difficulties of getting into colleges full of GIs, the atomic bomb ("Scientists have disproved the theory that the area of the explosion is unfit to live in").

Despite these larger issues, several yearbook developments are worth noting. Nineteen forty-one uses faculty photos, a piece of pioneering that does not catch on at once but will reemerge in 1954 and stay until the end of the school. Nineteen forty-eight (which has an unusually strong cover, red, with crossed American flags and the school seal) offers a page for autographs. By the early forties, too, the practice of using quotations with Senior photos seems firmly established. Here are some representative offerings for 1941:

> Not that I love work less but that I love fun more.

> A small man sometimes casts a long shadow.

> A perfect woman, nobly planned
> To warm [sic], to comfort, and command.

> Silence is golden.

> Give the world the best that you have,
> and the best will come back to you.

> The twinkle in thine eye, girl, betokens mischief.

Do these sound familiar? They should. It would be worth studying, this phenomenon of yearbook quotations, sources long lost, passed down from year to year like skipping rhymes in a schoolyard. In 1941, though, there was still a bit of original verse as well:

> When radios need fixing and no one seems to be near,
> Just call upon Charles Edward Brewster and you won't have a
> thing to fear.

Through the fifties, literature decreases and editorials disappear entirely, the latter to be replaced at last, I suppose, by the Message from the Principal. Underclassmen become more important; in 1955, for the first time, they appear in small individual pictures. The 1954 *Scroll*, like the 1928 one, stands out for its innovations: it is the first hardcover yearbook at Higgins, it has the first Principal's Message (the next one will be in 1958, after which it sticks), it includes more informal shots, some attention is paid to underclassmen, senior photos are bigger, and there are only five pages of literature. In 1955 the democratic impulse includes not only underclassmen and faculty but trustees, and literature has shrunk to three pages and appears under Activities. Nineteen fifty-eight introduces Senior Superlatives —photos of the shortest, tallest, loudest, and so on, and 1959 brings in one of the silliest among silly yearbook devices, those elliptical allusions (a bastard offspring of Senior Statistics?) whose significance is programmed to self-destruct after graduation: " 'Stearns' . . . talking . . . cough . . . orange shoes . . . Prexy . . . 'Snerd' . . . student store . . . rushed waiter . . . Sr. English . . . 'Guess I'll go over and sleep' . . . study agriculture." Another long-lasting innovation first practiced in the fifties is the inclusion of senior baby pictures. A number of these additions seem to reflect a joyful self-absorption last seen in the twenties.

Minor milestones punctuate the years from 1960 to 1975. Padded covers make an appearance in 1966 and sometimes thereafter; some years, 1965 and 1968 for instance, achieve a kind of sophistication by choosing a dominant theme, like "All the world's a stage." Literature turns on and off; one year it will be quite good, and another year gone entirely. At first there is some rather respectable stuff, though in the 1961 *Scroll* I am interested to note a poem that had appeared in my own yearbook over the signature of the plagiarist's elder sister. Nor is this the only case of plagiarism in literary sections; I notice that "What Is a Boy?" and "What Is a Girl?" have been popular thefts over the years and have slipped by inexperienced editors over and over again, though I wonder that some faculty sponsor has not caught on.

Perhaps the major changes from 1960 to 1975 are, on the plus side, increasingly creative and sophisticated photography and, on the minus side, a kind of impersonal standardization. In 1960 and 1961 section dividers are photographed at Higgins, not canned, for one (in 1960) shows a gradebook with familiar names, and the faculty section title page in 1961 shows their coat rack and abandoned mud shoes. In 1963 students have cut out and arranged full-length photos of themselves against backgrounds of giant books, basketballs, and pieces of chalk. The effect is good. Similarly, in 1960, there's a won-

derful picture of the basketball coach holding out his hands and jug-
gling on his palms nine players like marionettes dribbling tiny
basketballs in the air. In 1964 and for some years thereafter the endpapers of the yearbooks are color aerial shots of campus. (Once before, in 1956, photographic endpapers were used, gray and white
photos of the Institute and Tibbetts Hall; otherwise, they have been
plain, but good for autographing.) In 1973 and thereafter we find
poems, statistics, jokes, etc., printed over screened-down photographs—very striking.

The impulse to standardization may be the fault not of the student editors but of the yearbook manufacturers, who were perhaps
offering limited choices. From 1969 on, the covers are no longer of
home design and sometimes not very pertinent to Higgins, though
the 1970 orange and black cover is handsome. In these new covers
the class numerals very much out-loom the title, and no specific
reference to the school appears. In 1971 we begin seeing canned endpapers, the kind of misty scenes that banks put on checks. Despite
these superficial eradications of individuality, both class tone and
Higgins specifics survive. We can suspect, for instance, that class
morale was peculiar in 1972, when Senior Statistics include both
"Biggest Ambition" and "Most Likely to End up As," for three
seniors say they'll most likely end up dead and one says a widow. Of
course, what we may have here is an extraordinarily realistic class,
not an extraordinarily depressed one. Consider also the ambitions—
"olympic runner," "to be the first girl on the moon," "to own a horse
ranch"—paired respectively with predictions of reality—"motorcycle
bum," "earthbound," "housewife."

There is a late revival of Higgins tradition, too. The 1972 *Scroll* has
a shot of Higgins in 1905 taken by faculty member Peter Chase's
grandfather, and underneath it a 1972 shot taken by Peter with the
same camera. The title page in 1974 displays an oval photo of the
Institute with the school song printed below it, and farther on a
sketch of the Institute with an affectionate poem that I shall quote in
Chapter XV. The last *Scroll* has found a knight to put on the cover
and has risen to former heights with a translation from Virgil on the
first page: "And perhaps sometime it will be pleasant to recall these
things." The translator has tactfully omitted the force of *et, even* these
things.

The Scrawl

In 1938, when the *Scroll* had for about ten years been a yearbook rather than a school magazine, the student body once again felt the need for a periodical. Philip Keith was its first faculty advisor. Its title, designed to contrast with the formality of the *Scroll*, has that kind of "aw-shucks" humor that Higgins sometimes engendered. A poem in the 1939 *Scroll*, eliciting subscription payments, catches the tone all too well in its first four lines:

> *Maybe* The Scrawl *ain't no great paper;*
> *Maybe our writings aren't so hot;*
> *But to us up here at Higgins*
> *The scrawled up* Scrawl *means quite a lot.*

Probably, on second thought, we shouldn't denigrate that kind of humor, for it means that the school has succeeded in turning the genuinely unsophisticated into kids with enough self-knowledge to produce a deliberate hick act suitable for tourists.

I have before me the first *Scrawl* (September 28, 1938), two pieces of paper dittoed on both sides in blue ink, stapled together. A sketch of the new Institute adorns the top. The *Scrawl*'s purposes, says the editor, are fun (both for its editors and for its readers), notification of events, reminders of past events, advertisement of the school, and experience in publication. The first number is homey, including not only sports news but chatter about a recent storm and what it did, and a mock-Middle-English account of the janitor squashing a big spider; the second (October 12) includes an account, with names withheld, of a grudge fight in the gym, and the story of a local fire doused by volunteer students and faculty.

By the third issue, the *Scrawl* has settled into the format it is to keep for twenty-five years: colored paper covers with a student drawing on the front and perhaps ten pages of mixed sports, reports, announcements, gossip, and jokes, with now and then a bit of litera-ture. It came out twice a month. I see from my own *Scrawls*, the few I've saved, that we were enjoying a violent flirtation with colored dittoes, cover illustrations laboriously (I speak from experience) pieced together from red and green and purple masters. I think that ours may have come out only once a month. The contents have not changed. Editorials, if any, are intractably seasonal; we are exhorted to thankfulness in November, love in February, renewal of joy in April, nostalgia in June.

The *Scrawl* lasted, I think, until the mid sixties. From 1965 on I find no more pictures of its staff, and my brother, who was at Higgins from 1964 to 1968, does not remember it, though the 1972–73 catalogue says that it is published three or four times a year.

I wish I could report that Higgins alumni got their first impulse toward subsequent careers in journalism, art, or publishing from their experiences on the *Scroll* or *Scrawl* boards, but no evidence of such a connection exists. Even I, the writer closest at hand, did not produce a single word intended for either publication; having mistaken my vocation, I was instead drawing pictures for the covers, an activity that has led to absolutely nothing in later life. A less glamorous but more accurate view of our literary activities is that we wished to have newspapers and yearbooks, and therefore manufactured them as well as we could. People who live inconveniently far from cities or who don't have much money already know that they can make almost anything—it's not a revelation. And yes, as the first *Scrawl* promises, we did have fun. The first *Scroll* staff's modest hope that from the bending of the intellectual twig some good would finally emerge was apparently unfounded, while their suspicion that the magazine might be without value was excessively modest; the publications themselves were of inestimable value—compact, portable souvenirs of an extraordinary experience and a time of life that would seem in alumni memory particularly golden.

XI

LOVE AND OTHER UNSCHEDULED RECREATIONS

Nov. 7. Several love affairs getting serious in spite of expert treatment.

—"HISTORY OF THE YEAR,"
1932 *Scroll*

Higgins is located in a rural community. Students are taught to help provide their own amusements and are carefully supervised at all times," my father writes in a letter dated 6/24/41. Of course students are only too glad to help provide their own amusements, hence the constant supervision. As Hugh Smith once remarked, at that age they can't help doing things just to see what will happen. Higgins students were kept fairly busy through the week, and faculty drummed up whatever entertainments they could on the weekends, but there was still space for creativity. Some students found the entertainment provided by the school more satisfying than others did. "Pleasures were simple, but my need for pleasure was simple," says Ronald Bishop ('49), who came from a farm. Frank Whitehouse Anderson ('16) recalls as an especially pleasant memory just "going to the dining room at night in the dark, and watching the drifting snow swirling and howling by the windows." On the other hand, the lack of cinemas, roller rinks, shopping districts, and so on, could be disconcerting. Robert Reny ('51) remembers that as he arrived at Higgins another car drew up and let out a boy who took one look at the bucolic vista, freaked, and hollered, "Take me home! I'm not gonna spend a year in this place!" His parents took him home.

What students had to entertain themselves with was mainly one another. Since teenagers yearn to be with their peers, this was no mean toy. A principal preoccupation, always (though not for all students), was the relationship between the sexes. That is not to say that the relationship was necessarily amorous, though we shall get on to that shortly. Alumni are pretty much unanimous in asserting that boy/girl relationships were open and friendly, as indeed I always found them. One of the pleasant memories of my senior spring is cutting last-period study hall to sit by an open window in the back of the chapel with Peter Chase, unromantically chatting about a hundred things. "The boys," my unsentimental friend Bobbie says, remembering our friends twenty-five years later, and you can hear affection warm her voice, "the boys always used to say—." But here the recollection must end, because "the boys' " best witticisms were always too outrageous and libelous for publication.

Romance was inhibited (to understate the case) by the scrupulosity with which the girls were watched. Boys were much less closely supervised, which was partly practical and partly prejudicial. Beyond the important facts that girls can get pregnant (a very bad advertisement for a boarding school) and that there were fewer of them to watch, I think we are seeing here some sexist notion that the girls were more boy-crazy than the boys were girl-crazy, and therefore likelier to stir up that silliness called love. I find my father writing to the parents of one girl who is "primarily interested in boys" that "our work is to help her find things in life which are more constructive and more lasting." Under those two comparatives lies some philosophy so basic and so unnerving as to defy discussion. Further, Leon Williams ('28) remembers my father growling, as he observed perambulating couples, that he wasn't running a matrimonial bureau. One can see that the atmosphere at Higgins was not exactly nurturing for lovers.

"Teachers kept a careful eye on girls. We all had our sweethearts but for the most part our friendship was purely platonic," says Frank Whitehouse Anderson ('16). "I felt the school was too strict with boy/girl relationships—a faculty member sat in the small room we could see boys in," writes Frances Ward ('38). Pete Minott ('38) laughed when I asked whether relationships had been open, friendly, romantic, frustrating, steamy, or what: " 'Steamy?'—How could you do it when I went there?" "Steamy? At Higgins? You've got to be kidding," echoes Charles Cummings ('41). "Hard to be alone with a girl," notes a 1954 graduate. And I think that this did not change much in the periods of greater license, for a 1970 graduate complains that she was punished for kissing her boyfriend, when in fact she was whispering in his ear.

Of course couples were allowed to do some things—daylight things, group things. For instance, they could, and did, walk round and round the campus sidewalks, gaining thereby a little private conversation and perhaps a chance to hold hands. I would like to think that this Higgins experience encouraged conversational skills, but I suppose that a lot of it was inarticulate cooing. In the 1920s, amorous students got some consolation from religion; that is to say, boys and girls were allowed to attend Tuesday night prayer meeting at the Baptist church together, sit together, and walk home together. One 1926 graduate mentioned that the Institute pillars were good for necking behind on the way home. Myrtle Paine ('27) writes, "I suppose we were supposed to be religiously motivated, but that was the only social event allowed to a boy and girl, so we went more to hold hands behind the hymn book, and to request hymns such as 'And He Walks With Me—' ["In the Garden"], singing with anything but religious thoughts." It would have been fun to know what they were praying for. It's impossible to imagine that my father didn't know why his students were so pious on Tuesdays, so why did he let this go on? Maybe he was being kind, giving them a safe outlet. Maybe he liked the looks of a good Higgins delegation at prayer meeting and knew how to get it. Maybe he really wished to create in student minds a pleasant association with worship, like giving Sunday School treats.

"Socials," through the nineteen tens, twenties, and thirties, provided a romantic context of sorts. A pretty poor one, sophisticates claimed, but that still left a lot of Higgins students who thought it was hot stuff. Lucetta Doore ('14) recalls fiddle and piano music, with not real dancing but the Grand March and games that resembled contra dancing. (Walter Elden ['27] says that they were allowed to cross over but not to balance their partners on the side!) Ellis Holt ('27) liked socials and reports that

> At intermission time there would be cake and cocoa, or ice cream for sale. It was customary for the boys to buy refreshments for their girls, or any girl who would receive the offering. The socials were socialization of sorts and for me exciting enough to keep me coming back and looking forward to the next one. I did not even know how to dance.

Sometimes, says Frank Whitehouse Anderson, they could meet the girls in the dining room at night, under teacher supervision, and play cards and have ice cream and popcorn. And Lucetta Doore remembers another small mercy, that at noon recess the boys and girls could sit together in the double seats.

Besides socials, Ellis Holt says, "On some Friday evenings we had movies, using one projector which required intermission between reels and whenever the reel broke, with the pictures thrown onto a cotton sheet on the platform." Those Friday night movies were a curious dispensation. A number of alumni have insisted that one was *allowed* to kiss at the movies; that's a very odd rule, but perhaps it was true, for why have an activity so conducive to kissing unless kissing was understood to be permitted? Certainly not for the quality of the films themselves; they were awful. I suppose, though, that they were cheap (*Spawn of the North* cost $17.60 in 1941) and that we didn't have much choice.

The physical difficulties of getting films to Charleston make one feel that perhaps films are naturally an urban phenomenon and should not be transplanted; my father writes to a supplier in March of 1943 that if the film doesn't get to Bangor by Friday there's no getting hold of it, and that we couldn't help returning one film late because "the roads were blocked on Monday and Tuesday." By sixth grade or so, we film-starved local children sometimes were allowed to go to Friday night movies, where we sat up front and shot one another with rubber bands. I remember the grind and whinny of the sound starting up, the black numerals like Chinese writing that raced backward across the sheet, and our absolutely illogical sense of anticipation, but I can recall only one film—a gangster number called *Ruthless*, which rose to the refinement of an epigraph ("He who lives by the sword shall die by the sword") and undoubtedly declined from there on. Still, the Higgins students appreciated these as a kind of covering action. Neal Brown ('56) writes,

> Movies in the chapel, although per se lousy, were an exceptional treat, because in the dim sanctuary of flickering light and under the cover of projector noise—couples could do some serious necking and, perhaps, even some petting. Legend had it that one couple during my years at H.C.I. actually effected a well-planned sexual union during a Saturday night movie at the chapel. Considering the level of post-study hall passion which that couple exhibited openly in front of the girls' dorm on weeknights, I find it easy to believe the legend.

Until the removal of girls from Tibbetts Hall in 1937, the inaccessible proximity of the opposite sex must have been a terrific frustration and challenge. Students met it with some creativity. One 1926 graduate recalls that in fall and spring, when the screens were off, one could climb across the roof and into the girls' side, if the owners of key rooms were cooperative. (Nothing sexual, he assures us, just a friendly visit.) More ingenious yet was Ellis Holt's brother, who, when he found himself unsupervised, went to the girls' side and put paper behind the fuses, plunging the rooms into blackness. When he was through visiting, he took the paper out and went back to his room. (No wonder the fusebox was peculiar in later years. Mary Jane Keith reminds me that whenever you opened it to pull the main switch, one of two things jumped out, a foot-long electrical spark or a mouse. "When it was rewired some of the magic went out of my life," she quips.) The girls were ordinarily not quite so aggressive about the roof, but Martha Bragger ('35) tells me that once a year, when all the teachers were at a faculty dinner, a few of the most daring would sneak over to the boys' side. Otherwise, she says, there was a hole behind one of the bureaus. There (á la Pyramus and Thisbe) conversation and notes could be exchanged. Even solid walls could be useful, according to Ruth Sargent ('26):

> My room was just by the porch (2nd floor) and the wall between the sub master Hugh Smith on the boys' side of the building—my friend was a good friend of Hugh Smith so

when he was away my friend had access to study in his room if he wanted to. So we used to pound on the wall to get each other's attention. Then we would reach out the windows over the porch to pass notes, food, etc., to each other. . . . I might add that once I thought Mr. Smith was away and I pounded on the wall and knocked a picture off the wall onto his table where he was working. That wasn't ever mentioned to me but he did tell my friend.

One of my all-time favorite stories was sent by Ima Brown ('34). I cherish it for its depiction of frustration, ingenuity, and relative innocence. When constant chaperonage became more than they could bear, "the young man climbed the fire escape of the girls' dormitory to the girl friend's room and cut a small hole in the screen so that they could share a good night kiss. However they were caught in the act by the housemother who was on rounds." A 1941 graduate, male, also alludes to "kissing through the downstairs screens in the girls' dorm after dark." He does not mention cutting holes, so one imagines lots of smiling, cross-hatched lips.

Another opportunity of sorts occurred at evening study hall, though the boys and girls occupied separate classrooms and the girls were led out and shepherded to the dorm marginally earlier. Besides the writing and receiving of passionate notes, there was the walk back, if one could somehow manage to coincide with the beloved and escape observation. Carl McGraw ('36) cites that as the only opportunity for "smooching," though Miriam Sweet ('40) points out its difficulties: "If you wanted to walk home from study hall you weren't supposed to hold hands, to say nothing about a good-night kiss, or 'Growing Trees' as it was called." Says Merrill Clement ('43), "[Couples] would run ahead of Miss Mitchell to get a kiss before she caught up."

Obviously the way to secure extra time was somehow to leave early. Leroy Kennedy ('57) assures me that he and a few other boys used to leave study hall via the fire escape while their supervisor was chatting to the girls' supervisor during the girls' departure. Lorraine Archer ('57), long married to one of those others, says, "We did sneak a kiss each night after study hall. He would supposedly have a bathroom release from study hall but sneak out the fire escape to walk me to the dorm." Ormonde Brown ('47) tells a more risqué tale:

Serious sexual encounters were few but did happen. One stealthy couple used to have a regular session behind the Institute building just before study hall was over. Their timing was exacting because they had to be through before the boys headed for the smoker. They never got caught by the faculty, but once by an early smoker. She always made it back to the girls' dorm in time from study hall!!!

I have asked a reliable classmate exactly what the sexual situation at Higgins was in our time. Because, of course, I didn't know. In the first place, I had very much wanted not to know. In the second, no sane teenager would have reported sexual escapades to the daughter of the Chairman of the Board of Trustees. (As my friend Jeannie Philbrick kindly put it, I was branded as a snitch from the start. Possibly with justification, it occurs to me now—here I am, snitching furiously.) My classmate responded that although much of the student body was sexually active, consummation was reserved for weekends, when they were away from campus. During the week they wrote notes and set up assignations and generally got ready. Sex has never been so good since, she added—there's nothing like a whole week of foreplay.

We should not leave a discussion of boarding school amours without a word about student-faculty hanky-pank. One imagines easily enough the traditional crushes of female students or the lecheries of unscrupulous male instructors; a trickier and more unsettling business is the attraction between male students and female teachers. In vain (sometimes) the female teacher struggles against a crisis for which our culture has not prepared her—the flattery of being loved by a younger man, complicated by a desire to yield, when her job compels her to dominate. What's worse, if the boy is a senior, and he almost always is, then he begins to look old enough, compared to most of the student body; she loses perspective.

One spring, not at Higgins but at another boarding school, a perfect frenzy of romance swept the campus. A twenty-four-year-old dorm mother and an eighteen-year-old prefect spent so much time together in the stable, feeding her horse in a state of amorous befuddlement, that the dorm father threw her out. Another colleague—conservative, clean, engaged to be married the following summer—fell for a foreign student and went on romantic, melancholy picnics with him; she would pace her room for hours, saying tenderly to herself (and any friends who happened in), "Mi libro es rojo; my book is red. Mi vaca esta muerta; my cow is dead."

Nor is this folly exclusively modern—Lucetta Doore ('14) recalls a hapless teacher in her time who was interested in a boy named West and fell into a trap: "In what direction do your bedroom windows face?" she was asked in class and innocently replied, "West," to the loud delight of her students. An anonymous male respondent from the twenties loved a female teacher, who on one magical night let him hold her hand, under the blanket, on a hayride. And perhaps after all it is broadening for the students to have a little rehearsal for being in love with adults or for the teachers to be reminded of the intoxications of adolescent flesh.

I have so far said nothing about homosexuality, though perhaps readers will be expecting it. It was not an important issue at Higgins; in fact, mostly it never crossed anyone's mind. Now and then a few savvy students would snicker about some student or faculty twosome, but the real point was to show off their own sophistication. Two stories will illustrate the general level of obliviousness. Jake Bishop ('55), when he wrote, was still giggling about Hugh Smith's uneasiness at the close friendship between him and his roommate. He tells me that when it got cold, a lot of boys chose, for warmth, to sleep together in their narrow beds. "Probably contributed to Hugh Smith thinking we were queer!" he says cheerfully. The second story involves a genuine scandal: the discovery, in the emotional aftermath of the '56 dorm fire, that the Dean of Men had taken sexual advantage of two of his younger students. Though I listened down hot-air registers and subsequently resorted to *Webster's Unabridged*, I was hard put, with no previous knowledge, to make sense of what had happened. I was perhaps slightly, but certainly not radically, backward in this respect, for when this scandal aroused in my mother's breast a sudden desire to know what homosexuals, in fact, *did*, she was obliged to ask her best friend, who didn't know either but applied to a young faculty wife, who in her turn didn't know but got the information from her husband. All of these were educated adult women. (I shall say to my mother's credit that, having found out, she shared the news with me at once.)

Hazing, another unscheduled recreation, was a less constant affair than love. It was evidently lively in the twenties, somewhat modified in the thirties, and prohibited suddenly in the forties—the fall of '43 to be specific, according to a couple of graduates, though nobody has explained what happened then to precipitate the ban. In the fifties and later we see a slight revival. It seems to have been a rather freelance, spontaneous business mostly, no freshman beanies or anything of that sort. An initiation (largely a matter of whacking applicants, it appears) to the more specialized pleasures of the smoker was traditional until the GIs came to school and refused to put up with it. The majority of alumni felt that freshmen had been treated well, even cordially. Wilder Pearl ('37) put the benevolent view best: freshmen, as the youngest members of the family, were made to feel welcome.

But of course the more interesting reading deals with what happened on the occasions when hazing, in spite of general goodwill to newcomers, took place. My earliest report comes from Sabra Lee ('18), who says that in her time a freshman boy was paddled and his father made a great fuss about it. There was even talk of expelling the paddlers. In the midst of the excitement a boy named Willins tried to start a strike, rising up in chapel and saying, "Come on, boys. Follow me," but nobody did. The culprits were not expelled after all, and the only effect of the incident was a new nickname—One-Man Strike Willins. John Bradeen ('28), who attests to all kinds of hazing in his time, cites particularly going after a naked freshman with a broom and pushing him into a shower. His old roommate Ellis Holt ('27) has more lurid recollections.

> When the mood struck [upperclassmen] they might engage a freshman in a pleasant little game which required the freshman to bare his buttocks and kneel with his head in a pillow held by an upperclassman in his lap. The assembled upperclassmen would then take turns using a paddle on the bare buttocks whereupon the freshman would quickly look up and try to identify the paddler. That went on until he did so and then it was time for another freshman. . . . It was also customary that during one's sophomore year he got his pubic hair shaved off and his class numerals painted on his belly with iodine.

Ruth Dyer ('29), in her rhymed account of class history, alludes to hazing as customary, though her version is either (1) expurgated, (2) pertinent to female hazing only, or (3) both.

> Sophomore days began with ardor
> Three new students joined the ranks;
> Then began the sophomore giggling
> And the usual hazing pranks.
> They'd forgotten how they suffered
> Under twenty-eight's wild reign,
> Now they harassed poor green freshmen,
> Made them work with might and main;
> For they darned the sophomore stockings,
> Even stooped to tie a shoe,
> Made the beds, and did the housework,
> Just as any maid should do.

"Twenty-eight's wild reign," incidentally, is probably an apt description. The class of 1928 prided itself on being the worst in Higgins history, and with some reason, though in the end it seems to have been unusually rich in talent, enterprise, and personality. Three of its members were later Higgins institutions and appear elsewhere in these pages—Mabel Robinson, cook; Joe Roderick, coach; and Leon Williams, last Chairman of the Board of Trustees. We know that female hazing sometimes did get rough. A woman who graduated in 1926 reports, "My class of dorm girls were a very lively bunch. We were stripped and saddled, etc., the women teachers approved." "New kids were always given a bath," says Madeline Thurlow ('30).

Not all of the initiation was physical. Harry Nason ('27) reports a classic hoax, in this case turned back on the hoaxer.

> I remember one incident of hazing. I was sent to the hardware store for a left handed monkey wrench. Mr. Tracy was there. I saw him confer with Hollis Soule, the owner. Hollis gave me a wrench with a bill for the same to the person who had sent me. I'm sure Hollis gave "Pod" Applebee, a senior, the credit for the wrench, as I never heard any more about it.

Higgins also had a homegrown hoax, though doubtless spontaneous counterparts existed elsewhere. Avery Rich ('33) writes for his own book, *Growing Up Yankee*, an account of "Visiting Aunt May," a practice with which his brother Wayne in the late twenties was also familiar. He tells it with charm, but I shall merely paraphrase to avert copyright complications. Newcomers were told about a hospitable lady in town named Aunt May. Avery discreetly describes her as an excellent cook and friendly to students; other reliable sources suggest that "friendly" hardly covers the cordiality of her purported intercourse with Higgins students, and that food was not an issue. Could there have been two versions? In any case, her husband, "Uncle Frank," objected to her generosity. Initiates would be led off to a certain abandoned house at night, theoretically Aunt May's, where one of the boys would be hiding to impersonate Uncle Frank by firing off—pick your version—a cap pistol or a gun, and the initiates would flee for their lives.

On the whole, reports from the thirties are milder, though Miriam Sweet ('40) recalls that some boys left school because of hazing. Girls are being put into tubs of water and made to push pennies with their noses, and there is some feeling that upperclassmen are trying out authoritarian poses to see if they work. I have a pleasant story from Robert Houghton ('37).

> There was some hazing of Freshmen. The first snow that came they would get a ducking. I remember a Kermit Johnson, they took his pants off. He claimed he had a broken rib with no symptoms. He hurt so he couldn't go to church. Mr. Thomas, the Dean, asked me to sit in his room and not let him out during services. Just before dinner he wanted to know what they were going to have for dessert. I said ice cream. He was all well then.

After the 1943 embargo I find no mention of hazing again until what would have been the fall of '46, and by then it had lost much of its color and character. Ronald Bishop ('49), who entered as a small sophomore, convinced a gang of other sophomores who were leading him off to the boiler room that he really was one of them—his first great sales job, he says. In the fifties there was some hazing, though Neal Brown ('56) describes it as "mild and informal." Wayne Adams ('58) says he got "the broom treatment" but that it wasn't bad, and Leroy Kennedy ('57) recalls the custom of blindfolding a new boy while everyone ostensibly spit in a cup (really egg whites, not much improvement on spit) and then gave it to him to drink. Jake Bishop ('55) mentions a Kangaroo Court at which one hopeless boy, told to plead insanity, said, "I plead unsanitary," and was let off out of pity. None of it sounds much worse than what one had to endure on an average night at Baptist Youth Fellowship with the rambunctious Reverend Reedy. If he didn't make us drink spit or egg whites it was only because he didn't know that trick; he once duped us into sniffing ammonia, and he had a large repertoire of equally engaging practical jokes. By the sixties the girls' hazing is described as mild, and Kenneth Churchill ('61) says that male upperclassmen demanded that freshmen call them "sir." I have no hazing data from the seventies.

Higgins students in all periods possessed a particularly fine piece of equipment for hazing and other games: the Higgins family tomb. It sits in the middle of the cemetery, an abrupt little hill crowned with a granite obelisk. Into its side is sunk a heavy, studded iron door with a big ring for a handle. I know that it's heavy, because once during church a little boy named William Parris was allowed outside to play and he played with the tomb and snipped his finger-end off in the door. I don't think that the door can be locked, but it can certainly be sat on, and how could a freshman's tormenters resist doing that, the better to hear any emotion from their victim inside? Evidence suggests that in all decades it was used for storage of the live as well as the dead, and in the earliest alumni reference to it, Sabra Lee ('18) describes its use as a speaking platform for a burlesqued Billy Sunday sermon in the middle of the night.

Prank playing, on fellow students or on faculty, was popular at Higgins, as it doubtless was at all schools, and some of the tricks (knotted pajamas, foreign substances in beds) were standard issue. Others depended on naiveté or rural resources. Pete Minott ('38) told me about a boy who, having begged some suppositories for his hemorrhoids, was aghast and disbelieving at the instructions for use; Mozart Robinson hastened to assure him that of course it wasn't true, that he was really to take one orally each day before breakfast. Leone Dakin ('21) and her roommate spent a weekend on the farm and, noticing that sheep droppings looked a lot like the homemade dried-rose beads her friend Mildred admired, brought her some for stringing. Another anecdote involving Mildred, who was in fact much beloved, speaks well for the good-natured tone of these games.

Mildred was dropped, fully dressed, into a tub of water, whereupon her assailants (and the innocent Miss Dakin) lost their social privileges.

> We couldn't go to socials, couldn't go to church with our boy friends, couldn't go up to Farmer's Store, etc. With Mildred's help we wrote a song of four verses describing the event and punishment in a humorous way and set it to the music of our school hymn, "Faith of Our Fathers." Mildred was the best musician and pianist in the dorm. So she played it and we all sang it at the first social we went to after we got our privileges back. Mr. Tracy complimented us on the song and praised Mildred for being a good sport and playing it for us.

Now and then pranks played on faculty crossed into the vicious. Bonnie Wood says that in her first year teaching at Higgins the students turned on all the gas jets in the lab and strung piano wire neck-high for her. Myrtle Crocker ('46) remembers that one of the students beat up a teacher in study hall, with the audience urging him on, and the teacher resigned. There was never a lot of this at Higgins, but the potential is always there in a situation where the masses cheerfully regard the authorities as, however popular, a kind of natural enemy. It's even present in the joking. At our twenty-fifth reunion, David Jewett ('58) captured perfectly the tone of my high school years when he said of teacher Donald Doe, "After we knew he was taking nitroglycerin pills, all we wanted to do was push him downstairs and watch him blow up." Is it any wonder that from time to time a teacher fell apart? A 1941 graduate remembers that in chapel one day the teacher who was playing the piano suddenly lost control of herself and played "The Monkey Chased His Tail Around the Flagpole." She was not rehired.

But between male students and teachers, part of the bonding comes from horseplay and prank playing. Gerald Osgood ('38) phoned me from Atlanta to talk about his Higgins experience. He had roomed with Jiggs Thompson and gotten into so much trouble that Submaster Tilson Thomas had moved them into the first-floor room next to his. This meant that their lights were not controlled by the master switch, and when they, inevitably, failed to turn out their lights at 10 P.M., they would hear his angry footsteps coming down the hall. A couple of times they grabbed him when he came through the door and threw him down, Jerry said, but they had to hold him until he got over being mad. Once Jiggs let go one of his arms and he gave Jerry "an awful clout." They liked him very much—"A jewel"—and Jerry thinks that it was reciprocal. Twenty years later, David Jewett added ink to Coach Nick Hashey's study hall Coke, and watched him flash a terrible blue smile around the room until he lit on the culprit and slam-dunked him into the wastebasket. Reciprocally, in the sixties, when Derwin Emerson was a student, teachers liked to send him and his friends to the faculty lounge with blank notes (though the boys didn't know they were blank), a signal to the recipients to snatch the bearers into the room and harass them with fierce interrogation.

The favorite form of harassment in my own time almost passed beyond prank into theater, the performance done for the joy of it and requiring the faculty as audience but not as motive. I allude to the Romp, a close relative of the riot, but different in that it served no end and led to nothing but satisfaction in a job well done. Its very name, Romp, captures the way we felt about it. Romps were disruptions of varying length, involving noise and, if possible, darkness. Perhaps they had a touch of "we could if we would" about them—of "Look at us, we could take over the school, brush you aside like gnats, but we won't because we're so nice."

The boys romped oftenest and hardest. (In the twenties they had done something similar by slamming their iron beds up and down.) My friends used to say that Coach Hashey could sense a Romp coming on, and that he would let the boys watch late television and ply them with cake in hopes of heading it off. I think that he made them almost sorry to do it, but not quite. The king of all Romps was the O'Keefe Romp, named in honor of its subsequently expelled organizer. It was very much admired, and we sometimes talk about it yet when we see each other. These were the days of the new cinderblock Tracy Hall, and the missiles thrown were not the Indian clubs and jugs of the 1910 pro-gymnasium editorial, but chairs, bricks, and lead pipes. These flying objects could do little damage to the structure, but they could and did keep the faculty in their rooms and make the boys feel powerful. There was at least one nocturnal girls' romp, too, featuring silverware in the dryer and Coke bottles rolled down the stairs. This racket brought the faculty running, as it was supposed to do; I think the principal's wife came as well. And I remember an evening study-hall Romp when someone threw the master switch.

Respondents are sparse from the later years—alumni lists were not up to date—but Maria Bartlett ('75), one of my most valued contributors, sent me an account of a prank and thereby caused me to understand something important.

> At one of the school dances, someone took the pins out of the hinges on one of the huge front doors. Someone opened it and the door nearly fell. Of course the teacher in charge sent everyone home, but it was worth it. I think the general feeling when I was in school was a lot of craziness, particularly in the last year. We learned, but we made sure we had a good time doing it.

Until I read that, I had been rather stuffily thinking that the vandalism of the last few years contributed to the demise of the school. Now I think, rather, that the impending demise caused a lot of vandalism. What would you do, after all, if you had the sword of threatened closing perpetually over your head? You might very well turn tense and jumpy and kick the hell out of the buildings, both because you were going to lose them anyway and because you couldn't bear to lose them. It was, if you like, a small-scale equivalent of the generational malaise caused by nuclear threats.

Harassment and tricks were mostly, but not all, intramural. Merrill Clement ('43) assures me that students made things lively for the town on Halloween—"Students raised everything in town. The church bell rang all evening in between chases by Reverend Meader and teachers." Shameful to say, harassing Pentecostal camp meetings was a popular sport right through the forties, but at any rate the Pentecostals have got their own back now, for they are the current owners of Higgins. Milder recreations such as sleighing, nude bathing (men only, though Ernie Ross ['51] says girls were in the bushes, watching), girls sleeping out on the dorm roof (with boys creeping over to see it, says my informant ['70]), going to Bangor to the movies, picnics, trips to the coast, and "crust walks" (an early diversion involving snowy hikes to maple-sugar camps) are fairly predictable. So, perhaps, are hunting and fishing, but somehow in the stories they seem a part of the perpetual adolescent search for more food. (I except from that impression Ellis Holt's story of boys sneaking up on a skunk and whacking it over the head with a pole.) Leone Dakin ('21), for instance, recalls going to the kitchen for a private trout-fry when some friends had been successful anglers. I have mentioned the venison provided by Robert Houghton ('37). Jack Nicholson ('18) stole a farmer's chicken and then invited him for chicken stew. Finally, Robert Bearman ('46) writes:

> A student came strutting across the campus with a porcupine he had shot. Thinking that I could do as well I went to Black Bill and asked if I could borrow the shotgun to shoot porcupines. In his typical good nature he let me have the shotgun and one shell. I took a freshman in tow and headed across the road and into the woods, and behind a farm across from the Institute building. We were walking through the woods and into a clearing. A covey of partridge drummed out of the grass. One flew into a bush. I lowered the shotgun, squeezed the trigger. I went to the bush and picked up the grouse. This was my first ever successful hunting trip. (And to date—the last.) Then I realized that grouse season would not be open for another two weeks. I took the bird to Mr. Tracy and confessed all and asked for advice. He told me to take it to the cook and ask him to cook it for me. Which he did. The next weekend I again asked Black Bill if I could borrow the shotgun to hunt porcupine. In his usual good humor he explained to me that I might see a partridge blinking in the sun and could not restrain myself. I did not get the gun. After partridge season opened I got the shotgun again, but no birds.

"Blinking in the sun" I can guarantee as an accurate quotation; I would know it as my father's if (as Coleridge said of certain Wordsworth lines) I met it "running wild in the deserts of Arabia." For readers who may blanch at the notion of a shotgun being put into the hands of a boy who might or might not prove reliable, all I can say is that it's perfectly normal rural Maine behavior. People have to learn to use tools, right? My brother is amazed now when he recalls that one of his elementary school teachers needed a classroom Christmas tree and sent a third-grader out with an axe to fetch one in. The boy miscalculated a little and chopped his foot, but I don't think anybody made a fuss. Those things happen when you have to provide your own amusements.

XII

JOHN HIGGINS & CO.

*But, me thinkes, it shewes a kind of gratitude and
good nature, to revive Memories and memorialls of
the pious and charitable benefactors long since dead
and gone.*

—JOHN AUBREY

THE FOUNDER

The Reverend John Hamilton Higgins (1841–1910) is by now, as so often happens with monuments, overgrown with the lichen of myth and cliché, the edges of his personality blurred; but he is worth scraping for. I have before me three accounts of his life, not seriously contradictory: a kind of obituary in the books of the Free Temple Baptist Church of Charleston, written on the day of his death by his widow; "Life of John Hamilton Higgins," a four-page document distributed by his daughter, Ethel Beck, at the school's centenary; and *The Portland Sunday Telegram and Sunday Press Herald*'s April 25, 1937, feature on HCI and its upcoming anniversary. We shall try to read between the lines.

John Hamilton Higgins was born on May 28, 1841, in Charleston (his widow says Garland), into a large, poor, affectionate farm family. He was the seventh child—there would be nine—and the fourth of six boys. About his father, Amos Higgins, we know almost nothing. We know a little more about his mother, Sarah Hamilton Higgins, perhaps because of the nineteenth century's enthusiasm for maternal influence. She is said to have gone at night into the open and ill-roofed chamber where her sons slept to brush the snow from the boys' covers and tuck them in more tightly, praying that one of them would be a "Soldier of the Cross." (An infidel friend of mine suggests that a more practical woman would have prayed for a carpenter.) She is said also to have smoked a pipe and enjoyed gin when she could get it, details that incline me to trust the earlier picture of maternal piety; dishonest biographers would have suppressed the gin.

The family's poverty was considerable, though perhaps not much out of the ordinary for that time and place and family size. A classic story survives in which the boys took turns wearing the family's one pair of boots to church. These hardships seem not to have blighted their energy or spirits; "the Higgins devils," unhappy teachers called John and his brothers, finding themselves the first objects of that perseverance and quick-wittedness that would take such different turns later. One exhausted teacher, rather than giving John the usual beating, is said to have asked him with tears in her eyes, "What makes you act so?" and thereby effected a revolution in his behavior. Maybe. Subsequent events reveal a personality capable of a *volte face*, but Ethel Beck's account says only that he was a model boy "as long as she was teacher."

When he was sixteen he went to New York at the invitation of his three uncles, multimillionaire owners of the E.S. Higgins & Co. carpet factory at the foot of Forty-third Street. Two other brothers were also invited, and at least one, Alvin, went and became an excellent salesman, but his story pales beside that of John, who was a success on all fronts. In five years, that is to say by the age of twenty-one, he was superintendent of the factory. He invented a way to make one-dollar-a-yard carpet that looked almost like their five-dollar-a-yard carpet; his uncles made more millions. They polished and groomed him: he was required to carve at their table and plan the landscaping for their new mansion. He was making money himself. He was going to be like his uncles. One can imagine his delight at how his life was turning out, how many pairs of shoes he had, how he could keep track of his forks at a formal dinner.

In 1866 he married his cousin Frances E. Perley, a Maine girl, not a rich New York connection, and said to be very beautiful. Her death in childbirth a year later left him with several concerns besides his grief: an infant daughter, Fanny; a sister-in-law, Emma, whom he would marry in 1872 and with whom he would have the rest of his offspring; and a deathbed promise that he would "meet her in heaven," that is to say, that he would become a Christian, which evidently he was not then, despite his turn with the church-going boots. By the last of these legacies, Frances Perley Higgins altered history as she might not have done had she lived. Ethel Beck writes, "He and Charlie Tibbetts, who had followed him to New York, were gloriously converted in the old 42nd St. Baptist Church in New York," and two things in the statement require some consideration.

The first is Charlie Tibbetts, about whom we know too little, but who was certainly both one of the great blessings of John Higgins's life and a testimony to his character. A boyhood friend who stayed a friend, a rare thing in a life so full of radical change, he followed John Higgins to New York, and he seems later to have followed him home, though not, as far as I know, into preaching. Ethel Beck says that they were separated only once during their lives, while Charlie Tibbetts fought in the Civil War and John Higgins was exempt on account of manufacturing blankets for the army. (A good thing, says his daughter; he was afraid of guns, though "usually a courageous man," and fired one only once, hunkering behind a log with Charlie Tibbetts and reaching over to fire it on the other side.)

"Gloriously converted" is the other thing. What precisely that adverb denotes, nobody now living can tell us. Are not all conversions glorious? Was there shouting? Did fire come down? His widow's account says that he brought with him into the church nine others whom he had led to Christ; perhaps the glory lies in that. Or perhaps "Gloriously" means to suggest the thoroughness of it, for he was well and truly converted and his nine followers were a pale foreshadowing. If Saul of Tarsus is an overblown analogy, think at least of C.S. Lewis in his study, oppressed by God's insistent presence. This conversion was an event with ramifications.

With his conversion came an appalling suspicion that he had "got the call" to be a minister. Nobody who has not been hatched in the more excitable shoals of Protestantism can understand the dismay of that. From their earliest childhoods, fundamentalist children quail with dread lest they get the call, especially the call to be a missionary, the horror being the greater in proportion to their clear unsuitability for the job. Because the thing is, if you get the call you have to take it, and goodbye to all pleasure and ease and normality. Goodbye to it if you don't go, too; we all knew about Jonah. (Perhaps little Catholic girls who wish not to be nuns suffer something similar from the question of vocation?) So there was John Higgins fighting his awful suspicion, hoping that it was irrational, clinging to the prospect of life as a rich New Yorker. But he was uneasy enough—suppose it *was* a true call—to adopt a kind of halfway measure and pay the salaries of half a dozen ministers. That he could afford to do so suggests how much he had to lose.

Until 1874 he lived with this compromise and, one supposes, managed to hold at bay his suspicion that he was called. Then his daughter by his first wife died, and his conviction revived. The modern and/or secular reader will understand some of the connection between these two events—the reminder of his first wife's death and his consequent conversion, the loss of an excuse not to leave urban advantages for the child's sake. More important than either of these would have been the belief that until you do God's work, He will slap your toys out of your hand. John Higgins is said to have paced and knelt all one long night, struggling for the strength to give up the life he loved. By morning he was resolved to leave New York and go back to Maine to preach, a thing that he had never done or wanted to do, and for which he had not been trained. He was thirty-three.

Clearly the conviction that one *must* be a minister does not carry with it the desire or confidence to be one. Sheer principle must have led him through that first sermon in a schoolhouse, when, as he always said afterward, he would have been happy to have the floor open and swallow him up. His text was appropriate to his state of mind: "Now we see through a glass darkly, but then face to face." As it turned out, he was a natural orator. For the next seventeen years he made evangelistic tours around the state, later accompanied by John Hatch, a singer whom he had converted. He was by all accounts a spellbinder.

When he left New York he was already married to Emma Perley, his first wife's sister. Had he confided to her at their marriage the possibility that they would be changing what is now known as their lifestyle? In any case, she went with him to Charleston and settled down to producing her own family of six girls, three of whom, Florence, Ethel, and Alice, lived into adulthood. Sometime in the course of this domesticity Emma's father must have moved to Charleston from Gray, for Old Mr. Perley, as he was called, was to live on as the town eccentric (not a title loosely conferred in Charleston) for many a year after his daughters and son-in-law were in their graves. John Higgins was a great benefactor to his home town, for as well as founding the school, he built a hotel, an observatory (through whose telescope the courthouse clock twenty-five miles away in Bangor was said to be visible), and a glove factory.

In 1888 his uncle Elias, the carpet magnate, sent him an urgent appeal and provoked another crisis of conscience. The uncle was dying, the factory in trouble from incompetent management (did this provoke a little guilt?) and labor problems. He was offered any price to come back as general manager. Driven not by the temptation of business, I think, but by the duty he owed his uncle, who had been the making of him, John Higgins moved his family back to New York and ran the company for two years. Ethel Beck assures us that "The masterly manner in which he rehabilitated the business, crushed the labor organizations, which had been a constant menace, and placed every department in a sound and equitable basis of work and production was a revelation to everyone who knew of his accomplishment." Crushing the labor organizations does not sound quite the right thing nowadays, but at any rate he did it adeptly. He had not lost his knack for business. Had he lost his taste for it, one wonders? Was it hard to give up New York a second time? In 1899 he still felt the attractions of commerce enough to give Higgins students a chapel talk on how to "conquer a place for themselves in the world."

After he turned fifty, the Reverend John no longer felt well enough for strenuous tours, but he had energy enough to build up and nurture all the small churches in surrounding towns and to be the pastor of Charleston's Free Temple Baptist Church. At this time, too, he acquired a new project, without which I would not be writing his life. Dwight L. Moody, whom he admired, had founded the Northfield School; he would found a Christian school of his own. So he bought Charleston Academy, which already had a sound reputation in state education, from its shareholders. His uncles, whom he had hoped would take an interest in the project, failed him. Nothing daunted, he invested half his own fortune in the school, reorganized its courses of studies, and gave it to Colby College as a fourth fitting school, the earlier three being Coburn Classical Institute, Hebron Academy, and Ricker Classical Institute. Higgins Classical Institute was named and incorporated by act of the Maine Legislature in 1891. He paid for the Institute Building and Tibbetts Hall, and supervised their construction himself in 1901 after his contractor defaulted. This was a further strain on his already overtaxed constitution. His determination to keep Higgins tuition so low that no student should be denied an education was backed by his custom of writing a check at the close of each year to cover any deficit, a classic example of putting one's money where one's mouth is.

His second wife died in 1894 and three months later he married a third, Ellen Harvey McCulley, who was already the widow of a millionaire judge from Honolulu (and who would later yet, after John Higgins, marry another millionaire). The 1937 newspaper article asserts that she was "endowed with many graces of person and mind" and she must have been, though all living witnesses remember her merely as a fat, regal old lady.

He died at home when he was sixty-eight, in 1910. Accounts of his dying words are fairly consistent and therefore probably accurate. Besides, the preoccupations are right:

> I guess the Lord has my old house most pulled down here on earth, and my heavenly mansion most done. Don't let the minister get up and tell what I've done. I'm simply a sinner saved by grace. Churches and School Houses don't count, but I've got a building not made with hands, eternal in the Heavens. No matter what else you miss, don't miss the things Jesus wants of you.

His funeral was said to be the most impressive ever held in Charleston, and very likely the minister did "get up and tell what he'd done." He left an estate of $90,000, a school that would last another sixty-five years, and a life story so dramatic, so borderline incredible, that it rapidly passed into the twilight zone of myth and almost ceased to be believed. He is buried under one of three dozen modest, identical marble headstones in his family's portion of the Charleston cemetery, where, until the demise of his school, an especially virtuous young man was deputed each commencement to lay a wreath on his grave and recite his remarkable biography, while no-body much listened.

ELLEN MCCULLEY HIGGINS LEWIS

Although it may be that Higgins owed its existence to the Reverend John's first wife, who by dying effected his conversion, or to his second wife, who consented to follow him back to the relative wilderness, it was his third wife and eventual widow who made some mark on the school's daily life. Her career, in its own way, is as dramatic as his. Born Ellen Harvey in Kenduskeag, Maine, she managed during her eighty-two years to marry three very wealthy men, at least two of whom were celebrities of sorts. She herself was voted an honorary member of the Yale class of 1852 and was given an honorary membership in the First Maine Heavy Artillery. As her obituary observed, "In her life she lived much."

Her first husband was Lawrence McCulley, a justice of the Supreme Court of Hawaii. Mary Herrick O'Halloran (her grand-niece) tells me that the McCulleys were sent as ambassadors to Spain and England, and that they were well received in Spain but that Queen Victoria was so snippy that Aunt Ellen never afterward cared for the British. After thirty years in Hawaii, the now-widowed Ellen McCulley left her missionary work there and returned to Maine, where she married the Reverend John Higgins, who had just lost his second wife.

This was the mid 1890s. Neither the bride nor the groom was in the first blush of youth. Rather, they were two wealthy, distin-guished, strong-minded, aggressively Christian, middle-aged people. Though they had no mutual children, she called him "Papa." Besides her own income, Ellen brought with her one daughter and the mas-sive, ornate Hawaiian palace furniture that Mary O'Halloran remem-bers looming in what would some years later be the girls' dorm. The only story I have heard about the inner dynamics of their marriage is that for a while they lived at the hotel, the Trustee House, which the Reverend John had built, and that, miffed because Ellen wouldn't give any of her money to the school, he charged her room and board.

If she did not give the school any money, at any rate in her widow-hood she gave it a good deal of attention. She lived on the north edge of campus, after all, and school life went on under her eyes. It is hard to forget Sabra Lee's picture of the widowed Mrs. Higgins in her black dress and lace jabot, marshalling the nervous seniors for the most formal banquet of their lives. She preferred to spend her money, perhaps, in her own family, for she seems to have been fiercely clannish. She put Mary O'Halloran's uncle (her nephew) through college with a big allowance, offering him a choice of Colby, Yale, or Oxford. (He chose Colby as being the least terrifying.)

One other anecdote, long cherished in Charleston, has survived. On the occasion of her third marriage, to Frank E. Lewis, of Janesville, Wisconsin, Charleston women prepared a handsome wedding breakfast in her home. As she looked at the spread, her eyes filled with tears. "If only Papa could see this," she said. The preservation of that story is perhaps a subtle revenge for her readiness to hire her neighbors as servants *pro tem.*

However, the irreverent instinct to hunt flaws and to see her as pretentious is somewhat thwarted by her letter to the December 1922 *Scroll*, a response to a request for facts about her life. The tone of that letter—witty, lucid, endearing—could not be faked and gives us some notion of why three men would marry her. The letter makes her trips to Europe and Japan and her support of the Higgins ballteams sound of equal importance to her, which must have done good things for the collective student ego.

In Janesville, in her final bedridden years, she called a class of fourteen Chinese boys to her bedside weekly, keeping on with God's work. When she died, in 1926, there was a memorial service in the Institute chapel. Florence Sawyer sang "Faith of Our Fathers," Mrs. Lewis' favorite hymn. The 1926 *Scroll* quotes a wonderful tribute from the Janesville paper, and I shall quote from it, too:

> Fourteen young boys who came from the house where a woman of eighty-two had passed from earth, but where the body still lay—fourteen boys sobbing in evident distress over what had happened,—tragedy with which they had come in contact—was a tribute to the dead with which no amount of written or printed encomiums might attempt to compete. "Our Club Mother is dead," was the cry from these boys. . . . Her mind was attuned to all that was going on in this world, a scholar and observer, and she went answering the final sum-

mons with a life lived to its utmost in helpfulness to humanity and community. The boys who loved her had been weekly visitors when she presided at games and reading and none had a lighter heart than she. Chinese and Kanaka in far off Honolulu, where she was the wife of a high official of the old Hawaiian regime, when we knew that Archipelago as the Sandwich Islands, call her blessed. Woodsmen, and small farmers, and fisher folks in Maine will mourn her as do the boys in Janesville. It is something to have lived so that when the curtain falls, there shall be those who own they are in debt to the dead.

Assorted trustees drift in and out of these pages in other capacities—Hugh Smith and Vina Parent Adams as teachers; Leon Williams and Leone Dakin Nutting as students; Leon Thorsen as designer and trouble-shooter and overseer for the construction of Tracy Hall; Phillip Hamm as witty recorder of the last days; my parents; Harold Rich; Hollis Soule. There were dozens of others over the years, solid, earnest men and women (by an overwhelming majority men) who cared about the school and found students and rallied to crises and whose devotion left no individually identifiable mark. It is hard not to bring them out, dust them off, and parade them— distinguished Dr. Wyman who always came up from Boston for the August meeting and always thanked the wives for the luncheon by saying, "I feel as if I'd et right out of the horn of plenty"; Horace Ridlon, whose handwritten Trustee minutes over twenty years came to look more and more like Morse Code, who would lean over the head of his cane and snap a "No" out of his bulldog jaws with such emphasis that Dad and Hugh Smith used to say that he managed to trim a whole syllable off it.

Certainly E. Earle Herrick, who was Chairman of the Board of Trustees for a record thirty-four years, must have one anecdote before we consign him to oblivion. I was dismayed to have this story identified as an old chestnut, for I had it from his own niece, but I'll pass it on all the same, both for its own sake and because, since stories must begin somewhere, it may have been his after all. Her Uncle Earle, she said, was as close to a true, practicing Christian as one can imagine. A quiet, retiring man, he had turned down his

Aunt Ellen's offer of a college education in favor of half interest in Miller and Webster Clothing Company in Bangor. His reputation as a good Baptist and an honest man was such that a certain lumberjack, coming down from the woods each year for his annual spree, would stop by the store and leave all except his binge money in Earle Herrick's safekeeping. When he sobered up he'd come back and get it, and by this strategem he would be very much better off than his improvident peers. But the year that Earle Herrick was put on the school board, no lumberjack turned up. Or at least not until rather later, when he arrived broke and raddled, asking to borrow money to get back to his job. "Why didn't you leave it with me this year?" Herrick wanted to know. "I read the Bangor papers," said the lumberjack. "I keep up with things. And when I saw you'd *gone into politics* I didn't feel I could trust you any more."

But I shall fight down nostalgia and restrict my biographical attentions to one trustee, also a Higgins, and also, in his own way, star material.

FRANKLIN A. HIGGINS

Other members of the Higgins family made their contributions to the welfare and history of the school as well—for instance, Ethel Higgins Beck, daughter of the founder, who wrote the school song and put the kibosh on dancing for many a long year. Or Alvin Hamilton Higgins, the founder's brother, endowed with the Higgins family business sense, who according to his *Scroll* obituary in 1910 became "a king among salesmen" and a generous benefactor to the school. But next to the founder himself in importance was his nephew Franklin, who came as close to filling the Reverend John's empty niche as anyone could have, though perhaps in a very different style.

Franklin Higgins was born in 1867, the year of his Uncle John's remarkable conversion. Like his uncle, he was one of nine rural children, and like his uncle he went to New York at sixteen and made his fortune. Unlike his uncle, he kept his mind firmly on business, and when he retired from the John Arbuckle Company in 1925 and came home to live on his interest, he became not only a kind of founder-surrogate presence for the school but an embodiment of worldly *savoir-faire* for all of us.

As I look at a 1933 Alumni Day photo in which he is sitting in the middle of the front row with five other trustees and my father, I can see that he has not lost his metropolitan air. All those men have ties and suits and summer hats and polished shoes; all of them look respectable in the purest sense of the word. But somehow Franklin's panama is even more immaculate than the others as he dangles it easily between his tailored knees. His perpetual White Owl cigar rests lightly between the fingers of his other hand. He seems to have given cigars to three of the trustees, who look less at ease with them; dear old Dr. Weymouth, a rakish wildflower in his buttonhole, is holding his as though it might kick. All the other men are clean-shaven, but Franklin has a sweeping mustache, curled at the ends (in 1933 still dark at the center) and a Kentucky colonel goatee, ornaments that he wore until the end of his life; in this he resembles his uncle. His shoes are high-tops, slick as glass, for when he found a good thing he stuck with it. The only car I ever knew him to have was a black Model T Ford in top condition (Buddy Meader remembers Frank and his crippled brother John sitting in that car at football games in the forties and blowing the horn for applause), but his grandniece tells me that later there was a gray Chevy.

When I said "worldly" earlier I did not mean wicked—no wine, women, and song, though he does unexpectedly seem to have married his aunt. What I mean is polish, respect for money, and a saber-sharp sense of business. I remember my father saying that Frank, who was trustee treasurer for twenty years, had (properly, he admitted) scolded him for putting a three-cent stamp, just because it was handy, on something that could have gone for two. In fact, I'm told that he didn't think my father was much of a bookkeeper, and I can see that this might have been so, for although Dad later proved good at investment, he kept his calculations scribbled in notebooks upside down and back to front (not much like Frank's own copper-plate columns) and was probably soft with debtors. Students who had earned small sums, ninety-nine cents say, at woodchopping or other chores were obliged to repair to Frank's own house with a note in order to collect. Frank kept his New York connections fresh. Twenty years after he'd left he could tell you the best and cheapest place to get this or that, and pick up the phone and arrange it. "Cheapest" was important.

I find on page 92 of his treasurer journal a careful computation of the comparative value of wood and soft coal, including the relative weights of different sorts of dry cord wood (rock maple, beech, elm, etc.) and the degree to which a certain percentage of moisture reduces their value; he concludes that "good wood" at $6.00 a cord is worth about the same as coal at $8.50 a ton, but he adds a nervous query about the cost of handling wood, which he has not figured in.

But although Frank was a hard man, he wasn't unkind. Shine Higgins told me that once as a boy he had gone to Frank to borrow a gun for his father. "Why," said Frank, "I'd as soon let someone have my pocketbook as one of my guns." Then he called him back. "I didn't say I wouldn't do it," he said. Children were mostly afraid of him, for he had a booming voice and a force of personality like a typhoon. My mother has told me how patiently he worked to win my affection, and he won it thoroughly. I can see him standing on the site of a newly buried fuel tank, sweetly playing straight man, pretending that I must indeed be stronger than he if I could snap my bit of shale in half while he struggled with the slate I had given him. When I was seven and he was seventy-one, he sent me my first candy-from-a-gentleman, a gesture of appreciation for my having pounded a little boy who had been rude about him. More significantly, several alumni said that he had helped them through school, and trustee minutes demonstrate how often he lent the school money and then, though always in a most businesslike manner, forgave portions of the debt.

In 1948 he sold his great Victorian house at the town crossroads, the most imposing place in town, and moved to Dover-Foxcroft. He hunted, fished, raised pigeons, and listened to baseball games, filling in a score book himself as he did so. In the 1950s he gave Charleston money to build a new firehouse and library, and drove down every two or three days to supervise the work. According to his unusually detailed obituary in the *Bangor Daily News*, he smoked ten cigars a day, ate three full meals and a hefty midnight sandwich, and rose at 8 A.M., though his grandniece, who lived with him in the late fifties, remembers less food and earlier risings and bedtimes.

Having been only one day in hospital, Frank died less than a month short of his hundredth birthday. I had seen him, pink and unwrinkled as a baby, the summer before, when he lucidly discussed the problem of hiring household help, for he had been holding interviews. My mother wrote me about his funeral:

> The funeral was different (all planned by him). There were no flowers—just a red rose in his buttonhole. ("Waste of money— flowers.") At that he had something. There was nothing to draw attention from the main show. Mr. Nutter spoke and I wonder if Franklin told him what to say. It was o.k. anyhow. Then Shirley sang one verse of "Safe in the Arms of Jesus." It was all rather effective.

"Rather effective" is Mainese for a total knockout. His niece, Elsie Trask, said that perhaps Uncle Frank would have lived longer if he hadn't smoked so many cigars, but the rest of us doubted it.

XIII

PRINCIPALS

I only had one year at Higgins (1927–28)—loved
it—one of the most happy years of my life, between
athletics, school plays, and being allowed to escort a
girl to church on Tuesday nights. We held hands and
sang, "God will take care of you"—God and Mr.
Tracy did!

—RICHARD MERSEREAU ('28)

Being any sort of administrator can drive you crazy, but being principal of a private school is the fastest way to a nervous collapse. Private schools eat principals and spit their bones out. "You can't eat the orange and throw the peel away—a man is not a piece of fruit!" Willy Loman says, but he's wrong. Imagine the stress of it, standing *in loco parentis* to a hundred and twenty-five teenagers who don't go home at night, and for whom you are a person, even a target, of some significance. If you don't love them, how can you stand their noise, their silliness, their head colds, their wise mouths? If you do love them, how can you bear such multiplication of tears and agony and failures and deaths? And don't forget that the phone is always ringing, papers always need filling out, the trustees want accounts settled, new students must be inveigled in, teams need to be cheered, hands need to be held. Then there are the special circumstances: the dorm burning, the history teacher having a nervous breakdown, the pump freezing, the cook getting drunk and chasing automobiles with his pants off, war, and economic depression.

The Reverend
JOHN HAMILTON HIGGINS.

CHARLES CARROLL RICHARDSON
Principal 1891–96.

HENRY WARREN FOSS
Principal 1896–1903.

ARTHUR MILTON THOMAS
Principal 1903–06.

LINWOOD LEIGHTON WORKMAN
Principal 1906–09.

WILLIAM ALBERT COWING
Principal 1909–13.

HENRY G. BLOUNT
Principal 1913–1914.

HOWARD AUSTIN McLELLAN
Principal 1914–17.

GORDON ENOCH GATES
Substitute Principal
for fall term, 1918.

WILLIAM ADELBERT TRACY
Principal 1917–1948.

PHILIP EDWARD KEITH
Principal 1948–53.

The Reverend
CHARLES EUGENE O'CONNOR
Principal 1953–54.

The Reverend
LEON BURTON MEADER
Principal 1954–58.

PERRY GILBERT WORTMAN
Principal 1958–68.

FRANCIS STANLEY FOSS
Principal 1968–74.

PETER DONALD CHASE
Principal 1974–75.

Of the principals whom I have known personally, only Perry Wortman seems to have escaped without tooth marks on his psyche. My own father was extraordinarily tough, for he lasted thirty-two years, but at the end (he told me) he couldn't remember whether or not he'd rung the bells, and he was "just about cutting out paper dolls." Philip Keith left in ill health after five years of it. Charles O'Connor decamped to quieter waters after one year. Leon Meader, one of the best physical specimens I've ever known, was a mass of twitching coffee nerves when he resigned after four years. Francis Foss, who was principal for six years, apparently doesn't want to talk about it; he hasn't answered my letters. Peter Chase, who took the last tumultuous year, hasn't done a lick of academic work since.

I shall pass briefly over the principals of the school in its pre-Higgins days, both because they fall outside our scope and because we know very little about most of them. An 1897 *Scroll*, whose account of them is historically closest to the fact, mentions the following (I have supplemented slightly from other accounts): Samuel Sillsbee, who was head of Charleston Academy in its first year; the Honorable Elisha M. Thurston, a Colby graduate, who later played a prominent part in the abolition movement in Kansas and died there; A. W. Paine, a Colby graduate; David S. True; Mr. Buck, a Colby graduate, who afterward went to California and became a rich wholesale grocer; Mr. Brown, a Colby graduate, who later studied law at Chicago and became somewhat famous as an attorney; the Reverend John Johnson, "one of the brightest scholars of his time"; Mr. Jason Huckins, not a college graduate, later an assistant surgeon in the army; Mr. Frank Rowell of Dover; and Mr. Whitney J. Rideout of Garland. And we must not forget a Mr. Hinkley, who conducted the abortive theological school of 1836. Real Higgins principals, however, begin with C.C. Richardson, in 1891.

> *Name:* CHARLES CARROLL RICHARDSON
> *Principal:* 1891–96
> *Born:* 1860
> *Education:* Colby College B.A. 1887, M.S. 1891 Phi Beta Kappa.
> Brown University
> Newton Theological Seminary
> *Academic Specialty:* Physics, Chemistry, German
> *Wife:* Georgia Norton

Children: Ruth, Mark, Rhea
Died: 1955

Though he was only thirty-one and still a bachelor when he took Higgins—he married and started his family during his tenure there—C.C. Richardson was already a man of some administrative experience, for it was his third principalship. Just before he came to us he had been at East Corinth Academy, one town south. A photograph taken, I should judge, in middle age, shows a bald, plainly dressed, earnest-looking man who is frowning a little at the camera but whose mouth looks accustomed to smiling, as his hands look accustomed to hard work. Despite his training in science, he taught Latin, Greek, Higher English, and a Sunday School class. This versatility is reflected in the curricular richness of his school, for courses in his time included natural science, math, drawing, instrumental music, painting, telegraphy, Biblical literature, and typewriting. He acquired a telescope from Paris for astronomy, a microscope for botany and physiology, and a supply of charts, globes, and maps.

After he left Higgins Richardson moved out of state; he appears to have done graduate study beyond the M.A. at both Brown University and Newton Theological Seminary, but to have left both without degrees. From 1902 to 1930 he was superintendent of various Massachusetts schools. At seventy he became submaster, for three years, of the University School at Bridgeport, Connecticut, where his son Mark was head. A year before his death, he wrote to Colby College, protesting that *he*, at ninety-four, was the oldest living alumnus, not some other chap whom they had wrongly identified as such.

Name: H. WARREN FOSS
Principal: 1896–1903
Born: 1869
Education: Kent's Hill
           Colby College B.A. 1896
Academic Specialty: Science, English, History
Wife: Lottie Butler
Children: Lillian, Barbara
Died: 1957

H. Warren Foss, Higgins's second principal, is familiar by sight to generations of Higgins students who borrowed his portrait (though they didn't know it was his) from the attic for class plays. Students who have used it will remember a calm, intelligent, slightly ascetic face in rimless glasses. The portrait was much prized for mystery-comedies because its eyes seemed to follow one, a good trait in a headmaster.

At Colby he seems to have been something of a personage—tennis doubles champ for two years, yearbook editor, class vice-president, junior and senior exhibitions participant, and so on. Senior Statistics tell us that he was five-feet, nine and a half inches tall, weighed 145 pounds, favored the Baptist Church and the Republican Party. He planned to be a lawyer, was prone to lecturing, never lost his temper, and was considered a washout in the romance department. (Like Richardson, he came to Higgins single and started his family there, so perhaps he improved.) His college nickname was "Fossil," and odds are on that it followed him to Higgins, or was rein-vented there.

Ethel Beck said, in the centennial handout on her father's life, that "Mr. H. Warren Foss and William A. Tracy have been the most outstanding principals of the school, being contributing factors to its growth and success." One wishes that she had been more specific. We can at any rate note that he had a relatively long tenure and that he was head during those exciting days when the Institute and Tibbetts Hall were being built and a new school was emerging like a butterfly from a chrysalis. Also, she may have had in mind his rather distin-guished subsequent career, for after Higgins he was headmaster of the Master Kelley School in Cambridge for fifteen years and the Agassiz School for thirteen. In 1925 he came back to give a chapel talk at Higgins, telling students that "in these days of automobiles, radio, and jazz it is refreshing to visit a quiet New England town that places a premium on sane thinking. . . . Charleston is such a town." He retired to Mt. Vernon and died at the age of eighty-seven.

Name: ARTHUR MILTON THOMAS
Principal: 1903–06
Born: 1858
Education: Colby College B.A. 1880, M.A. 1883
Academic Specialty: Chemistry

Wife: Carrie Odionne
Children: Helen
Died: 1945

When A.M. Thomas came to Higgins he was already middle-aged. I note in his biographical records at Colby the birth of a daughter, Helen, who should have been nearly old enough to attend Higgins during his regime, though we do not know whether she did so. Of his life before Higgins we know only that he had been president of his senior class at Colby, where he had sung tenor for the glee club, and that he had already been principal of Ricker (1885–1901), where he had had the reputation of being strait-laced. He seems to have been reasonably well liked at Higgins, for the Thomases are described (after their departure, a vote for sincerity) as having met students in the fall with "welcoming smiles." His wife kept the students happy by reading to them between supper and study time— *Ramona, The Prospector, The Little Shepherd of Kingdom Come*. It was Thomas who permitted students with a grade of 85 or higher and no absences to skip examinations, and who was responsible for the planting of fifteen trees on Arbor Day. From Higgins he went to Kennebunk High for three years and then became submaster of Farmington State Normal School, where he spent the final twenty years of his career.

Name: LINWOOD LEIGHTON WORKMAN
Principal: 1906–09
Born: 1878
Education: Coburn Classical Institute
              Colby College B.A. 1902
              Harvard University M.Ed. 1927
Academic Specialty: Science, Math
Wife: Mary Alexander
Children: Edmund, Linwood, Jr.
Died: 1966

Higgins was Linwood Workman's fourth academic post, and I think his only principalship. At Colby he had sung second tenor for the glee club, played first violin in the college orchestra, and led the Mandolin-Guitar Club. Yearbook statistics tell us that he was five-feet, eight and a half inches tall, weighed 132 pounds, and was both Baptist and Republican. His peers seem to have perceived him as somewhat full of himself. I quote from the 1902 Colby *Oracle*:

> Self Estimate: I'm glad I'm Workman.
> Others Say: "Go 'way back and sit down."

It is only fair to point out that his purported conceit had some justification in subsequent events.

His Higgins career seems to have been successful enough. Students observe, in the December 1906 *Scroll*, that he has made some good changes in the courses of study and that school spirit is strong. And it was Linwood Workman who in 1908 instituted the madly popular Athletic Association Fair on Washington's Birthday, later moved to November.

After he left Higgins he went to Massachusetts, where in 1912 he became head of the Department of Household Physics at the State Normal School at Framingham, Massachusetts, a post that he held until 1948, when he would have been seventy. He was co-author of a book called *Testing and the Uses of Test Results*. The Colby archives tell me that in 1939, with the help of his wife and their younger son, he subdued and tied up a burglar who had invaded his house. The press photo shows the three of them looking eager and holding lengths of clothesline.

Name: WILLIAM ALBERT COWING
Principal: 1909–13
Born: 1878
Education: Higgins Classical Institute
            Colby College B.A. 1904
            Massachusetts State M.Ed. 1931
Academic Specialty: Math
Wife: Helen Shockford
Children: Cleal, Charles, William Thornton, Roy, Margaret,
            Robert
Died: 1963

Bill Cowing was the first Higgins principal who was himself a graduate of the school. From Higgins he took his already noteworthy athletic ability to Colby, where he was a mainstay in sports for four years—football captain for two years, baseball captain for three, All-Maine football and baseball for four years, and holder of the college record for the shot put. "He holds first mortgage claims on all the C's," jokes the 1904 *Oracle*.

When, after selling insurance and teaching at Deer Isle and Jonesport, he came back to Higgins in 1909, he was the father of two small boys. His third and fourth sons were Higgins babies.

He was by all accounts a popular head, friendly and well-disposed toward the students. Accounts of school events in his time sound happy; it was he who succumbed to a petition for a school holiday one October day in 1909 and arranged a picnic for the entire school. Lucetta Doore ('14) writes, "During the time Cowing was in charge everything went well. He was a good man for the school, being well educated and friendly, also had good order." Another 1914 graduate has sent me a whole anecdote.

> Here is an amusing incident that gives a little insight into the kind of man Prof. Cowing was. A few of us girls used to study together in the coat room. (We didn't have to remain in the regular study room if our ranks were high enough.) One morning, a mouse appeared. One of the girls screamed. Pretty soon, we heard steps coming down the stairs and then a knock at the door of the coat room. Just as one of us started to open the door, one girl knelt to look through the keyhole. There was Prof. Cowing at the door. All he said was, "If there's a mouse in there, chase him out." I feel sure he had hard work to keep from grinning.

After he left Higgins he dallied briefly with two other schools in Massachusetts before settling down at West Springfield High in 1916 for the thirty remaining years of his career. In the spring of 1940 he wrote to my father, giving him a tip on a boy who might go to Higgins, so his loyalties seem to have stayed in place. He became a thirty-third degree Mason and a member of the Massachusetts House of Representatives. He died at the age of eighty-five.

Name: HENRY G. BLOUNT
Principal: 1913–14
Born: 1883
Education: Bates College B.A. 1906
Academic Specialty: Unknown

Wife: (1) Name unknown; (2) Augusta Parker Briery
Children: No information
Died: 1948

Henry Blount has left fewer tracks than any other Higgins principal. It seems probable that he was the same H.G. Blount who was principal of Corinna Union Academy in 1906–07, and who not only coached their football team but was its captain and one of its best players, according to Keith's history (p. 170). That H.G. Blount also played first base on the baseball team in the spring. Our Blount seems to have come with a wife, for there is a reference in the December 1913 *Scroll* to a Mrs. Blount who teaches French. What subjects he himself taught, if any, we do not know, but he was interested in wireless telegraphy and installed a wireless station at the school, so perhaps he was a forward-looking man. Photographed with the football team—we do not know whether he helped to coach it—he looks bright-eyed and alert, but Lucetta Doore ('14) says that he was "a shy man and not very good at getting along with young people." Perhaps his shyness in the presence of young people accounts for his having stayed only one year, or perhaps the burning of the first Tibbetts Hall in January of 1914 gave him enough of prep school complications.

He has been overshadowed in student memory by Cowing on one side and McLellan on the other, both genial and popular men. We know nothing of his subsequent career except that in 1948, in his mid sixties, he married a woman named Augusta Parker Briery; what happened to the first Mrs. Blount we do not know. The 1914 Commencement issue *Scroll* says, "We regret the loss of one of our teachers, Mrs. H.G. Blount." We do not know whether she got pregnant, went mad, died, or left him. Any of the last three might have caused him to seek a happier environment. He died eleven days before his eighty-fifth birthday.

Name: HOWARD AUSTIN MCLELLAN
Principal: 1914–17
Born: 1877
Education: Coburn Classical Institute
        Colby College B.A. 1909
Academic Specialty: Science

Wife: Vera Anderson
Children: None
Died: 1937

Howard McLellan is the first principal who emerges so completely from the mist of the past that we know his Higgins nickname—Old Sittin' Bull, his students called him, says Sabra Lee ('18), on account of his Indian blood.The handful of his students who survive speak of him with great affection. Certainly my father and Hugh Smith both liked and respected him very much indeed, and neither of them was ever a hair-trigger liker or respecter. Leah Colbath ('15) in the April 1915 *Scroll* writes: "Again I can see the kindly face of Prof. McLellan, who as he himself always expressed it, never meant to be 'disagreeable' to any of us." Little glimpses of personality emerge from other *Scroll* allusions—a picture of him sitting at football games and perpetually whittling on a stick, or telling his General Science students, "Will you please chew gum in some other class."

One of my respondents objected that he was "too gullible and trusting to maintain discipline," and there may be something in it, for when my father arrived in 1916, the students had already used up four submasters in the course of a year or two. Still, such discrepancy in opinion may be in some measure resolved by Hugh Smith's recollection that McLellan was a "character" who thought it was funny to act dumb when he wasn't. His Colby yearbook teases, "It takes a good while to say it, but he says 'jest' what he thinks."

After he left Higgins he worked at Oakland High School for a year and then went to be Superintendent of Schools at Island Falls, Maine. In 1927, asserting that he preferred teaching to administration, he went to Pemetic High at Southwest Harbor to finish his career. There, one morning in the fall of 1937, he was lighting his kitchen fire with kerosene when he somehow ignited himself and was so badly burned that he died a week later. Some former student wrote a memorial poem, from which I quote the following assessment of McLellan's impact:

> You taught your boys and girls
> That figures were to earn an
> Honest living, not to be distorted,
> Bent to further selfish ends;
> That English was a pure expression

Of the soul, not simply words that
Readily lent themselves
To lustful purposes.

"To know him was to love him; to have known him is always to remember him," concludes the dedication of the 1938 *Scroll*.

Name: GORDON ENOCH GATES
Principal: Substitute for fall term of 1918
Born: 1897
Education: Colby College B.A. 1919
     Harvard University M.A., Ph.D. 1920, 1934
     Colby College Honorary Dr. of Science 1948
Academic Specialty: Biology
Wife: Helen Baldwin
Children: Evelyn, Alice
Died: 1987

Gordon Gates spent the summer of 1918 on Cape Cod, taking a postgraduate-level course in marine invertebrate zoology; he had been certified as unfit for military service because of poor eyesight and hearing. In that fall of his senior year he was at Colby early, helping the matron, a tough veteran of Civil War nursing, clean the girls' dorms. Suddenly a delegation of Baptist ministers appeared, asserted that it was his patriotic duty to become principal of Higgins (for my father had been drafted into the army), and carried him off with no discussion of salary. Was this sort of thing usual then, I asked him. Certainly not, he said, but "almost nothing at all was *usual* during those World War I months. The country was being ravaged by a flu epidemic in which many died! Quarantines were imposed, even churches were closed." So that fall he found himself, rather than pursuing his studies on schedule, facing a mischievous student body not much younger than himself, with a staff consisting of a University of Maine sophomore who mostly stayed out of sight when things got hot, the wife of a trustee (Mrs. Hubbard), and a local girl who had gotten an education and come home. It was a lively and desperate term. In the end—a fine irony—he pacified the boys by instituting military training.

As soon as the Armistice was declared and the trustees had procured my father's release from Camp Devens, Gates headed back to

Colby without, he says, even waiting to report. As it turned out, the military had taken over Colby and he hadn't missed much except a chance at the flu. He went on to a long and distinguished career in zoology, becoming a world authority on earthworms, traveled and taught widely, and fled on foot over the mountains from Burma to India to escape the Japanese army. "GEG must have learned a few valuable lessons while at Higgins," he writes, "but what they really were, he will not try to determine at such a distance in time."

> *Name:* WILLIAM ADELBERT TRACY
> *Principal:* 1917–48
> *Born:* 1889
> *Education:* Ricker Classical Institute
>   Colby College B.A. 1915, Honorary M.A. 1944
> *Academic Specialty:* Math
> *Wife:* (1) Florence Preble; (2) Brenna Blaisdell
> *Children:* Ann, William, Jr.
> *Died:* 1969

Born the youngest of four in a penniless but relatively educated family of farmers and teachers in northern Maine, my father was himself precisely the sort of promising rural boy that he spent his life educating. He managed high school in three years and pushed on through Colby, dropping out for a year to work in a sawmill and on the river drive until he could pay for the rest of his undergraduate education.

He had meant originally to go on to law school, but he started teaching at Higgins to raise money for it and that was it—he was hooked. When he came to Higgins he was twenty-eight and the school twenty-six years old; it would outlast him by six years.

His discipline was legendary, and indeed he was known to his students and staff as "Black Bill," from the portentious darkening of his face in anger—a kind of reddish black, one graduate aptly described it forty years afterward. Sabra Lee ('18) told me the story of Dad's first study hall at Higgins when he arrived as submaster in 1916:

> I well remember the 1st day he had a study room. He had a
> math class down front and about 30 of us kids in there for a

208

study period. We started whispering and talking as usual, and the math class wasn't paying attention. There was a gavel on the desk left from a meeting the previous night. Your dad banged the gavel and said, "I'll declare a three minute recess so that those not interested in the class or not in here to study may leave the room. However you'll come back at four o'clock and make up the work!" Then he walked over and looked out the window. Well, nobody left the room and from then on he had no discipline problems in his classes.

Having established order at one dramatic swoop, he seems never to have lost it again. Carl McGraw ('36) tells me that Dad occasionally took a study hall "and never had to look up from his reading to maintain quiet, whereas some of the younger teachers (e.g., All-American hammer thrower Don Favor, who was well liked) could not maintain order even by patrolling the aisles constantly." Nothing is so potent as reputation, except perhaps the ability to turn black.

His attitudes and policies were pretty straightforward. I've heard him say a hundred times that he thought of all Higgins students as his own youngsters, and he meant it, too. What he wanted his own youngsters to do was work their hardest, build their characters by the practice of integrity in daily life, purge their minds of foolishness and muddy thinking, and dazzle their opponents with as much fast footwork as honor would allow, but no more. My father's strongest allegiance, I suspect, was neither to the educational process in general nor to his job in particular, but to Higgins as an entity, a kind of earthbound, lovable, demanding deity. The year after the Institute burned, he turned his whole salary back to the school; he was provided with food and lodging, and alumni will recall that a suit lasted him a long time.

I have been much struck by the liveliness of love and terror that still comes across in his old students' recollections of him. For all the terror, few if any seemed to dislike him; for all the love, nobody felt like taking liberties. In short, some people thought he was a candidate for sainthood, and nobody thought he was anybody to mess with.

Several things contributed to the terror. One was a reputation for omniscience and omnipresence: how was it that, said to be out of town, he could materialize in the midst of wrongdoing? A Charleston graduate in the class of 1940 told me a lovely story about cutting school with her friends to go skating one day when Dad was supposed to be in Bangor. "It's Mr. Tracy," they joked as each car went by, and suddenly it *was*. Another terrific weapon was what one anonymous respondent called "fixing one with a good glare." The third and most potent was his tongue. As Sir Thomas Browne said of scholars' tongues in general, it was "sharper than Actius his razor." Not *exactly* an acid tongue, Pete Minot ('38) said kindly, but Mr. Tracy "could make you humble with a minimum of words."

For the love, too, there was a good basis. For one thing, he had charm, or charisma, if you want a trendier word. He could almost literally charm birds out of the trees. Infants and animals would fall all over themselves with delight and cooperation, and not just the susceptible dog, but all animals—sheep, cats, raccoons, horses, cows, the lot. Their confidence was justified by his kindness and interest. One of my favorite childhood anecdotes was my mother's tale of Dad putting down a piece of donut for a passing rodent and saying, "Nothing is going to go hungry in my house, not even a mouse." This kindly interest extended up the chain of being to adolescents— especially to adolescents. Ruth Merrill ('40) remembers his pleasure at her making her own evening gown for Senior Banquet; Margaret Bishop ('44), his soothing management of her collapse at discovering that she was about to give her commencement speech two days earlier than she'd planned, with no family at hand; Nettie Hillman ('41), his cutting chapel short on the day her boyfriend left for war, because she was crying so hard. Impassioned testimonials from graduates give us some notion of what intensity he provoked: "Except for my own family, I think I loved, admired, and respected your father more than any other man I ever knew."—Leone Dakin ('21); "The turning point in my life was the day I looked into his gentle, knowing eyes and he said I could come to Higgins"—Ormonde Brown ('47); "His philosophy permeated my whole life"—Harriet Lord ('30); "I will never forget your Dad as long as I live for what he taught me"— Robert Houghton ('37); "I was always in awe of him, but I've loved him as a father for all these years"—Harry Nason ('27).

Besides character, math was his subject and he was good at it. He always said that there were only two students he hadn't been able to get math into, and it was a great point of pride that MIT told him they'd take anybody he sent, no tests necessary. I should add that he taught math along with doing everything else—being principal, handling the finances, recruiting, playing guidance counselor, coping without professional secretarial help, and sometimes coaching. Finally all this wore him down. "How is the world using you? I am just getting two years older every year," he writes in a 1945 letter. I fear that being the father of a four-year-old may have contributed.

After he retired in 1948 his reputation as a terror lingered on. This was a bit of a burden to me as a Higgins student in the mid fifties, but we both found some of its effects funny. "*I'll* come over to your house and see you," I remember Jane MacDonald saying to me in our freshman year. "*I'm* not afraid of your father; I'm not afraid of hardly anybody." My friends who braved the house found his generous side. He kept a giant can of potato chips just inside the kitchen door for easy access by hungry teenagers, Bobbie Simpson in particular, and only last summer Marlene Robinson reminded me that he used to drive her home after basketball games to save her a long walk in the dark. In his retirement, besides raising my brother and me, he played the stock market, gardened expansively, ran back and forth to Aroostook County to cope with the family farm, and developed a fine knack for comic verse.

His death in 1969 resulted from several internal systems running down, though emphysema was the official culprit, an unjust end for a nonsmoker. In the summer of '68 he was too ill to accept an honorary Doctor of Pedagogy offered him by Ricker College, but he made his longish deathbed memorable by crawling out of it, against all odds, to go partridge hunting a couple of months before he died. His nurse had worked at the insane asylum and took most things calmly (in her earlier days as a Higgins housemother she would sometimes forget and refer to the students as "the patients"), so she carried his oxygen tank and his gun, while my mother drove around the back roads amazed at the folly of it all. I would like to report that he bagged his game, but he didn't. He did get a shot at a partridge, though, the nurse standing behind him to catch him when the gun kicked. He was seventy-nine when he died.

Name: PHILIP EDWARD KEITH
Principal: 1948–53

Born: 1900
Education: Higgins Classical Institute
             Colby College B.A. 1926
             University of Maine M.A. 1942
Academic Specialty: Chemistry, Physics, English
Wife: Evelyn Lancaster
Children: John, Mary Jane
Died: 1964

An outstanding athlete and scholar, Philip Keith devoted his talents to Higgins for twenty-six years; his length of service must not be measured by his relatively brief tenure as ninth principal. Indeed, it might be said that of all the principals he was the most thoroughly a Higgins man. Hugh Smith tells me that when he first went to Higgins as submaster, Punk Keith, then a senior, was his only disciplinary backing in a tough dorm full of naked, noisy boys. Moreover, Keith is said to have scored the first basket for Higgins in the first state prep school basketball tournament.

At Colby he played basketball, was varsity catcher, and made All-Maine tackle; in his senior year he was captain of the "best [foot]ball team in recent years." A fine student, he rightly resented his professors' expecting him to be below average academically because he was an above-average athlete. Despite the fullness of his college life and his work in the Colby bookstore, he kept drifting back to Higgins for weekends, as students sometimes did in those days. By 1927 he was back full time as a member of the faculty. His two children were born, bred, and educated at Higgins, and lived in dormitories most of their growing-up years.

He was a quiet man, deeply contented with a book and a pipe, fond of music, poetry, and drama. He had a long fuse, his daughter tells me ("lost his temper once every ten years"), and a strong sense of honor and duty. He liked to fish, but refused to own guns. No name has been mentioned more often than his as an excellent teacher—dedicated, fair, knowledgeable, patient, and kind. He taught English literature as well as chemistry and physics, and was famous in his time for the theatricality of his laboratory demonstrations. "He was smart and could criticize an author in a book. When he answered a question you could get a good answer," says Robert Houghton ('37).

"Superb instructor, great personal example," says a 1937 graduate. "He was our idol—Evelyn too," adds Betty Roundy ('30).

But his was a complex personality, for he was also the owner of the famous foot, trained on generations of erring Higgins posteriors. A story sent in by Charles and Frances Higgins Wilcox ('41) catches the formidable side of his nature:

> I heard . . . that Mr. Keith was at the school in Charleston when a "bull" or "cow" got loose and everyone was trying to catch the creature. After failing to get a rope on the animal or corner him, Mr. Keith ran after the creature and tackled it as he used to do to quarterbacks in football. He held it down until they could get a rope on it. So all the boys, in hearing this, were thinking, "Don't mess around with Mr. Keith."

In sports—and he coached endless years of basketball, baseball, football, even girls' sports and semi-semi-pro—his fiercer side took over. Willis Parker ('39) says, "Punk Keith never smiled during a game, unless the blood was running. He believed in clean, hard play—no quarter asked nor given." The blood to which Willis alludes was football blood, I think, but there was once a student baseball player who missed a fly ball and ran straight off the field to the dorm to escape Coach Keith's chewing-out.

His wit is well represented in the old *Scrolls*, where students loved to quote his classroom jibes.

> Mr. Keith in Chemistry class: "You people go into the laboratory with an open mind all right. The only trouble is that you come out that way also."

> Keith: "I don't mind if a student looks at his watch once in a while, but what gets me is to see someone take out his watch and shake it a few times and then put it up to his ear."

> Keith: "Better get your head off the windowsill, Mr. ——, there've been a lot of woodpeckers this year."

As principal his top priority was good faculty salaries, for he felt that from a strong faculty all other good things must follow. Sports were important, too, and he went out of his way to find strong players; I well remember the massive backs of his football teams hulking across their benches. Always anxious about fire, he rewired the boys' dorm, drilled a new well, had the smokestack fixed. And—this is particularly lovable—he got the girls a washer and dryer.

The brevity of his principalship was the result of waning strength and health. His was the bad luck of being caught behind an un-naturally long-reigning predecessor, so that when he came to office he was already drained by twenty-one years of very active service. Students from his regime as head think well of him, saying that he was a man of high principle and that the school was clearly in good hands, but recollections of him are not nearly as vivid as when he was submaster: the weight of new duties and problems have to some degree submerged him. After his resignation in 1953 he lived for only eleven more years, during the first seven of which he taught at Presque Isle, Maine. He died of arteriosclerosis in 1964. In 1966 the Higgins library (Tibbetts Library) was renamed the Philip E. Keith Memorial Library, an appropriate but perhaps inadequate gesture. He was, as the Colby *Oracle* said when he graduated, "a living monu-ment of the old Greek ideal of a strong mind and a strong body."

Name: The Reverend CHARLES EUGENE O'CONNOR
Principal: 1953–54
Born: 1909
Education: University of Maine B.A. 1931 Phi Beta Kappa
             Yale Divinity School
Academic Specialty: Public Speaking
Wife: Mildred Guay
Children: Jean, Marilyn, Patricia
Died: 1987

Charles O'Connor came to Higgins from the University of Maine, where he had been director of the Student Religious Associa-tion. A quiet, scholarly looking man, he gave the school a certain tone. "Jupiter Pluvius is frowning upon us this morning," I can remember his observing when it rained. Alumni memories of him are pleasant, though not vivid. "Likeable," "low-key," "religious," they say of him. My own liveliest memory is of his heroic behavior when a large and unstable female student fainted at a public event, a basketball game I think, and he picked her up and carried her out while everyone watched slack-jawed, for he was rather a slight man and led a quiet life. During his year at Higgins he developed a cross-country team that participated in the regional interscholastics at the University of Maine; he had himself been a track man at Maine, holding the state broad jump record for ten years. And he must have done some effective college guidance, for four graduates received scholarships from good colleges. His message in the *Scroll* is immediate, articulate, and more religious than those of subsequent principals.

He left Higgins to be Student YMCA Staff Member of the Student Christian Movement in New England. Later he was Dean of Men and Financial Aid Officer at the Massachusetts Bay Community College in Wellesley. He has written me a very kind letter in which he describes Higgins as "a truly great private Institute in the best New England tradition."

Name: The Reverend LEON BURTON MEADER
Principal: 1954–58
Born: 1908
Education: Wheaton College B.A. 1935
                Providence Bible Institute
                University of Maine M.Ed. 1964
Academic Specialty: History, Bible
Wife: Mary Jacobus
Children: Leon Jr. (Buddy), David, Neil

Leon Meader was my own principal as well as my minister for my first twelve years. A handsome, genial outdoorsman, woodsman, canoeist, he had been a college wrestler and would sometimes show the boys fancy moves. When I saw him three years ago neither his good looks nor his vigor had waned in the slightest and he was still making canoe trips in northern Canada. Long nicknamed "Bull" (from Bull of the Woods, i.e., foreman of a lumbering crew), he was delightedly called "The Bull" by his students, who, ignorant of the name's origins, thought it fit his strength and rampant masculinity.

When he came to the principalship he was already a familiar and popular figure, for he had been for fourteen years minister of the local Baptist church, where he was particularly prized for the dignity with which he conducted weddings and funerals. Having also taught part-time at Higgins for many years, he was familiar with its habits and quirks. Indeed, the fervor of his loyalty to Higgins sports was a local legend. In 1953, when he had left town to be principal at Monson Academy, grown men had wept; Charlestown was glad to see him come home.

He was the last head of what I might describe as the old Higgins; he was also the last principal who tried to operate as a one-man band, that is to say, without office staff or guidance counselors, while teaching classes himself. His style of principalship I take to have been somewhat like Bill Cowing's—friendly, lenient, with order at the perimeter but room to wing around inside it.

He was popular with his students, aside from the obligatory, ritual antagonism that one was supposed to feel then for one's principal. "Bull was a wrestler and a socializer. I enjoyed having him physically participate with the students, showed he was not better than us," says John Thibodeau ('57). Neal Brown ('56) remembers that "He was visible to students, personable, and a blend of toughness and gentleness." From the State of Maine Senate Chamber, Michael Pearson (a freshman in 1956–57) writes, "I liked him. I remember the night that I had supper at his table and quietly asked him if it was all right to go swimming at the reservoir and he quietly told me it was against the rules so I should be careful when I did it so that I wouldn't get hurt and then winked at me. . . . He was a big man but kind and very understanding. I think he remembered what it was like to be a boy." Leroy Kennedy ('57) still admires Meader's having been man enough to apologize to him after a mistaken accusation.

For all the goodwill of his students, he could not have had a very pleasant four years, for he was plagued with ill luck, disasters honestly beyond his control. Only the malignity of the stars could have dealt him the conflagration of the boys' dorm, the jailing of his Dean of Men, and the death of one of his best seniors in an auto accident. It is to his credit that he stayed genial. In the tradition of C.C. Richardson, H. Warren Foss, Linwood Workman, and William Cowing, he went to Massachusetts after he left Higgins, and Charleston was the poorer.

I think, in balance, that there are no four years in the history of the school when I would rather have been there. Having been raised by a monumentally efficient authority figure, I have ever since preferred my authority a little tempered, and those were agreeable years, full of good feeling, a nice balance between tradition and liberty. I was happy in them, I got an education sufficient for my subsequent needs, and I am grateful to have had with Leon Meader the last blooming of an unbroken forty or fifty years of Higgins tradition.

Name: PERRY GILBERT WORTMAN
Principal: 1958–68
Born: 1911
Education: Colby College B.A. 1933 Phi Beta Kappa
           University of Maine M.Ed. 1947
Academic Specialty: Chemistry, Education
Wife: Ruby Jardine
Children: Edward

When Perry Wortman was approached about taking the principalship of Higgins, he had been for many years principal at Crosby High in Belfast, and he was notoriously opposed to the existence of private schools—"I didn't see what they were good for," he told me. Nevertheless, offered a job at Higgins, he took it, for he couldn't resist the challenge of restoring to power and glory an institution that he perceived as being in a sad state of decay. I have this from his own lips. Why did the trustees seek out and solicit an anti–private school man to run their private school? My guess is that they knew him personally and understood what he could do, that he was tough, capable, determined, stubborn, an iron man who could get a grip on the situation and keep it. Certainly he hit the ground running, for I have a carbon of a letter he sent to his public school colleagues sometime between his contract-signing and his arrival at Higgins, announcing his defection and soliciting students for his new school.

A good man can bring Higgins back, even financially, by improving the school and doing good recruitment, say his letters to Harold Rich and my father. The hitch, he knows, is that he must modernize the school and its curriculum, and he dreads the chorus of "we've always done it that way." Now I must confess that had I been around I would have sung in that chorus myself, for I loved every tatter of Higgins just as it was and deplored all the outward manifestations of renewal: the steel engravings coming down and the cartoon virtues going up; Chapel imperceptibly changing into Assembly; my beloved brown walls turning a too-jolly green; my prep school with day

217

students undergoing a horrid metamorphosis into a high school with boarders. Yet fairness, and hindsight, oblige me to admit that, judged by any standard but sentimentality, he gets very high marks indeed: he set himself a colossal goal and he achieved it with exemplary efficiency. And make no mistake, he did love that school—his slide collection bears testimony: all the seasons, every year's Christmas decorations, each line of graduates, dozens of pairs of feet at the sock hop. There's no doubt in my mind that Ethel Beck would have added him to her list of Great Headmasters, and I am constrained to do the same.

His improvements to the buildings and grounds bordered on the astounding. Here is what he did, and without increasing the school's total indebtedness during his ten-year term: made the gym wider by twenty feet, longer by the depth of the old stage; added lockers and changing rooms; paved a new parking lot; finished the inside of Tracy Hall—closets, ceilings, etc.; built a principal's house; made outdoor basketball and tennis courts; drilled a new well; turned two small houses across the street into faculty housing; made more rooms for girls, as well as a kitchen, toilets, and showers, where the old principal's apartment had been; restored the library to its proper function; turned the old model classrooms in the Institute basement into classrooms for business subjects; redid the labs; made a new principal's office in the bay windows of the first floor; installed a guidance counselor in the old principal's office; planted ivy on the Institute and Tracy Hall; abolished the open sewer; and had the athletic field mowed all summer so it wouldn't be so stubbly in the fall.

The rather young faculty whom Perry Wortman found waiting for him at Higgins have weathered well in education this past quarter century, for they were bright and dedicated, but I think that he may have wished they were a little more experienced and less full of bounce. He has never told me that, but I have a dim recollection of several female faculty members singing for me, when I was home on vacation, a secret song that they had written to relieve tension. It was like the M-O-T-H-E-R song, only it spelled W-O-R-T-M-A-N, and I remember only the start of it: "W's the worry that we cause you; O is for how old we ought to be." We can draw some conclusions from that.

Enrollments in his time were strong. The class of 1968 graduated a record sixty-one. Students called him "The Riveter" (or sometimes

"The Woodpecker") from his habit of driving home his scoldings by the staccato thrusting of his index finger into the culprit's chest, no matter how massive. His students agree that he was tough, but good, and full of sound advice. "A short man in stature but a strong man in character," says David Lassell ('60). Tough is not to say insensitive. Doreen Dugal ('66) was impressed and touched that he wept without apology when he came to tell his students of John Kennedy's assassination.

Several students noted in Wortman a kind of professionalism new to them, an interest in standardized tests, statistics, and college admissions. ("Education is my life," he had said in an early letter to Harold Rich.) Several reported very gratefully that Mr. Wortman gave them college guidance that opened new possibilities. "Did the most for me of any one man—suggested Nasson College," says Gary Green, who was a postgraduate in 1961. I have only a small sampling from this period, but respect runs high.

In the end, not only did he change Higgins, but Higgins changed him, persuading him of the worth of private education. So what had begun as a public-school man taking a private school ended as a private-school man leaving a much more public school than he had found, and all I can say is that they seem to have been good for one another. Those were the most rewarding ten years of his career, he says, though not the easiest.

Name: FRANCIS STANLEY FOSS
Principal: 1968–74
Born: 1930
Education: Higgins Classical Institute
University of Maine B.S. 1956
Academic Specialty: Education, Math, History
Wife: Shirley Dixon
Children: Gwen, Jill, Eric, Kimberly

Stub Foss was the third principal to have been, like Cowing and Keith, a Higgins alumnus. He graduated in the class of 1949 and took a postgraduate year in addition. For all five years he played football, basketball, and baseball. Two years after he finished college he was back at Higgins, coaching and teaching.

As submaster under Perry Wortman he was very popular with students, who felt that if he batted them around a little (an activity in the best Higgins tradition), he was doing it out of affection and for their own welfare. "Young and nice," one graduate calls him, and says that he played sports for the fun of it. The class of 1967 had this to say:

> The SCROLL is proudly dedicated to a person for whom everyone has the greatest admiration and respect. As a teacher and friend of the students of Higgins Classical Institute, he has done much to instill in them those qualities which will best suit them for their roles as mature, useful adults.
>
> His understanding, patience, and wisdom have suited him well for his guidance work, and any problem, large or small, gets the same friendly, intelligent considerations. His abilities are also exhibited in the capable leadership and guidance he has given to the Varsity Club and athletics.
>
> We know him as a person whose principles and integrity have served both him and each of us as a guide in our education and daily life. For all these things, we proudly and gratefully dedicate the 1967 SCROLL to our friend and teacher, Mr. Francis S. Foss.

We have here a picture of an intelligent, efficient, and well-liked submaster. What could have gone wrong when he was head? The school somehow came to pieces in his hands, for there is no gainsaying that he got from Perry Wortman a decently well populated school with its buildings and grounds in good order, and six years later he handed over to Peter Chase a shambles of an institution with holes in the walls and a boarding population that made up for its sparseness with its rowdiness. Still, we must fight the impulse to light on him as a scapegoat and take as charitable a view as possible; these things are inevitably complicated. Certainly the times were against him—all this will be dealt with more fully in Chapter XV—and he seems to have struggled with them. Getting the state to send Indian students was a good idea of his and should have worked better than it did. His students perceived him as trying to save the school, and on the emotionally fraught night of the January 31, 1974, meeting to discuss closing the school, they rose and gave him an ovation for his efforts. I wish that I had his perspective on all of this—perhaps I should have pressed him harder—but I can understand that he'd rather not think about it, for it was his school, his town, and it would be a bitter thing to be implicated in its downfall. Probably not more than one principal in twenty could have brought Higgins through those difficult times triumphant, and I don't know that we can blame Stub Foss overmuch for being one of the other nineteen.

Name: PETER DONALD CHASE
Principal: 1974–75
Born: 1935
Education: Beals College Assoc. Degree 1956
       University of Maine B.S. 1964
       University of Wyoming M.S. 1968
Academic Specialty: Accounting, Math, Science
Wife: Sylvia Archer
Children: Amy, Danny

Peter Chase came to Higgins in 1964, went away to get his M.S. in 1966, and came back in 1970. He taught math, science, and organic gardening, and acted as submaster (or assistant principal as it was called by then). He advised and taught the photography club and the science club. "He cared about learning," says Michael Gallant ('71), citing him as a good teacher. His colleagues and students alike seem to have thought very well of him. The 1966 *Scroll* is dedicated to him for his patience, understanding, leadership, and untiring efforts.

The drama of his accession to head will be presented in more detail in Chapter XV, but this is it in short. When it appeared that the school would after all reopen for 1974–75, and that it would need a principal, Peter Chase was asked to take the job. He refused, saying that he wasn't what the school needed, that he could take care of staff, budget, stability, but that what Higgins needed at that point was an expensive entrepreneur, and he wasn't it. Had he known Ethel Beck's famous line, I suppose he would have said that he was not the man the Lord had raised up for Higgins. So the trustees set to work hunting someone with the necessary spark and decided on a Mr. Dix from South Carolina. Dix went back to settle his affairs at home, but delayed his return to Maine, delegating responsibility to Peter, item by item, and on the nineteenth of August sent word that he wanted nothing to do with Higgins after all. So Peter, despite his protests, was the fourteenth and last principal of Higgins.

If honesty, earnestness, purity of purpose, and an unpretentious highmindedness had been enough to save the school, Peter Chase would have done it. He was in and out of our house all summer, plotting strategy. One picture sticks in my mind: my mother and I had just brought in clean clothes from the line and dropped them on the kitchen table for sorting when Peter came in for a conference. We were a little abashed at the nature of the laundry, but Peter sat down and swept our underwear aside with as much honest unconcern as if it had been a pile of breadcrumbs; he was aiming to talk about the school.

But of course he was right—an expensive entrepreneur was what we needed, and it might have been too late even for that. Given the unpleasant job of closing the school, he did it with honor—relative solvency, a decent academic program, *standards*. Leon Williams says it was more like the old Higgins than it had been for years, that Peter deserves as much glory as I can get on paper for his valiant finale. We could hold our heads up. Maria Bartlett ('75) says,

> Mr. Chase was principal the last year. I think there were very few people, if any, that didn't like him. He was very easygoing, but like the Emersons expected good behavior and your best try in everything you did. I think that the desire to do well for a teacher whom you wish to please gets much better results than the fear of punishment from a teacher you don't like.

The last *Scroll* is dedicated to him.

XIV

LOSSES

It all came back to me the other day when I was
looking at that picture, and I thought, my God, we
were two kids together, and I was only two years
older than Grover was, and now I'm forty-six . . .
Can you believe it? Can you figure it out—the way
we grow up and change and go away? . . . And my
Lord, Grover seemed so grown-up to me.

—THOMAS WOLFE
"The Lost Boy"

F or some people, prep schools are all frivolity and clipped lawns, islands of peace to which they look back with longing from their beleaguered adulthoods; their adolescent woes, lively enough at the time, fade out in retrospect. We like to think this enviable state of affairs normal, and indeed a school may well enjoy a dozen consecutive years between calamities, graduating successive classes untraumatized by war or tragedy. (And of course at the other end of the spectrum, some people have suffered major losses and assaults in childhood and come to their high school years already burned.) But for many of us, adolescence is the period in which we and our peers first find ourselves living with accelerated risks, for we are old enough to drive, to fly, to hunt and play dangerous sports, and old enough to be sent to foreign countries and be shot at. Who would dare say that the bereavements we suffer in youth are not a principal part of learning, or that disaster is not a crucial, recurrent motif in the fabric of a school's history?

War is the most obvious hazard to life, for boys in their late teens are prime age for soldiers. War's larger issues interest historians, and its personal impact is the stuff of literature. In between, not very much regarded, are such institutions as Higgins, which suffer change and deprivation and the loss of sons in their own peculiar ways. I have never forgotten a story told to me by Addison Green one night at the Smith Faculty Club: After World War I, a friend of his father's, in England, was called by his old school, which begged him to come and talk to them, saying, "You're the only one left from your class; *you must come back and tell us what our traditions were.*" On the way to citing the Higgins war dead we shall look briefly at other effects of world war.

The sudden deaths of one's friends and teachers are only personal history, but nonetheless cataclysmic for that; no moment is more educational than the one in which we realize that if our friends, astonishingly, can die, then so can we. Boys and girls who die in their teens have no time to make their mark on the world in ordinary ways. They leave no progeny or inventions, they write no books, they found no schools or businesses. It is through death itself, by dying out of sequence, that they make their mark on the lives of their companions.

The only war whose effect on Higgins I know very much about is World War II. Of the First World War we know only that the principal and submaster were called up, leaving the school for one tumultuous term in the charge of a senior from Colby, a sophomore from the University of Maine, and the wife of a trustee. There were no sports then, and not much discipline until the introduction of uniforms and military drill. We have no record of deaths. We do, however, have from the December 1922 *Scroll* a poem called "Our Soldiers," which may be said to record a kind of loss, for unless I misread it, Part II is about a returned vet still suffering from the shock of battle. Its coolness takes even me a little aback, but perhaps "buck up and quit that" was a normal post–World War I response to shell-shock.

> *Tilly was a sodjer brave,*
> *His work was grave success,*
> *But now he's back in school again,*
> *He surely is a mess.*

> *You'll hear him in the evening,*
> > *You'll hear him in the night,*
> *His duty always by him,*
> > *And he commands with might.*
>
> *You'll wake as day is dawning*
> > *And hear a dreadful noise,*
> *And you'll say, "What is the matter?"*
> > *"I'm commanding of my boys."*
>
> *He seems to think his duty,*
> > *Away up here in school,*
> *Is the same as when he's wading*
> > *In the foamy, bloody pool.*
>
> *Now, people, please believe me,*
> > *And call me not a fool,*
> *When I say it is no joke*
> > *To have soldier boys in school.*

Of World War II we know more, for we are richer in documents and recollections. The incidental deprivations that change the texture of life are well recorded. For instance, I find a letter to the Augusta Rationing Board begging a permit to buy fifteen pairs of shoes for the basketball team. Another letter, however, makes us wonder whether the team was worth shoeing, for Dad writes to a Mr. Thompson (a graduate, I gather), "I should hate to think what that basketball team you had would do to our present quintet." The big boys are gone. Evening study hall, that Higgins hallmark, had to be called off in the winter because of blackouts. Says Merrill Clement ('43), "We had a piece of cake or a small dish of fruit for dessert. Milk was poured in your glass on the table. Seconds on anything was rare. . . . We were in a war and money was scarce. Food was rationed, etc." My father kept two cars, one his and one the school's, in order to get enough gas to take students to the doctor and a few away games. As well as new deprivations, new duties ensued: students and faculty took their turns at the local observation post (Ester 7). The Higgins canning center turned out the fourth highest total production in the state. And it goes without saying that war generates extra paperwork; anything the government has a hand in naturally does. "We have no local police station. What do you expect me to do about those fingerprints mentioned in Sec. B of Instruction I?" my father growls at some Augusta authority circa 1942.

But these things are pinpricks. The real losses are human. "I am sorry to see our boys going away," my father writes in 1943 with characteristic New England restraint. The girls were sorry, too, and less restrained. Eunice Merrill ('44) writes, "When we got that news Dec. 7, 1941 you never heard such weeping. The girls all had boy friends or brothers who would be called to serve." The boys themselves may have been taking it more calmly. Robert Bearman, who would have graduated in the class of 1946, says,

> I did not graduate from Higgins. My personal emotional commencement happened a few days after I left Higgins. I was lying in the top bunk at the Naval training center in Bainbridge, Maryland. The lights were out. I looked about the darkened barracks and the tall grey windows, with light seeping in from the outside. And thought to myself, "It's just another window in another dormitory," and promptly went to sleep.

There were practical ramifications, besides the emotional, to those boys going away. Principals took on a new task, writing pleas for deferment until graduation.

> This is to certify that W— B— of S. Portland is a student at H.C.I. in Charleston, Me. He is in the 2nd semester of the school year. School will close Thursday, June 3rd, 1943. I hope that he may be permitted to finish the school year. (4/5/43)

Enrollments became harder to calculate than ever. "Students seem to be coming in very well," my father writes in an undated letter from the mid forties; "Of course, we can't be too sure we have a student even after he has registered." In a 1943 letter he notes, "We have been very fortunate at Higgins in our registration but next year will be a difficult year for all prep schools."

The loss of students was difficult enough, but teachers got drafted, too. I find a long letter to Local Board explaining why Rodney Coffin shouldn't be taken away: he's teaching plane geometry, solid geometry, trig, aviation, and a science course. He is in charge of eighty boys in the dorm. "If we are to continue our type of education we must have instructors. If we are not to continue our type of education, why the war?" This clever piece of rhetoric did no good. Rodney Coffin went off to the army, leaving the family piano with us for safekeeping, which some years later led my parents to buy their own and subject me to lessons; the cruelties of war go on and on.

The 1944 and 1945 *Scrolls*, both of which have black covers (black for the first time among those I have seen), include lists of men in the service. The 1945 list shows 208 names. Eight boys should have been graduating that year. Two others, one each from the classes of 1946 and 1947, have joined up even before their senior year. The class of 1940 has the largest number, thirty-five, followed by 1938 with thirty-two (three of whom are already dead, and one a prisoner of war). Nineteen-nineteen is the oldest class in that list to have sent men (two), though the shorter 1944 list (113) shows two men from the class of 1913. I do not find the names of any women.

The memorial plaque to men who died in World War II is gone from the front hall of the Institute, and though Faith School kindly let me explore the attic, I could not find it there. But a penciled list in my father's handwriting exists, on the first page of a small brown notebook that also contains notes on school insurance, suggestions, and teachers' records. It is headed "Dead" and reads as follows:

Robert Moore, 4/19/44
Owen Towne
Alfred Crabtree
Parker Crabtree
Shirley Carter
Freddie York. England
Irving Dunning May 26—
New Guinea T. Sg. Air Medal
& 5 Oak leaf clusters
Wm Russell
Clarence Dow
Elmer Tower
Donald Barker

Between Russell and Dow he has written "Chaisson?" and scratched it out, and indeed Gilbert Chaisson ('43), although starred as Killed in Action on the 1945 list, is still alive and well and a retired U.S. Customs Port Director. About some of this list oral tradition still exists. Freddie York ('38), for instance, was the first Higgins casualty, and he must have been among the first to enlist as well, for he joined the RAF and was shot down in England. My father remembered how cross everyone was when he told them that Freddie wouldn't come back (the consistent accuracy of his dire predictions never made him very popular in the family either), for Freddie was constitutionally drawn into the thick of the action, no way to survive a war. You can see the devilment and optimism dancing in his senior-photo grin. ("He has determination and courage. He is a boy who will accept responsibility and carry it out to the best of his ability," Dad had written earlier in a general recommendation.) The Crabtree brothers came from a family of four boys, three of whom were killed and the fourth sent home. Once I knew how all three had died, but now I only remember that one was in the Bataan Death March. Donald Barker was torpedoed in a Japanese prison ship. Clarence Dow was the only Charleston casualty.

Robert Bearman mentions a Chapman who was killed in combat, but I have no record of him. Archie Hatch ('38) is listed as a prisoner of war, and Wilson Francis ('38), who had been pitching for the Cincinnati Reds before he went into the service, lost his occupation to a leg wound. Of the other wounds and imprisonments we have no record, but there were others. Some Higgins vet in occupational therapy kindly made me a little red, white, and blue bracelet, which I still have.

"We have about 160 students but they are rather young. I am looking forward to the close of the war and our group of older students," my father writes in one of his undated wartime letters, and indeed, after the war, the vets came back in great numbers. Our first two had been prisoners of war, and wounded, Evelyn Keith remembers. One of them had been a tail gunner and had bad spells of tail-gunning in the night, when he had to be sat up with. Twenty-five percent of the dormitory space was set aside for veterans, but an attempt to buy an extra house for further dorm space failed. Some boarding school regulations must have been a shock to men so experienced, but perhaps they were no worse than military discipline.

I gather from John Moore ('47), who had left school at sixteen to join the Merchant Marine, that besides the educational advantages of going to boarding school, one of the attractions was the chance to be with people his own age, and I would speculate that the relative placidity of boarding school routine would have been soothing, a great dose of the normalcy that they might not have survived to see again.

The GIs, Dad and Hugh agreed, were never any trouble; the trouble was with the sophomore boys, who were driven by the sight of them into frenzies of attention-getting behavior. (Anyone who has taught high school will understand why it was the sophomores.) Ormonde Brown ('47) writes,

> I've always been amazed as to how well the faculty handled the mix of students while I was in school. They had to deal with the thirteen year old freshmen who had never been away from home to the worldly veterans who had seen battle, death, and mankind at its worst. The rules were the same for everyone. I have always felt it worked because the teachers were excellent and all of us, non-veterans and veterans alike, learned to respect them.

Problems were principally financial. Five bales of additional blankets, army surplus, were ordered. I find a number of letters to the Veterans Administration asking if Higgins might not collect a full year's tuition for boys who have done a short year with special tutoring on the side, or whether vets might not pay slightly higher tuition to help with the hiring of an extra teacher, for Higgins has added a course that gives vets two years of algebra in one, a special English course in grammar and composition, and a special accelerated French course. (At Coburn, Hugh Smith and Doris Harding taught extra math courses at 7:30 A.M., he for free, though he paid her.) "I want it distinctly understood," my father writes, "that we will do exactly what we are doing for these veterans even if we do not receive any extra tuition. We cannot afford to do this but it is not the veteran's fault that he is behind in his courses."

"School is going very well but, of course, it isn't the old school," Dad had written in the letter already quoted about the youth of the student body and the feebleness of the basketball team. And of course it was not quite the old school after the war, either; in fact, I think it never was again.

Civilian deaths, perhaps, deal teenagers a greater philosophical shock than military deaths, which at least fit perceived laws of cause and effect: if your friend goes to war, he may be killed. But if he merely goes to the store, goes swimming, goes home for the weekend, you expect him to come back. When he doesn't, that's an eye-opener.

What exactly do the deaths of our peers teach us, besides pain of new and astounding proportions? First, obviously, they teach us about our mortality, about the fragility of the human body. We understand that old people (that is to say, people over thirty-five or forty) die, but youth seems a guarantee of durability. Young bodies look deceptively tough. It takes time to realize that not only our houses but our very handkerchiefs can outlast us, that a feather or an eggshell endures past the flesh of the ornithologist who collected it. Our mothers told us that Higgins student Norma Nelson, who died in 1949, had cancer as a result of being hit with an icy snowball, an odd but potent diagnosis. We said to ourselves, incredulous, "An icy snowball? That's all it takes?" and even in our preadolescent minds some notion of accountability began to stir. Somewhere there was somebody who'd thrown that snowball, right? Probably somebody who hadn't expected it to have any repercussions.

We also learn that we're playing with no safety zones. Looking at the memorials in Appendix B, we can imagine the impact of the deaths. Christmas Day? Miriam Libby died on *Christmas Day*? How could that happen? How could Sadie Higgins die in the spring of 1909 when she should have been valedictorian that June? Dorothy Russell died in 1923, in her freshman year, quite unprotected by her devoutness or by her virtue in taking care of her motherless siblings. And Bozo Scribner, who could tame a raccoon, make a star, fly an airplane—couldn't he stay alive? Can't we be saved by piety or wit or magic?

Our fumbling attempts to make sense of the cosmos when our classmate David Gray died in 1958 come back to me, and I hear again some wild adolescent theoretician arguing that one dies at one's appointed minute, that if David had not fortuitously been in a car when his minute came, he might instead have fallen downstairs, perhaps at home—and how (the speaker finished earnestly) would his family have liked *that*? Not much, we agreed, but we weren't comforted. We tried on all the available platitudes, but none of them fit very well, and in the end we could only grope for conversational topics that didn't hurt (we never found any) and wait to see whether time, as rumored, had any medicinal effects. I remember, too, seeing the other boys as they stood in their overcoats in front of the dorm, and thinking how old they suddenly looked. When we meet now, we never speak of all that—not, I think, because it's too unimportant, but because it's become to each of us too intensely private a memory of initiation.

I suppose that the ultimate philosophical horror was raised by Michael Surtees's death in 1944. To summarize material more thoroughly recounted in the appendix of memorials, Michael was an immensely popular sixteen-year-old English refugee who was boarding at Higgins with his two younger brothers. One February Saturday he was shoveling coal to earn extra pocket money when a great chunk broke off the frozen coal pile and crushed him. The irony is obvious: he had come to America to be safe (indeed, to be safe from falling objects). His parents had done the right thing, the school was trying to nurture him, and his own behavior was beyond reproach. So how could this disaster happen? It horrified a student body already somewhat inured by war to the deaths of contemporaries. Is man, then, unable to escape his fate? What kind of God plays a joke like that? More than any of the other dead, Michael became a grain of sand in the metaphysical shell, an irritant that had to be coated with layers of reflection and nostalgia and memorial scholarships before we could tolerate it.

Such events teach us not only about fragility but about resilience. The business of ordinary living goes on, however much we regard its doing so as a vulgar affront to our pain. We outlive the crisis, and then, perhaps, we are inoculated forever against surprise and outrage at the nastier turns of destiny. It takes a lot to make us shout, "But it can't happen!" We know that it can, and suspect that it will. "After the first death, there is no other."

XV

LAST DAYS

Higgins Classical Institute
Is my school.
I am a Knight.
Orange for the setting of the sun.
Black for the darkness of the night.

—ANON.
1973 Scroll

lthough its end was lingering, the final collapse of Higgins came on suddenly. Perry Wortman's Higgins in the 1960s had seemed a place of vigor, expansion, and hope. Phillip Hamm, secretary of the Board of Trustees (to whose lively and explicit minutes we are much indebted) writes after the February 1, 1962, meeting, "Throughout the reports and the planning a general atmosphere of optimism for the future of Higgins prevailed." Although the boys' dormitory was not expected to be quite full for 1962–63 and a few day students from Bradford and Hudson had withdrawn and gone to other schools, the trustees were not displeased: "There is a general feeling in the towns involved that Higgins ranks very very hard, a reputation that the trustees highly approve." By the next year the boarding population was back up, building and repairs were going on at a great rate, and school finances were comfortably in the black.

But in 1957 the Maine State Legislature had enacted a significant and, for Higgins, sinister piece of legislation, later to be known by the especially appropriate acronym SAD, for School Adminstrative District—the SAD Act. More formally, it is Chapter 364 of the 1957 Acts and Resolves. Its intent was to encourage, indeed strong-arm, small schools and communities into what it called "larger and more efficient administrative units," the point being to achieve better and more uniform educational opportunities, not to mention more uniform tax rates and state subsidies. Reorganized districts would be rewarded with supplemental state aid, whereas "the full program allowance" would not be given to "unnecessary small schools." Further, when a SAD district had been issued its certificate of organization, it could demand and receive the title to any property or building of any community schools that fell within its bounds, "notwithstanding any other provision in the charter of said school district or community school district." About the only friendly sounding section of the whole act (to my prejudiced ears) was the provision that persons between the ages of five and twenty-one living at lighthouse stations could go to any public school in the state without paying tuition.

The ramifications for Higgins were obvious: towns would go into SADs; towns would not pay tuition to boarding schools; students, indeed, would not be driven to boarding schools by the unavailability of public education. Towns could, however, make contracts with academies for their students as a group, excusing only those students who needed to go someplace else for a particular vocational course.

The first reference to School Administrative Districts that I find in the notes of the trustees appears in the June 27, 1966, minutes (though Leon Williams tells me that Clyde Russell had argued for a union perhaps two years before). A committee would be meeting with East Corinth representatives to see whether Higgins might not be offered up as the site of the district school, or part of it—because, clearly, there was going to be some trouble about getting students. All those students whose towns had been paying tuition would be obliged to pay out of their own pockets for coming to Higgins when they found themselves living in a SAD district, and the whole point of Higgins had been to educate boys and girls without that kind of money. Enrollment had peaked at 265 in 1964; now, though still over 200, it was going down.

But by March of 1967 the trustees' interest in a district had cooled. Higgins ought to remain private, though of course it would be delighted to go on educating Charleston students if they still wished it. Higgins would simply have to recruit more out-of-state students. But out-of-state students were affected by the times, too, for colleges were increasingly willing to accept and offer remedial courses to ill-prepared students who would once have needed a postgraduate year at boarding school. By 1971 the number of postgraduates had dwindled from perhaps thirty-plus to three.

In this desire to keep Higgins private we see the dawning of a major philosophical difficulty that the trustees would struggle with from then on. What could be done to save Higgins without its ceasing to be Higgins? To keep it as it was might be to lose it, for there was a feeling in the air that the evolutionary direction of education in Maine was leaving Higgins and its kind behind, obsolete as dinosaurs. But if it were changed to a public school, a junior high, a group foster home, a haven for the learning disabled (all possibilities that rose up at one time and another in discussions) and its survival thereby ensured, wouldn't Higgins itself be destroyed in the interest of preserving a name and a set of buildings? These were difficult and by no means rational issues, and it is no wonder that as the crises build we catch whiffs of dissension among the trustees and elsewhere.

In a report dated February 9, 1968, presented by the Committee on Instruction, its chairman, Clyde Russell, defined for the trustees the problem upon which Higgins was increasingly to founder:

> Higgins is in a position in which it is difficult, if not impossible, to operate efficiently. All over Maine, schools are being consolidated in order to make possible a program that would be impossibly expensive for small schools. We are trying to operate in Charleston a kind of SAD for Charleston, Swans Island, and Glenburn, in which the majority will not go on to college, and in which we have to offer at least two more or less vocational courses. We are, also, in competition with other college preparatory schools, attempting to do a good job of getting our graduates into good colleges and keeping them there. If we could concentrate on either objective, we could be more efficient, or if we could have an enrollment of 300 or 400, we could be.

This meeting was also the first one in some years at which Higgins had been threatened with a budget in the red (by $6,000), "due to less income than anticipated."

That report, and situation, is an interesting and unconscious echo of Philip Keith's description of the difficulties of the academies a hundred years earlier:

> During the period the academy tried to meet the popular demand for more practical courses for those who were not continuing in college or university by adopting subjects such as bookkeeping, surveying, navigation, chemistry, and agricultural arts, while at the same time, retaining the courses of study which were designed for college or university preparation. In spite of these changes the number of students constantly declined, and, as the period drew to a close, the financial affairs of this type of school were in a sad state. Those that remained in operation were becoming poorer with the passage of the years, and the high school law of 1873 seemed to be but the final blow to all but the strongest of this type of institution which had so gallantly fulfilled its purpose. (HEPC, p. 62)

As it turned out, the trustees' negotiations with East Corinth came to nothing; East Corinth became the district headquarters for SAD #64, while Dover-Foxcroft was made headquarters for SAD #68, the district to which Charleston belonged. Charleston students were allowed to attend Higgins unless they required some specific course of study that Dover offered and Higgins did not. Glenburn students, too, whose obvious neighbors did not seem willing or able to take them in, stuck with Higgins, as did the islanders, especially the Swans Island group, though in the end, Leon Williams tells me, even Swans Island went into a union.

By 1969, SAD #68 was proving even more of an impediment than anybody seems to have anticipated. The minutes of the May 20, 1969, trustees' meeting note that district representatives are "agreeable" to having Higgins educate Charleston students, but they want certain requirements met. The secretary records with quotation marks that the directors of SAD #68 are giving the trustees "an audience." (At the audience the school was informed of the district's dismay at the turnover of teachers for upcoming fall semester; Principal Foss, whose first year it was, explained that some faculty had defected because his new rules would have involved them in more extracurricular, after-hours duties.) Aside from a little anxiety about recruitment of students, nothing in the minutes suggests impending disaster. Indeed, the minutes for June 1970 seem in some ways promising, despite a cash loss the previous year of $12,500. Student inquiries are coming in. Repairs are going ahead. There is one ominous note, however: the trustees *vote* to open the school in the fall. Heretofore this has been taken for granted.

Two months later, the minutes of an Executive Committee meeting clarify the school's considerable difficulties. Boarding students have suddenly become almost extinct—only twenty-two boys and twelve girls are registered for the dorms in the fall, dorms that were designed for ninety boys and forty-five girls. It looks as though the school can expect another $13,000 shortfall. Should one dorm be closed? A lively discussion of dorm-closing ensued, in which "at times the conservative forces were led by Leon Thorsen, and the slightly less than conservative by Leon Williams." The dorm stayed open. Furthermore, the principal reported (evidently as reassurance) that nineteen students who wished "no regimentation or rules" would not be coming back; from this one can infer a good measure of chaos.

This 1970 plunge into disaster certainly marks the beginning of Higgins's last days. (Nineteen seventy was not a good period for prep schools. That same August, for instance, Coburn and Oak Grove saved themselves by mating the former's endowment with the latter's campus.) In November of 1970 Higgins was obliged to issue a press release stating that it *would* finish the current year, contrary to "numerous rumors" that it would close. Perhaps word had gotten out that at the September trustees' meeting Chairman Leon Thorsen had estimated a $70,000 debit by June 1971, or that the trustees had begun to consider selling some of the school's less crucial property.

The chairmanship of Leon Thorsen is worth noting, for it came in the midst of the Leon Williams regime and was intended as a solution to communications problems between Principal Foss and the Board of Trustees. Perhaps, the trustees thought, some antagonism between their personalities prevented Foss from talking to Williams about the problems that he certainly must have. Perhaps another chairman would elicit more confidence. But another chairman did not. Next, the trustees tried meeting monthly, in smaller, less intimidating, groups. How were things going, they'd ask Foss. All right, he'd say. This was not a situation in which Maine taciturnity was very constructive. To an outsider, and in retrospect, it seems amazing that one side or the other did not break out of this impasse.

Why, for instance, didn't the trustees fire a principal who would not talk to them about the worst crisis in the history of the school? Well, at least Foss was familiar with the situation; that was in his favor. He was himself a Higgins man, a graduate, teacher, submaster, principal—perhaps some superstition á la Ethel Beck about God's Chosen School still clung round, or at any rate he must have been perceived as having more motive to fight for the school than an outsider would. Furthermore, though the trustees were intelligent, devoted, and generous, they were not so experienced in hiring new principals as one might suppose, and perhaps were reluctant to bring it on themselves. Since my father left in 1948 they had twice promoted submasters and three times invited in people already known to at least some of them.

Why, on the other hand, did Foss not resign earlier? He had told the trustees when he was hired that he did not propose to work a twenty-four-hour day. Finding himself drawn into a crisis for which a thirty-six-hour workday would have been none too long, why did he persist? Stubbornness, I suppose, would have been one factor. Nobody likes to give up, and perhaps Stub Foss liked it even less than most. Having coached Higgins football teams, he may have viewed overwhelming odds as the normal course of events. "So far as I'm concerned," he says in a 1971 newspaper interview, "this school is not closing down." You can almost hear his teeth grind. Perhaps, too, it was impossible for someone who had grown up around Higgins to imagine on the deepest level of belief the impending possibility of its nonexistence.

Tension grew through the winter of 1970–71, for the trustees had offered SAD #68 an option to buy Higgins for a district junior high school. Hank Moody of the *Bangor Daily News* wrote a sympathetic article on February 18, 1971.

> Prospects of something gained, something lost hang with the option open to School Administrative District 68 (Dover-

Foxcroft) to take over the property now under the banner of Higgins Classical Institute by March 15.

If the school district decides to take advantage of the option, which it could do by assuming the debts of the private school, it would gain much needed space for a junior high school, though officials consider it poorly located.

The something lost would be the private school itself and what it would mean in terms of traditional and educational innuendos that would go out of being forever.

His article goes on to quote Chairman Leon Thorsen's opinion that the school's "cause" has waned, that its purpose has drifted. Selling the school was the first choice of the trustees, but if that failed, they proposed to rally somehow and keep going. In the end, SAD #68 turned down the deal by a hefty majority. Among other difficulties, Higgins was on the edge of the district; Monson children, for instance, would have had to ride thirty miles one way to get there.

Another Hank Moody article of the same period (2/12/71) quotes Leon Thorsen as saying that if Higgins stays in business, "We're going to dig deep down into a hidden pocket and try to make it go," but "Where that pocket is, I don't know." He found one such pocket in his own pants, for Leon Williams tells me that Thorsen helped the school with $5,000 that he never got back. Various other pockets were being explored. Higgins had begun to talk, for instance, about its mission to the "extreme" student—that is, the student so extremely good or extremely deficient that he or she required more attention than could be given in a public school. At the same time, just in case, it was courting the town of Glenburn, whose students, not having been snapped up by crowded adjacent towns, might be obtainable by contract, a more stable arrangement than had been in force. A five-year agreement under which Glenburn would send Higgins all its ninth- and tenth-grade students (fifty to seventy-five in all) was sugared by the promise of placing two Glenburn trustees on the board. Glenburn's acceptance of the contract, though it played a part in the final disaster, was probably the only thing that kept Higgins going another four years.

The May 4, 1971, trustees' meeting seems to have been giddy with relief. A unanimous and hearty vote of confidence was given to Principal Foss. Foss hoped that the trustees would take an interest in all the details of the school, and the trustees hoped to be revivified by the "inspiration of the Glenburn townspeople." In a final burst of goodwill, the trustees voted to give the Glenburn school an apparently superfluous safe from the Institute, Glenburn's "having been rendered *un*-safe by burglars." The high spirits of that last little joke testify to the tone of the meeting. Further, a special Joint Board was formed in 1971 to take over certain functions of the trustees re curriculum, hiring and firing, and rules for day students. It consisted of two directors from Glenburn, two from SAD #68, four Higgins trustees, the two superintendents, and the Higgins principal. I am told that in the end the Joint Board contributed to the downfall of the school. The regular Board of Trustees was still responsible for the plant, the finances, and the boarding students.

The Glenburn contract by no means meant that Higgins's troubles were over, merely—and that was enough for the moment—that its end hadn't come. Here is a list, in no particular order, of the expedients that were considered and tried, or considered and dropped, or considered but never quite followed up. Some worked, but not well enough. Some didn't work at all. Higgins did sell some of its holdings, two buildings across the street (extra faculty housing), and it sold stumpage off its woodlot. It tried—unsuccessfully—to rent out the school for meetings and conventions. It took in as many Indians as it could get, the Bureau of Indian Affairs having promised to pay $1,600 per pupil, but a change in administration complicated collection and made necessary a legislative act before Higgins could have its money. An advertising agency was retained but fired after six months; it threatened to sue the school. Recruiters were hired and quit. Redistricting was considered and dropped. A plan to fill the girls' dorm with state wards—foster children of high school age— seems not to have been followed up. An alumni fund drive didn't raise peanuts. I don't know what became of Foss's scheme to have businesses offer scholarships to needy students; perhaps the businesses were disinclined. A plan to cater to the learning disabled, whose parents pay high fees for good service (a plan kicked off by a search for the learning disabled already at Higgins), came too near the end to reach fruition. Of the various schemes, my own favorite was the plan to have vocational students build a house which could then be sold, but that never made it out of the trustees' meeting.

In the midst of all this tension and suspense, what was going on with the students, the people at real center stage while the trustees were dashing about in the wings? Theirs seems to have been a curious state of mind, as well it might. On the one hand, they were rowdy, vandalistic, full of hoaxes and excesses. It is hard, of course, to know how much this behavior was attributable to a general sixties hangover and how much to Higgins's own crisis. Certainly the drug problems and the demise of the dress code were period phenomena. An overall restlessness, discernable in assorted Higgins documents, was likely both. Mock bulletins (sometimes signed "The Phantom") survive to announce, "The Junior Class trip to South Viet Nam has been postponed until the middle of July"; "Found four joints in the bathroom. Will the owner pick them up at the car out front with the blue lights on top"; "The riflery club apologizes to the owner of the maroon Chevy ½ ton pick up for shooting out the windows." In the 1974 *Scroll*, Senior Superlatives include School Skippers, Complainers, Fender Benders, and Most Daring. Anonymous poetry in that year's *Scroll* is revealing, too, and some of it is fun as well. Here is a poem about day student woes:

> BUS RIDE
> *This crowded bus does cramp my style,*
> *Month after month, mile after mile.*
> *Beans and coins fly through the air*
> *Jelly sandwiches in my hair.*
> *Seats are crowded, two's & three's,*
> *Wrinkled coats and bashed up knees.*
> *The road from school to home is far*
> *Oh, how I wish I had a car.*
> *Free from scratches and from dents,*
> *Then I'd go for my license.*

Another poem on the same page complains about the condition of the buildings: "No guard rail on the creaking stairs / Dust and paint chips everywheres." "Dust and paint chips" is putting it kindly, for when my mother and I assessed the school in the summer of 1974 we also found broken furniture and holes in the walls and ceilings "everywheres," plus a general sense of energy run amok. One destructive act will have overtones for alumni who ever felt my father's basilisk stare snap them into line: his photograph from Tracy Hall was returned to my mother for safekeeping after students had poked its eyes out.

Maria Bartlett ('75), that invaluable correspondent and saver of memorabilia, shared a rumor that helped me picture the desolation of the seventies:

> A lot of students believed the dorms to be haunted. The girls' dorm in particular. I was told that once all the lights in the girls' dorm turned on at the same time. I believe one of the dorm students told me. Another friend said they used to hold seances. I'd be interested in hearing any other stories of the ghosts of Higgins.

But amidst all the dust and paint chips and rumors and hauntings a fair lot of school spirit still prevailed. If students couldn't enjoy the pride of riding high with a winner, at any rate they could work up affectionate loyalty for an underdog. A third anonymous poem in the 1974 *Scroll* is properly accorded a whole page, where it appears just above an unusually fine drawing of the Institute (though possibly not contemporary, for the gym seems to lack Perry Wortman's addition on the front). I am especially taken with the poignancy of the last four lines, but there are points of interest throughout.

> *Through the years I've come to love*
> *The things that Higgins is made of*
> *The dormitories and study halls*
> *The stairways and the many walls*
> *The beauty of the summer lawn*
> *The ivy that I look upon*
> *The gym where I've watched many a game*
> *Would hardly ever be the same*
> *If through the rough formalities*
> *Hard facts and technicalities*
> *I had to lose Higgins just because*
> *The finances had so many flaws*
> *I'd hate to see the school close down*
> *And be sent to another town*
> *Where I'd be lost and separated*
> *From the place where I'm situated*
> *I belong at HCI*
> *Keep her open, don't let her die*

To look towards the school and see
No one in the vicinity
No kids, or cars, or faculty
Would surely be a catastrophy
Tight shut windows, locked up doors
No pitter-patter on the floors
I love this school and what she stands for
Even though we have no bands or
Other things that some schools do
To my dear Higgins I'll be true.

On January 31, 1974, a meeting in the Higgins chapel seems to have brought pro-Higgins sentiment to an all-time dramatic high. Present, according to Phillip Hamm's fine notes, were "Williams, Thorsen, [Brenna] Tracy, Ritchie, Popham, Newman, Meguier, Hamm, Dogherty, Dinsmore, Principal Foss, and a packed chapel of students, teachers, townspeople from Glenburn and Charleston, Selectmen from Charleston, Town Manager from Glenburn, SAD #68 Board members, members of the Glenburn School Committee, Supts. Savage and Smith, friends of the school and perhaps a few enemies." The meeting was called in response to a Joint Board resolution to close the school, which had been presented to the Board of Trustees. And indeed things looked bad; Leon Williams had personally lent Higgins $10,000 to keep it open that year, taking third mortgages on the buildings. Further, the Glenburn School Committee had voted to dissolve the contract with Higgins. (The contract, however, had been made with the townspeople, not the committee, and so the vote was not considered binding.)

Peter Chase remembers that his math class had started a letter-writing campaign in favor of the school's staying open, and that Chairman Leon Williams came into the meeting holding up a packet of those letters, saying, "I'd made up my mind the school would close; these have changed it." Pastor Overlook of the Charleston Baptist Church had sent a supportive letter, too, which my mother (then a member of both the Board of Trustees and the Joint Board) read aloud. She and others had letters from students and parents in both Charleston and Glenburn, asking that the school stay open. Townspeople had sent petitions. A financial report argued that Higgins might survive economically if the girls' dorm were closed, and although in 1971 Leon Williams's suggestion that this be done was "shouted down" at a trustees meeting, for various reasons that the secretary thought it more delicate not to repeat, a public show of hands at the 1974 meeting judged the idea no longer too extreme.

Representatives of assorted student categories spoke on behalf of their constituents: all Charleston students but one wanted the school open; Glenburn students stood in favor of it, 67 to 6; all boarding students but one wanted it open, and that one, said his representative, didn't like school anyway. An out-of-town girl rose and asserted that she didn't want to go anywhere else. A mother of three Higgins students said that her children might have dropped out if they'd gone elsewhere. A senior girl wanted the school to be there for her successors.

For a while, the meeting degenerated to bickering and finances. Glenburn berated Higgins; Higgins growled about Dover; East Corinth tried to lure Charleston into SAD #64. Remarks were made about personality conflicts. Then, in a burst of highmindedness, the faculty announced that they would forego a salary increase for the next year; they received a standing ovation. On the heels of this, a student asked for an expression of feeling about Principal Foss's performance at Higgins, and the crowd was on its feet again with applause.

At the executive session that followed, the trustees voted to keep the school open through 1974–75, to request 100 percent rather than 90 percent of the state-allowable fee from Glenburn and SAD #68, and to close the girls' dorm, moving the girls into Tracy Hall as soon as "security hardware" could be put on the doors.

The summer of 1974 was one long, heroic, last-ditch attempt to put the shambles of Higgins back together—to keep it alive if possible, but, if not, to ensure that it it died with dignity. The *Bangor Daily News* (3/27/75) speaks, looking back, of that summer's "large volunteer efforts" by townspeople to "do some of the maintenance at the school which otherwise would have to have been paid for." I have remarked before upon the cordial relations between school and town, and it was never so much in evidence as then, save perhaps at the building of the gym or the rebuilding of Tibbetts Hall. So far as I know, no further documentation of that summer's work exists. I remember the deplorable state of the school at the beginning of the summer, as Peter Chase (into whose capable hands the summer needs of the school had fallen after Stub Foss's resignation) showed my mother and me around. After that, I remember only the all-consuming projects in which I was myself involved, so I must beg forgiveness for describing one of those as representative while other labors go unmentioned. They did not go unappreciated.

Tracy Hall seemed to be the heart of the desolation. The lounge (or reception room, as we were wont to call such places at Higgins), which one saw first on coming through the front doors, would have made a kennel look homey. Sixteen years earlier we'd furnished it with maple chairs and brass lamps, good mainstream reception room furniture, and dedicated it to the memory of my friend and classmate, David Gray. I don't know what happened in those sixteen years, but of course school furniture does not last forever. In any case, the sight of that room was provoking financial anxiety and despair in every breast. Other people's despair tends to make me short-tempered, so in a fit of bravado I announced privately to my mother that I, singlehandedly, was quite capable of redoing that entire room for two hundred dollars, so what was all the fuss about. She countered that in that case she would be happy to put up the two hundred bucks, and I was in for it.

My snapshots of the results remind me, most of all, that the refurbishing was far from singlehanded. Furniture was the major problem, of course. I threw myself on the mercies of Joe Hagelin, trustee, carpenter and good neighbor, and the result was half a dozen thick pine benches (four six feet long, two eight feet) to line the walls. We painted them cherry red and then I went begging to the townswomen with lengths of blue denim or ticking and long rectangles of foam that I had detached with a straight-edged razor from discarded Higgins mattresses. I think that only one woman declined to cover bench cushions for Higgins. A pedestal table had survived the wreckage; this too we painted red. Surrounded by four bentwood chairs we found in the dining room and with a checkerboard on top, it made an inviting game table. Somebody got us a lovely piece of carpet, so big that we didn't even have to splice, though Ernie Parmenter was standing by to show us how. The Charleston Public Library gave us discarded books to fill the shelves on either side of the picture window. At some point, my father (like Maria Bartlett and me, a hoarder) had acquired two scalloped wooden valances from a Howard Johnson's, which, nailed together and painted red, just fit across the window top, and we made pillow-ticking drapes. At this point I had been such a scrounger, beggar, and scavenger that I had about half the money left, so I laid it out on glass and posters. I can make out an odd mix in the snapshots, and distinctly representative of the times—Andy Warhol's *Marilyn Monroe, Superpig*, a Victorian photo of a chain manufacturer, Rackham's Alice in Wonderland and the hookah-smoking caterpillar, antique bicycle and auto ads, and a Magritte; another poster that I can't quite make out could have been a black-and-white drawing of plant life. I am told that Superpig was the favorite.

The other major excitement of the summer was the attempt to hire a new principal. Peter Chase, the assistant principal, was approached by the trustees. He looked a promising candidate—popular, intelligent, steady, acquainted with the ways of the school—but he declined, feeling that Higgins required for its resurrection something more of an entrepreneur. After a search that did not, I think, produce a record number of candidates, the trustees hired A. David Dix from South Carolina. His credentials looked lively if not especially entrepreneurial, for he had attended (according to the trustees' minutes) "a number of local colleges in West Virginia, . . . also Florida, and two summers at Colby in Maine." He cited as his fields English and Geology, with majors in Elementary and Secondary Education and Social Studies. Perhaps a certain twitchiness of resumé, the number of colleges attended and majors attempted, combined with his statement of philosophy (i.e., that changing a person's mind is the greatest challenge in education and the thing that education does) should have given someone pause. But hindsight is easy and candidates were limited. I find no record of his hiring, but the June 10, 1974, minutes allude to Principal Foss, and those of July 25 to Principal Dix.

I am told that Mr. Dix was given his keys and no further help by his burned-out predecessor. Peter filled him in as well as he could. At least half a dozen new teachers were needed; applications were coming in and needed to be reviewed; administrative duties piled up. Mr. Dix went back to South Carolina to see his family. As his absence dragged on into weeks, he kept in touch with Peter by phone, delegating business item by item. By mid August no faculty had been hired. On August nineteenth a Joint Board/Trustees meeting was scheduled, for which the new principal was definitely coming back—for which, indeed, he was supposedly en route when he phoned Peter and asked him just to start the meeting. While the meeting was in progress Muriel Mason, the school secretary, was obliged to announce to the trustees and board members that she had just received a phone call from erstwhile Principal Dix, who was really still in South Carolina and wanted nothing more to do with the school!

It is history now that Peter rose to the occasion and put Higgins's last year together. Feeling that it was bad policy to delude teachers about how hard they'd have to work (a not uncommon boarding-school hiring policy), he announced to his staff that it would be the worst year of their lives, that he'd own them body and soul. After that, he knew, any mercies would look good. Jack Walsh, a new teacher and himself a Higgins grad, had come early that summer with his wife and daughter and was full of good ideas. I remember his planning that the island kids would teach everyone how to make nets, and Peter remembers students in the Walsh apartment paring apples, though he can't recall whether for art or food.

I don't know whether it was the worst year of the faculty's lives, but it may have been the worst of the principal's. Few administrators remember 1974–75 (that year of drugs, alcohol, and general uproar) with pleasure, but the fragments of memory that surface in conversation with Higgins's last principal have a nightmare quality. He recalls purple drugs in the girls' quarters, marijuana growing unbeknownst to the faculty in their plant pots. One boy broke into the fire house and stole radios out of the fire trucks and stashed them in the school bus. A girl went catatonic in class and required so much attention that a second girl, envious, put her arm through a windowpane. All the Indians lay down on the floor one night and declined to go to study hall. One teacher bailed out in midyear and another couldn't get up in the morning by himself. The students were given paint to do their rooms, and one of them painted around his furniture. Alarms set in faculty rooms to detect coed escapes and entrances were not foolproof, for one boy who climbed down knotted rope supplied by his girlfriend would have escaped notice had not a third student set off the alarm. These recollections are not exhaustive, only representative.

All authorities agree, however, that it was very far from being the worst year in the life of the school. Leon Williams is passionate in his conviction that, though Peter consumed himself in doing it, he gave Higgins a glorious end, with high academic standards and paid bills. "It was more like the old Higgins than anything we'd seen in years," he says. We can tell from the last *Scroll* that such high-class activities as archery, riding, chess, and photography flourished. Peter fired his accountant and kept the books himself, from a manual. The October 21, 1974, trustee minutes note that for the first time in years most of the trustees understood the financial situation, and they are grateful to Peter for his clarity.

Judging by his report to the Joint Board and Trustees on March 25, 1975, the final blow that undid Higgins came, not out of any 1974–75 difficulty, but out of errors from the year before. The miscalculations, which involved hot lunch costs and the prorating of heat, electricity, insurance, and custodial salaries between instructional and dormitory costs, meant that Higgins owed rebates to "sending municipalities" to the tune of $9,637.12. Further, it had already rebated $3,770.96 to SAD #68 and Glenburn on the basis of another 1973–74 miscalculation. The total of $13,408.08 had to come from school assets, not from operating costs. The sale of the woodlot and remaining securities would leave almost no reserve for future emergencies, and emergencies are to a school as ants to a picnic. Besides, says his report, apparently "the days of boarding schools are coming to an end." SADs are supplying sophisticated educations; postsecondary schools are taking unsophisticated students. "The only remaining function appears to be to take island youngsters who have to go to a boarding school or youngsters so intolerable that their parents or foster parents have to get them from under foot." And there's a classic vicious circle: without the dorms, the staff would have to be reduced; with reduced staff the day students would fall away; with the day students dwindling, staff would be cut back again, and so on. Even a major repair could close a school so precariously balanced, and a midyear closing would be bad for everyone. The last principal concludes sadly, "If I could see some ray of hope for the survival of HCI, I would urge that we continue to struggle. I do not see that ray."

No one can envy him the making of that recommendation, which he describes as the hardest thing he ever had to do.

After hearing his report and holding some general discussion, the trustees went into session. My mother, as vice chairman, was obliged to conduct the meeting. The vote to close Higgins was six in favor, one opposed, and one member plus the chair abstaining. A committee to sell the property was formed.

On April 29 the trustees met with representatives from the Faith School of Theology of Brooklin, Maine, a potential buyer. Then sixteen years old, Faith School had a good reputation; it was known to pay its bills and maintain its property. Faith School and the trustees seem to have come quite promptly and amicably to an agreement. In the end, no actual sale took place, just a kind of legal tap dance. To whom, after all, could Faith have given the money? Rather, the new owners assumed outstanding debts and conceded certain benefits—free tuition for qualified Charleston applicants to the theological school, and the administering of a trust fund (composed of assorted scholarship monies, stocks, and bits of cash remaining to Higgins) for the higher education of Charleston students. The trustees decided to protect the grandfather clauses by a simple shift of board membership—the Higgins trustees would resign and Faith people be elected to take their places.

One effect of this arrangement has proved unpopular with alumni, though it looks good on paper. That is the preservation of the name Higgins Classical Institute to refer to the K–12 Christian school. Alumni blanch at the sight of Higgins jackets in white and black rather than orange and black, and when a current student says that he or she goes to Higgins, they want to shout, "You can't—it's dead!" I myself supposed at first that the trustees had given in to an ill-considered fit of sentimentality, like taking a dead pet to the taxidermist, but I see now that their motives were practical.

It's interesting and a little comforting—if there's any comfort to be got—to see how things great and small go full circle. Toward the end of Higgins, *Scroll* submissions are anonymous again, football dies out, two dormitories merge back into one. Rural Maine students once again dominate the school population, only they're day students, not boarders. And finally, under the new regime, religion comes back as the governing force. Perhaps the Reverend John wouldn't have minded too much.

In any case, and like it or not, the physical Higgins belongs to Faith School of Theology now. They sing the Lord's praises a little louder than we did and adhere to a stricter, more bundley dress code. They keep the campus looking good. They seem to be happy. I hope they love the place, for all they've got their sights on a better world. Handsome big signs on some of the dorms give them Biblical names—Jericho, Eden. Certainly the latter makes perfect sense to me; I grew up always supposing that Higgins was the Earthly Paradise.

XVI

ECHOES

Was I scared? Hell yes. It was new and I was confused. Not homesick, just confused. That Institute building was utterly confusing. It was so big and looked alike everywhere I went. I soon got over that. And today as I prowl through the acres of buildings in Houston, I think of, occasionally, the tiny Institute building. —ROBERT BEARMAN ('46)

In those years, in the early twenties, it seemed like we had a lot more snow than we usually do now, and every once in a while, usually about twice during the wintertime, they'd get together a big hayride. . . . [O]ne of the farmers would get a hayrack and take the wheels off and put on the bobsled runners. So we'd fill that up with hay and put in blankets and everybody'd get in under the blankets and we'd take off on a ride out—oh, maybe on the Bradford road or one of those roads—and we'd ride about maybe three or four miles and stop at a farmhouse where they'd have either hot oyster stew or lobster bisque or some hot dish for us. We'd stop in and eat and then make the trip back. It was usually on a full moon night and it was beautiful because . . . the horses had the sleigh bells on so you had the jingling of the sleighbells and everyone would sing all of these songs, and I think that was the most fun. —ANON. ('26)

Pleasant memories abound in this soul and body about Higgins. The smoker—Hollis Soule's store—the smell of hot muffins and bread coming from the kitchen—the weekends with Crit Cummings in Maxfield—picking potatoes—football trips—polishing cars—the swimming hole—the MCI rivalry—the basketball tournaments and speaking contests. Above all, I enjoyed the people—Ma Hillman, a gentle, talented lady—Mr. Van Horne, the janitor—the teachers, Mr. Tracy, Mr. Keith, Miss Brown, and Miss Estes being my favorites. The people really made the school. Mrs. Tracy—always a pleasant lady. The Fotters—John Keith, Mrs. Keith (a great sport booster). All contributed to the wonderful Higgins experience. There was nothing like it in the world. —ORMONDE BROWN ('47)

I had always lived in the country, so even having a bathroom was new to me. Being around so many people was different and something to get used to. Also we had seldom got to go to church and hadn't studied the Bible, so that this was all new to me with Chapel and Bible classes. I had also never had a man teacher. —ELIZABETH CHASE ('46)

Old Asa Mace came out of Aurora with one tie and he didn't know how to tie it. Someone tied it for him, and he slid it down each night. By June the knot was as big as the head of a pin. —PETE MINOTT ('38)

I recall Mr. Lancaster in science class telling how trees change their size as they grow. Kelsey Lord remarked that the maple tree he could see out the window hadn't changed since he had been in school. Mr. Lancaster commented, "It will probably change some before you graduate."—PHILLIP HAMM ('35)

I wonder how many who went to school at my time remember the little piece on the girls' bathroom door—it was shiny and not very clear or big—that we used for a mirror, day after day. I was very glad years later to visit that hangout to find someone had purchased a real mirror. —VERA TURNER ('40)

The class of '14 took a play to Exeter. The truck we went in broke down and we had to spend the night in the Grange Hall. As we returned to Charleston the next morning, Chapel was already in progress. As we entered the room the pianist started playing, "The Morning Light Is Breaking—the Darkness Disappears."—LUCETTA DOORE ('14)

The cooks were a man and wife. He made beautiful biscuits and I used to open the oven and grab the corner ones and throw in a square of butter and run for the swinging doors as he was after me with a knife 15 inches long!—LUCIEN GREEN ('32)

Bob Rosey, one of my friends from Bangor, taught me how to ski with harnesses. This was indeed a great thrill after having started skiing on barrel staves at the age of five or six. I also recall with great pleasure Roland Hutchinson and I making the ice cream on Sunday and running the freezer over so that we would have to take a quart out before the freezing could be completed. I am sure that Ma Hillman knew what we were doing, but we repeated this operation Sunday after Sunday . . . .

Several of my friends at Higgins had more spending money than my Dad earned during a week at that particular point in time. However, this did not bother me because I felt so fortunate to have the opportunity to be there and take advantage of this opportunity to obtain a high school education. —WILMOT OLIVER ('39)

Higgins Classical Institute—what a great name! We always felt that it was a cut above a public high school. The students [were] smarter, the curriculum stronger, the teachers better, and if you wanted to go to college—Higgins was the place to be. (I later learned that we were woefully lacking in things like science labs compared to current public schools in the later years.) —KEITH STANLEY ('59)

When Bonnie Wood first came to Higgins to teach, she had occasion to take a girl injured in sports up to the school doctor, Linus J. Stitham, in Dover. "You coaching down there?" he asked her. Yes, she said, not giving any extra information away, she was coaching some. A few weeks later a boy who was building mouse cages for her bio lab damaged his hand. "And you teach shop?" Stitham asked. Biology, she admitted. That winter she was skiing with some students when one of them was slightly hurt and subsequently got wetter and colder than she thought was good for him, so she dragged him to Dover, still in his ski clothes, and into Stitham's office. "My God," he said, "and you play with them, too."—ANON. ('58)

Bert and I were wrestling in our room one day. We were making a lot of noise and perhaps ruining some furniture. I had Bert down and was sitting on him when I felt a hand on my shoulder. Thinking it was a classmate I said, "You're next and you'll get the same." It turned out to be Mr. Coffin. I nearly died but he gave me only a reprimand. —GILBERT CHAISSON ('43)

I stayed out and picked potatoes to earn money so I could buy clothes for school. Boy, making up four weeks of homework isn't easy. —KENNETH CHURCHILL ('61)

A lot of the students when I was there were about the same type of people that I was. There were a lot from the coast whose parents were fishermen and lobstermen. And some of them were farmers in all the areas around, kids from neighboring towns. I don't know of any kids that you'd say were rich, spoiled brats. I think some kids came from Bangor, but there was no high hat stuff going on, I think no [one from] out of state when I was there. If anybody got snooty or high hat we'd just ignore them. It was just a nice place for a kid to grow up in. . . . No rapes or anything like that going on. Girls were real friendly—Lord knows if there'd been a character like that around he would have showed up, but the girls were respected and treated that way. —ANON. ('26)

Was I happy? Oh, yes, I was happy. I was my own man. I didn't have any brothers or sisters to bother me. And I became a somebody on campus; whether I was a big man in anybody else's mind or not didn't make any difference, I was in my own mind. —RONALD BISHOP ('49)

Yes, Higgins was the only school I ever did feel a part of. —INEZ CAREY ('61)

It was a warm, sunny June day in 1956; and graduation occurred outdoors in front of the Institute building. It was a typically bittersweet occasion when one reluctantly abandons old friends and institutions for the excitement of finding new ones. My family was there, of course; they listened patiently and with ill-concealed pride as I stumbled through my turgid valedictory. After the goodbyes and final wellwishes to my friends, I said my farewell to HCI. I remember that particular event well. I was to drive home in my brother's new Buick Century, which he had parked by the temporary dining hall between the Baptist church and the Institute building. I remember sitting in that car surveying the campus in a moist-eyed reverie of four pleasant years, while the rest of our family caravan impatiently tooted their horns to get me on my way. It must have been 5 minutes before I came to my senses and reluctantly pointed that Buick home. My last glimpse of HCI was the HCI sign in the rearview mirror. —NEAL BROWN ('56)

I used to like staying late in the fall and taking the activity bus home. I always enjoyed just walking to the General Store, around the grounds and the football field. I loved being in Charleston that time of year. The air was so cool and clean and crisp and the trees so beautiful. Sometimes it seemed as if time had stopped somewhere around 1949 and just refused to move on. —MARIA BARTLETT ('75)

I think of them, Sabra and Vina and her aunt and uncle we used to board with. We played in the snow and I walked the pasture fence. Why do we have to leave our most interesting youth? . . . Does Charleston look the same? I have coasted all the hills. —DORIS SPENCER ('18)

APPENDIX A
CLUBS

I am defining "club" rather loosely as a group of people who come together regularly to engage in some activity—club, that is to say, as a Glee Club is a club, though it may not have officers and keep minutes. Hence I am taking the liberty of including such alliances as the orchestra and the students who put out the school paper. Due to lacunae in the collected publications, I have been obliged sometimes to guess whether an organization was active during the missing years. And if an activity chances not to be mentioned in the *Scroll* or the catalogue, I have no way of knowing about it.

Clubs are listed in order of foundation, from the first literary society to the diet club of 1974–75, and it is interesting to watch the changes in fashion over the decades. That the earliest societies were literary and intellectual probably reflects popular trends at least as much as it does the tastes of the student body at Higgins. Indeed, we may discover the turn-of-the-century vogue for (usually exclusive) high school literary organizations without looking farther than the popular fiction of that period. (Thus, the heroine of *Emmy Lou: Her Book and Heart*, by George Madden Martin, 1901, receives an invitation to join the Platonian Society and looks at it "as an Athenian might have regarded an invitation into Olympus.") Perhaps if the Philopean ran true to form, the brevity of its tenure at Higgins may be accounted for by the school's militantly democratic atmosphere.

By the 1920s, organizations that were going to last a long time (e.g., the French Club, the Orchestra) had emerged, and these would be added to for the next twenty years or so. Higgins had moved into the stable middle period that formed the frame for chapters II and VIII.

Of more interest yet is the proliferation of short-lived clubs during the last five or ten years of the school. The desire to make any activity—dieting, weightlifting, cooking, bowling—into a club was, I suspect, an early symptom of our culture's current obsession with "networking," but other factors may be more peculiarly Higgins's— for instance, a high level of nervous student energy in the suspense-filled last days of the school, a faculty desire to avert mayhem with any conceivable kind of organized activity, and perhaps the shifts in interests and expertise that result from a rapid turnover of staff. Why ever it happened, the evolution from literary society to diet club seems fraught with gloomy portents of the decline of the American intellect. "Frivolity!" and "triviality!" we old grads can sniff. We can feel smug, provided that we don't look too closely at our own scrap-books. I remember that my mother had a late-thirties snapshot of the French Club up to their knees in the ocean, squealing, on their annual outing. They were probably not squealing in French.

PHILOPEAN, 1894–95.

This exclusive literary society was probably of several years' duration, though I have found reference to it only in the 1894–95 catalogue. Such student literary societies, with membership by invitation only, were a standard feature of high school life in that period.

THE SCROLL, 1897–1975.

The longest lasting Higgins institution, the *Scroll* is discussed in more detail in Chapter X.

DEBATE, 1898–1911, 1947–50, 1960–69, 1971–74.

Debate at Higgins began at least as early as 1898. The first de-bating society was male (future principal William Cowing was in it) and required initiation; in 1903 it was christened "Omicron Delta." The forties edition was called "The Higgins Forum." It seems, too, to have been a male organization, but perhaps that was by chance or conditioning, not legislation. From 1960 on, the debating club had no special name and was coed.

BASEBALL ASSOCIATION, *Spring of 1898.*

TENNIS ASSOCIATION FOR LADIES, 1899–?.
> This seems to have been defunct by 1905, but we cannot say when it died out. In 1970–71 there was a coed *Tennis Club*.
> Tennis was mostly played without benefit of organization.

HIGGINS TRAVEL CLASS, 1905–06.
> This was a literary society for girls. They traveled by reading.

ATHLETIC ASSOCIATION, 1907–59.
> I think that the AA disappeared for a couple of years here and there during each decade, but it was more on than off. I have the association's notebook for the period from the late teens to the mid twenties. Anyone could join for three dollars, and alumni got a special rate of a dollar fifty. The AA oversaw the duties of managers and captains, the eligibility for school letters, and the famous annual fair.

THE LITERARY SOCIETY, 1907–08.

YWCA, 1907–15, 1919–21.

KAPPA PHI BETA, 1908–09.
> A girls' society designed to promote social life and parliamentary law. In 1924 the *Girls' House Club* took up the cause of social life (though not, perhaps, parliamentary law) and lasted until 1930.

TIBBETTS HALL ASSOCIATION, 1909–10.
> The boys organized this association to make money, buy magazines and papers for their reception room, and generally improve the quality of dormitory life. In 1921–22 a similar organization called the *Radio Club* existed; I think that the radio in question was Hugh Smith's.

HIGGINS CLASSICAL INSTITUTE DISCUSSION CLUB, 1911–15, 1919–27.
> Boys only.

OPEN PARLIAMENT CLUB, 1913–20.
> Girls only.

SEWING CLUB, 1919–20.

RADIO CLUB, 1921–22.
> See *Tibbetts Hall Association*, 1909.

GIRL RESERVES, circa 1920–49.

I am guessing at the date of foundation. A 1924 allusion to Girl Reserves makes it sound already well entrenched. According to the 1928 *Scroll*, this popular and long-lasting organization was the teen version of the YWCA. Their meetings included "social, religious, and service topics," and judging by the minutes, they were keen on picnics and other forms of refreshment. The 1926 *Scroll* mentions their marching to church one Sunday in their uniforms, which I suppose may have been blue and white, their colors. Their candlelight initiation ceremony is said by those who experienced it to have been very moving, and certainly some of the ritual is elevating. The injunction from the old treasurer to the new, for instance, as the books are handed over, begins, "The keeper of the treasury cares for something more precious than gold—the faith of friends."

GIRLS HOUSE CLUB, 1924–30.

See *Kappa Phi Beta*, 1908.

ORCHESTRA, 1922–68.

I find the first reference to a Higgins Orchestra in the April 1923 *Scroll*. An undated photograph seems by the costume to have been taken at about that time. An orchestra or band existed from then on, instruction and talent permitting, until 1968. In 1949 the musical group seems irrevocably to have become a *band*. That is to say, although it occasionally referred to itself as an orchestra, strings were out and, bass drums and tubas were in. The peak year of the band was 1954–55, with forty-six musicians, orange-and-black uniforms, and Charles Danforth directing. Just after that came a period when anyone who fancied directing put on a uniform and tried, experience not essential. But the band survived even that and lasted, at least off and on, into the late sixties.

HIKING CLUB, 1925–34, 1943–50.

The hiking club was for girls, who often walked prodigious distances and won varsity letters. The club was a godsend when the Institute burned in 1930 and students had to be got outdoors for structured activity while the cooks set up lunch in the quondam study hall.

HINCLIN SUNDAY SCHOOL CLASS, 1927–28.

"H" *CLUB*, 1930–34, 1957–59, 1963–75.

An organization for students who had earned varsity letters, it was in fact called *Varsity Club* in its last incarnation, and sometimes "H" *Varsity Club* in its earlier ones.

ARCHERY, 1931–32, 1933–34, 1972–75.

BOYS' GLEE CLUB, 1933–49, 1955–56.

There was, as well, a male quartet in 1953–54. After 1950 the chorus was usually coed.

GIRLS' GLEE CLUB, 1933–49, 1951–52, 1955–56.

A female quartet existed in 1952–53. And see note above.

FRENCH CLUB, 1936–52.

There were perhaps a couple of one-year lapses in the duration. The club was both large and active, going on outings, writing to French pen-pals. In 1938 a pen-pal assures the Higgins French Club that "Monsieur Hitler" will never take France, for France has the best-organized army in the world in point of "morale et technique."

HI-Y, 1936–37.

KNITTING CLUB, 1936–37.

HOME-EC CLUB, 1937–42. AS FHA, 1947–75.

In 1947, the Home-Ec Club went national, as a chapter of Future Homemakers of America.

THE SCRAWL, 1938–63.

A biweekly student newspaper.

CAMERA CLUB, 1939–40, 1942–43, 1946–47, 1958–59, 1970–72, 1974–75.

This club was particularly dependent on the incidental skills and interest of the faculty. From 1970 on, it was called the *Photography Club*.

CHEERLEADERS, 1940–75.

I may be in error about the earlier date. The first cheerleaders I can find are pictured in the 1941–42 catalogue. Earlier yearbooks and catalogues make no mention of this activity, but then, neither does the 1941 *Scroll*, so who knows?

SCIENCE CLUB, 1940–41, 1958–59, 1963–66, 1971–72.
The 1958–59 installment was called *Science Seminar*.

DRAMATICS CLUB, 1942–43, 1952–53, 1964–66, 1971–75.
Foggy territory here. Sometimes the yearbooks show a group called "Dramatics Club," sometimes they show a group that puts on one-act plays without labeling themselves. I have used both. For many years all the drama was done by the junior and senior classes or by a combination of faculty, students, and townspeople.

FUTURE HOMEMAKERS OF AMERICA, 1947–75.

LATIN CLUB, 1948–53.

BAND, 1949–68.
See *Orchestra*, 1922.

GLEE CLUB, 1950–51, 1954–60, 1962–68, 1971–73.
The Glee Club (or *Chorus*, as it was called from 1962 on) included singers of both sexes. From 1965 to 1968 there was a "select chorus" as well.

NATIONAL HONOR SOCIETY, 1950–75.
For some account of this society, see Chapter VIII.

STUDENT COUNCIL, 1953–54, 1964–75.

MAJORETTES, 1955–56, 1966–69.

OUTING CLUB, 1957–59.

DORM COUNCILS, male and female, 1958–59, 1961–64, 1966–73.

MUSIC APPRECIATION CLUB, 1958–59.

ASSEMBLY COMMITTEE, 1959–60.
From 1962 to 1968 called *Chapel Committee*, which appears to be a triumph of traditional terminology over concept.

FUTURE TEACHERS OF AMERICA, 1961–63, 1965–66.

LIBRARY ASSISTANTS, 1961–75.

MATH CLUB, 1961–63.

CHORUS, 1962–73.
See *Glee Club*, 1950.

CENTRAL MAINE LEAGUE SPELLERS, 1962–68.

PEP CLUB, 1962–63, 1965–69, 1972–75.

CHESS CLUB, 1963–70, 1972–75.

VARSITY CLUB, 1963–75.
See "H" *Club*, 1930.

GIRLS' RIFLE CLUB, 1965–66.

NATIONAL RIFLE ASSOCIATION, 1965–66.

COOKING CLUB, 1967–68.

DIRIGO, 1967–75.

GYMNASTICS CLUB, 1967–68.

ART CLUB, 1969–72
In 1967–68 called Art Class, but listed as an activity. Judging from photographs, this club was involved in making, rather than merely appreciating, art. An excellent idea, it must in some measure have compensated for the lack of art classes.

BOWLING CLUB, 1969–71.

RIDING CLUB, 1969–75.

RIFLERY CLUB, 1969–74.

SKI-DOO CLUB, 1969–70.

PHOTOGRAPHY CLUB, 1970–72, 1974–75.
See *Camera Club*, 1939.

SKI CLUB, 1970–71.

TENNIS CLUB, 1970–71.
See *Ladies' Tennis Association*, 1899.

WEIGHTLIFTING, 1971–72.

COLOR GUARDS, 1973–74.

ELECTRICITY CLASS, 1973–74.

FOREIGN LANGUAGE CLUB, 1973–75.

GUITAR CLUB, 1973–74.

NATURE STUDY CLUB, 1973–74.

DIET CLUB, 1974–75.

APPENDIX B
MEMORIALS

Here follow Higgins's civilian deaths. In apology for unpleasant detail I can only plead a regional predisposition. I read somewhere once that Maine people can't resist telling gory or ironic stories of death ("He'd only had that tractor twenty-four hours when it tipped over and crushed him"), and it's true—we can't. How else would I, a child at the time, have known some of these things? Ah, the stories I could tell you about children who were impaled on pitchforks eighty years ago, or drownings in full sight of a helpless crowd!

There is some danger that a detached and skeptical reader, faced with assertions that the deceased were all especially bright and lovable, will remember that sainthood is always conferred after death and suspect some posthumous rise in value. Yes, of course it's necessary to say something decent about the dead, but I assure you that as far as I know the praise is perfectly accurate. The notion that the good die young may after all have something in it; it would certainly go far toward explaining the state of the world. In any case, our ancestors believed it, and we have no reason to believe that they were greater fools than we.

With some difficulty I have decided to exclude students who died after their graduations, however shortly after, for what is the statute of limitations to be? Clearly one really ought to include here Gerry Cormier ('52), who drowned so soon after his graduation that emotional involvement was still at a pitch and two or three carloads of students as well as some faculty assembled for his funeral. If we include Cormier, we can scarcely leave out Earle Dunham ('43), who died only a little later in the summer after his graduation, having, while bending to pick berries, dropped a pistol that hit a rock, fired, and shot him through the heart. What then of Eugene Lyford ('97), whose losing struggle against lung disease the Higgins student body followed through his letters until he died in April of 1898? And if Lyford qualifies, what about Charles Merrill Treworgy ('16)? He died in December of 1922, but the April 1923 *Scroll* gives five closely packed pages to his obituary, including a three-page letter from Professor Herbert C. Libby of Colby College (where Treworgy died in a dormitory fire). I have answered these questions by arbitrary exclusion. I have also excluded teachers who were not employed at Higgins in the year of their deaths. This is not a large sampling, but we may note a tentative historical phenomenon. Through the twenties the dead are all girls (except for Lyford, above) and the causes of death are natural. From the forties on (I find no deaths in the thirties), the dead are male (except for Norma Nielson) and the deaths are accidental.

1909—SADIE M. HIGGINS, who was to have been valedictorian of the class of 1909, died suddenly during spring term. The *Scroll* alludes to "her last sickness," but not to its nature. Her fellow students seem to have been extraordinarily fond of her—"one of our dearest classmates," they called her.

1910—MIRIAM K. LIBBY (or perhaps Marion Libby—two allusions in the *Scroll* differ, as do the recollections of Charleston neighbors) died in her freshman year, on Christmas day. She was the only child of Katy and Lewis Libby, of Charleston, and was said to have been unusually bright. She died of appendicitis, the symptoms of which were not taken seriously until too late. Since neighbors have a vague recollection that her death had "something to do with puberty," I imagine that her symptoms were misattributed to that cause.

1921—ANNA EDNA FLEMING, who died on April 24, 1921, during an operation for an internal tumor of some sort, had been Preceptress (nowadays Dean of Women) during that school year. She is still remembered fondly by alumni as a good Latin teacher, and is of particular interest to me because she was engaged to be married to my father. She had been a classmate of his at Ricker and was thirty-one at the time of her death. Her memorial photograph in the *Scroll*, in academic attire, shows an intelligent, attractive, down-to-earth face, and I think that her feminist sensibilities may have been well developed, for Hugh Smith has told me that she used to distress my father by refusing to let him pay for her dinner even after they were engaged. She was completing her degree at Colby during the time she worked at Higgins.

1923—DOROTHY RUSSELL, a Charleston girl, died in February of her Freshman year. The April 1923 *Scroll*, which announces her death, does not say what she died of, but it gives us some notion of her life. She is described as a "quiet, earnest, Christian girl," and the writer asserts that all who knew her loved her. This is, I suspect, a tactful way of coping with a girl whom not many students would have known well, for her mother was dead, and she had for some years been helping her grandmother raise her younger brothers and sisters.

1938—FLORENCE PREBLE TRACY, my father's first wife, a teacher of languages at Higgins, died very suddenly in the fall of 1938. Dressed for her Eastern Star meeting in Corinth, she was waiting for the trolley when she began to feel so bad that my father rushed her to the Bangor Hospital. She died, Eleanor Mills says, the same night. She has been cited by a number of alumni as an especially good teacher, and I gather from a couplet in the January 1922 *Scroll* (her first academic year) that she was held in some awe as a linguist:

> P stands for Miss Preble, from Colby she comes,
> And they say she can speak in twenty-nine tongues.

She was, at the least, proficient in French, German, and Latin. (The amorous effect of Latin proficiency upon my father might bear looking into; my mother, as well as Anna Fleming and Florence Preble, taught that language.) Her nature seems to have been pleasant and affectionate, though not perhaps assertive; I recall hearing that her mother, who lived with her, would not "let" her cut her hair. My father, I know, found old Mrs. Preble overbearing, though I don't suppose she overbore *him*, and he was obliged to go on living with his mother-in-law for the duration of the year, or at any rate until he could find something else to do with her. A scholarship in Florence Tracy's name was given each spring thereafter to a junior girl.

1944—The day MICHAEL SURTEES Died was a world-class bad day at Higgins, probably one of the worst half dozen in its history. Rumors of collapse echo down the years—his brother Peter screaming, Mary Jane Keith hiding in the closet, my father sitting on his hat. For irony, heroism, and gruesomeness it was unsurpassed by any Higgins deaths before or after.

For one thing, Michael himself was special, not just because he was deservedly popular, not just because he was junior class president that year, but because he was our own English evacuee, whom we were keeping safe. He and his younger brothers, Timothy and Peter, had sailed to Quebec (chased by a submarine all the way, they assured us), and then traveled on to Massachusetts to spend the war with the Reverend J. W. Greiss, who, like their father, was an Anglican clergyman. Complications in the Greiss family and their friendship with a Higgins trustee had made our school seem a logical solution for the boys; English boys were used to boarding schools anyway. Michael and Timothy came the first year, which would have been the fall of 1942, Peter a year later. The two younger boys were still in grammar school.

February 19, 1944, was a cold, bright Saturday. Everyone was going about his own business. My father was in Bangor. So were Mary Jane and Evelyn Keith. Mr. Van Horne, the janitor, was in the heating plant. Outside the heating plant, Michael and another boy were shoveling coal. This was not Michael's regular job—in fact, he probably didn't have one; he was earning some extra money to take a girl to the movies. There are tricks to shoveling frozen coal, but Mr. Van Horne had explained them: you have to break the coal down from the top if you don't want a cave-in. "The coal pile was only from 7 to 10 feet high," my father wrote to Michael's guardian. "I believe the cause of the accident was a piece of coal breaking off and starting to roll down, then breaking a second time and pitching over onto Michael." What pitched over onto him is not quite clear from the letter, but Robert Bearman ('46) remembers looking at "the high frozen section of coal that fell on him," and when he paced it off for me as he remembered it, it looked a dozen feet long and six feet thick. The coal would have fallen on the other boy, too, or perhaps instead, but Michael pushed him out of the way, thereby contributing the final element to his drama: heroism.

Michael was taken to the Bangor hospital, where he died two hours later. His death certificate in the Charleston Town Clerk's records lists shock, a compound fracture of the pelvis, and a fractured spine as causes of death. All that day and the next, people came back from errands in Bangor or back to school from the weekend and had to be told. Evelyn Keith, the submaster's wife, who knew Peter and Timothy pretty well, drew the harrowing task of telling them. The whole basketball team, she says, was waiting in the corridor and at the sound of Peter's screams ran in and carried him off to distract him. Timothy was distracting himself by refusing to believe her.

Higgins had a memorial service on the same day as Michael's Massachusetts funeral; it was in the gym, the biggest place, because the whole town wanted to attend. Margaret Bishop ('44) says the students were allowed an afternoon off when the service was over. They were a student body unusually accustomed to death, given the year, but they took it hard. It had happened on campus and it was an effect almost without a cause, neither a military death nor the result of careless driving. Brad Brown ('47) writes, "When Michael was killed it made me realize that all of us at HCI were as bonded as the most close knit family. It was as if we had lost a brother."

Of course the 1944 yearbook was dedicated to Michael Surtees, but Robert Bearman informs me that "in a moment of melancholy" a group of students dedicated the Smoker to him as well, though no plaque marks that transaction. Judging by the importance of that smoky hole to the male students of Higgins, I imagine that Michael would have appreciated that honor most of all. And of course his memory was officially revived for another thirty years of Last Chapels by the giving of a scholarship in his name. A long poem by Robert Cameron ('45) on the editorial page of the 1944 *Scroll* struggles to express the prevailing welter of emotions and philosophical difficulties. He concludes:

> *But we cannot direct our destinies,*
> *And so he died in Maine on such a date:*

He died because he saved another's life—
Example of the irony of fate.

Even for those of us who came too late to know him, his story had a kind of mythic pull, a hint of grim and romantic possibilities in the working of the world, and all the ironies of an Oedipus Rex's flight from Corinth brought down to familiar circumstances.

1945—A new boy named CARBONNE, from Portland, died in an auto accident in the fall of 1945. None of the alumni who mentioned the accident could remember his first name. It was not a time when death was in itself much of a novelty, I think.

1948—ROLAND S. FOTTER, who earlier in March of 1948 had seen his basketball team win the prep school tournament, was killed in an auto accident during spring vacation. A Colby graduate, he had for four years been coaching at Higgins, teaching algebra and Latin, and living with his family in the boys' dorm. He was always well loved, and his star must have been particularly high just then because of the tournament.

His car was hit by a truck, which knocked it into the ditch and kept going. He died on the way to the Bar Harbor hospital. Details not included in the newspaper but recited in my presence have stuck in my mind—his son Lee, who was ten, flagging down help in the dark; the three-year-old saying in surprise, "Daddy's asleep, he's snoring."

The school grieved very much. Earle Stevens ('48) recalls sitting at the head of the casket and imagining that he saw Roland breathing, remembering him saying that he was going to win the championship if it was the last thing he did. The senior class honored his memory by setting their class ode to his favorite song, "Now Is the Hour."

1949—NORMA NIELSON, who would have graduated in 1951, died, I was always told, of cancer resulting from an injury; she was held up to us in our childhoods as proof of the pernicious effects of ever, ever hitting anyone with an icy snowball. This diagnosis seems a little suspect now. The 1951 *Scroll* is dedicated to her.

1952—FRANCIS K. (BOZO) Scribner died on July 5 in the summer before his senior year. I speak from the perspective of someone half a dozen years younger when I say that he always seemed a magical sort of person, endowed with attributes and skills that nobody else had. For instance, he had tamed a raccoon; it would sit on his shoulder when he rode his bicycle. Moreover, he could use a jigsaw, and once out of goodwill produced for our grade-school nativity play a star so professional, so yellow and perfectly proportioned, that it was impossible to imagine its having been made by anyone we knew. It seemed only fitting that he could fly.

I mean, of course, in a plane, but that was amazing enough, that he had an airplane in high school and was a working pilot of some reputation, carrying mail and supplies and sportsmen back and forth to wilderness camps. He was flying some sportsmen out of camp when he went down and burned at Desolation Pond. The sportsmen escaped, and I remember a lot of local indignation that they hadn't managed to get Bozo out of the plane as well. Everybody liked him and everybody was upset. Indeed, he was enough of a personage that Bud Leavitt, the sports writer, did a piece about his death for the Bangor paper, commenting on his kindness, thoughtfulness, and courtesy, his general lovability. "What a full life he lived for a boy!" he writes. "In many ways it was the equivalent of at least two lives."

His class chose a clever memorial, a school sign for the front lawn, so that as long as the school lasted, Bozo's name swung in the air over the campus.

1958—DAVID GERALD GRAY died on January 17, 1958, in his senior year. He was seventeen years old. His last day was a cold, sleety one, with ice skimming the puddles, but things were pleasant at school—it was a Friday, the school paper came out, we were looking forward to a basketball game. The last thing he did was go with some friends, after classes, on what is so often miscalled a joy ride.

David was a fine student, outstandingly bright, and he wore his intellect so gracefully that we almost didn't notice, or didn't remember. He was constitutionally incapable of unkindness, as far as I know, and he was witty and a cut-up—he once hung out a second-story window by his fingertips to enliven a Latin class. Everyone liked him a lot, and something about him made you feel that things couldn't go too far wrong if he was around. I remember the Dean of Girls pacing the reception room floor the night he was killed, saying, "That nice, nice boy! Why, there wasn't a nicer boy in the school."

Thomas Wolfe's Lost Boy, Grover, calls him back for me a little, but so, I must admit, does John Knowles's Phineas and Holden Caulfield's brother Allie and every other lamented youth in literature short of Stephen Dowling Bots. David died almost thirty years ago, and judging by all the available evidence, internal and external, his friends and family are never going to get over it.

1962—DAVID RONALD WORCESTER was drowned the summer before his senior year. I am missing the yearbooks that would tell me what he did with himself at Higgins, but a classmate remembers him as "a real nice kid," and the 1963 *Scroll* dedication uses the unexpected phrase "with deepest respect." His is the last death of which I have any record.